Freemium Economics
Leveraging Analytics and User Segmentation to Drive Revenue

Freemium Economics
Leveraging Analytics and User Segmentation to Drive Revenue

Eric Benjamin Seufert

AMSTERDAM • BOSTON • HEIDELBERG • LONDON
NEW YORK • OXFORD • PARIS • SAN DIEGO
SAN FRANCISCO • SINGAPORE • SYDNEY • TOKYO
Morgan Kaufmann is an imprint of Elsevier

Acquiring Editor: *Andrea Dierna*
Editorial Project Manager: *Kaitlin Herbert*
Project Manager: *Malathi Samayan*
Designer: *Matthew Limbert*

Morgan Kaufmann is an imprint of Elsevier
225 Wyman Street, Waltham, MA 02451, USA

Notices
Knowledge and best practice in this field are constantly changing. As new research and
experience broaden our understanding, changes in research methods or professional practices,
may become necessary. Practitioners and researchers must always rely on their own experience
and knowledge in evaluating and using any information or methods described here in. In using
such information or methods they should be mindful of their own safety and the safety of
others, including parties for whom they have a professional responsibility.

To the fullest extent of the law, neither the Publisher nor the authors, contributors, or editors,
assume any liability for any injury and/or damage to persons or property as a matter of
products liability, negligence or otherwise, or from any use or operation of any methods,
products, instructions, or ideas contained in the material herein.

Library of Congress Cataloging-in-Publication Data
Seufert, Eric Benjamin.
  Freemium economics : leveraging analytics and user segmentation to drive revenue /
Eric Benjamin Seufert.
    pages cm
  Includes bibliographical references and index.
  ISBN 978-0-12-416690-5 (alk. paper)
1. Pricing. 2. Bundling (Marketing) 3. Marketing. 4. Demand (Economic theory)
5. Consumption (Economics) 6. Computer software industry—Case studies. I. Title.
  HF5416.5.S48 2014
  658.8′16—dc23   2013037659

British Library Cataloguing-in-Publication Data
A catalogue record for this book is available from the British Library

ISBN: 978-0-12-416690-5

Printed and bound in the United States of America

14 15 16 17 18   11 10 9 8 7 6 5 4 3 2 1

For information on all MK publications,
visit our website at www.mkp.com or www.elsevierdirect.com

For my mother

In praise of *Freemium Economics: Leveraging Analytics and User Segmentation to Drive Revenue*

"Eric Seufert provides comprehensive, analytical insight into the what, why, and how of building a successful freemium business. Whether you're building a free-to-play game or freeware SaaS product, *Freemium Economics* is an excellent resource to increase chances of success."

—Ryan Hoover, PlayHaven

"Eric Seufert's *Freemium Economics* covers every aspect of freemium software design and development, from the core concepts of "freemium economics" to marketing. This book is a must read for anyone developing freemium products."

—Michail Katkoff ("The Deconstructor of Fun"), Scopely

Contents

Acknowledgments

This book represents the combined efforts of a number of people.

To the reviewers, Michail Katkoff, Kenton Kivestu, Ryan Hoover, and Stanislav Beremski: without your input, this book would be of far lower quality. Your help is greatly appreciated.

To Thorbjörn Warin and Jon Jordan, who helped me convince a publisher that a book about the freemium model would be not only salient but timely: without your assistance, this book would not exist.

To the book's illustrations and diagrams artist, Vladimir Šipka: your contributions to *Freemium Economics* are invaluable. Your speed and good nature in taking revision requests significantly reduced the stress of the writing process.

To my girlfriend, Päivi Pütsepp: your patience with my weekly—and, as the deadline approached, daily—writing sessions allowed the book to receive the attention it deserved.

To my family: your love and encouragement inspired me to pursue a lifelong dream.

And to the publisher, Morgan Kaufmann: without your early support, the long journey out of which this book culminated would likely not have been undertaken.

Thank you, all.

Author Biography

Eric Seufert is a quantitative marketer with a passion for blending real-world problems with large amounts of data, econometric frameworks, and analytical systems. His professional specialty lies in programmatic statistical methods and predictive forecasting for freemium products.

Eric received an undergraduate degree in finance from the University of Texas at Austin and an MA in economics from University College London, where he was an Erasmus Mundus scholar. Eric joined Skype immediately out of graduate school and subsequently held marketing and strategy roles at Digital Chocolate and at Wooga, where he is now the head of marketing.

Originally from Texas, Eric currently lives in Berlin. In his spare time, Eric enjoys traveling, writing, and performing stand-up comedy.

Introduction

Freemium Economics is a survey of the freemium business model from an analytical perspective: the book aims to dissect the model and explain how its component parts contribute to its success in software products. The freemium model has become the dominant means of generating revenue on mobile devices. *Freemium Economics* was written to provide an instructive and, more importantly, holistic overview of how freemium products generate revenue, keep users engaged, and grow.

This book serves to formalize the commercial and logistical principles that accommodate the successful application of the freemium business model, both in the abstract and within the context of software development. This book is not a product development guide; it does not prescribe a certain set of actions or best practices to take under concrete circumstances when developing specific products. Rather, it establishes a theoretical framework, informed by both economic principles and the practical realities of software development, that can be applied to the process of building freemium software products.

The scope of the material covered in this book is broad because the book is written with no particular audience in mind. *Freemium Economics* is not dedicated solely to prescribing an approach to analytics or catalyzing virality in product design or outlining user experience best practices; rather, the book is meant to inform an individual's understanding of how the freemium model generates revenue for products priced at $0. While understanding the structure of freemium components—how an analytics stack tracks data, or how virality can be quantified, for instance—is important, the interaction between those components is much more significant in terms of revenue relevance.

Dedicating chapters of the book to fairly esoteric topics, such as analytics and quantitative methods, is not to render experts out of generalists or to make the book accessible to practitioners of those subjects. Rather, the book covers a diverse set of subjects because the freemium business model is sophisticated and requires at least a basic level of savvy in a set of disparate competencies.

The goal of *Freemium Economics* is to provide the reader (whose occupation, experience, and goals with the freemium model are not assumed) with an understanding of why and when a product should be released at a price point of $0. After finishing the book, the reader should have a firm grasp on the following elements of freemium software development:

- The prerequisites to success in the freemium model, including the size of a product's addressable market and the product's ability to scale;
- Data-driven product development, facilitated by a robust analytics stack, clear and informative reporting, and a basic understanding of quantitative methods;
- The core principles of choice and product catalogue strategy in monetizing freemium products and how freemium products should be structured in order to optimize each user's "lifetime customer value"; and
- Freemium product growth facilitated through virality and paid user acquisition.

Chapter 1, "The Freemium Business Model," begins with an overview of the basic components of the freemium model, each of which is elaborated on individually in later chapters. The chapter expands into a discussion of three economic principles—price elasticity of demand, price discrimination, and Pareto efficiency—and the role each one plays in building and measuring freemium products. The chapter ends with case studies of three high-profile freemium software products: Skype, Spotify, and Candy Crush Saga. These case studies set the stage for discussing aspects of the model in later chapters and are meant to bring various elements of the freemium model to the fore of the reader's mind for later consideration.

Chapter 2, "Analytics and Freemium Product Development," discusses the role of analytics in the freemium model and its importance in not only developing a freemium product but maximizing its revenues after launch. The chapter begins with a definition of the term "insight" within the context of the freemium model and then progresses into an overview of an analytics stack—the combination of software and hardware elements that allows for product data to be stored, analyzed, and reported—and the ways in which the stack interacts with a freemium product. The chapter ends with a discussion of data-driven product design and how it is best implemented in the freemium development process.

Chapter 3, "Quantitative Methods for Product Management," is an introduction to various quantitative concepts that can be used to measure the success of freemium products. The chapter begins with an overview of the analytical techniques and concepts that can be used to measure products, such as exploratory data analysis, probability distributions, and visualization, and their proper interpretations. The chapter then segues into an overview of A/B testing and its role in data-driven product development, followed by an explanation of regression analysis. The chapter ends with a discussion of user segmentation and the means by which the statistical and quantitative techniques previously discussed allow for freemium product developers to tailor the product to the preferences of each user.

Chapter 4, "Freemium Metrics," expands on the foundation laid in Chapters 2 and 3 by providing a practical set of guidelines by which analytics and quantitative methods can be used in a freemium product's development process to iterate upon and improve it. The chapter begins with a definition of a freemium product's "minimum viable metrics" (the minimum set of metrics that must be tracked by a freemium product to facilitate data-driven improvements) and then proceeds into a detailed description of each of the four broad categories contained therein: retention, monetization, engagement, and virality. The chapter ends with an outline of a practical, instructive strategy for using metrics to inform product development.

Chapter 5, "Lifetime Customer Value," is an overview of one of the most important concepts in freemium design. The chapter begins by defining lifetime customer value and its significance in the freemium context. The chapter proceeds into descriptions of two methods of calculating lifetime customer value: the spreadsheet method, using spreadsheet software to estimate a rough yet accessible lifetime customer value metric, and the analytics method, which algorithmically tracks lifetime customer value. The chapter ends with a discussion of the lifetime customer value metric in an organizational role and how it can be used to make decisions.

Chapter 6. "Freemium Monetization," dissects the various forces at work in the dynamic between freemium products and users and offers a strategy for optimizing revenues while maintaining trust and goodwill with the user base. The chapter begins with an introduction to choice theory and an explanation of the different monetization roles users fall into in a freemium product. The chapter then expands into a description of the role data plays in forming a monetization strategy, including a definition of data products and the means by which they can contribute to freemium revenues. The chapter ends with a discussion of "downstream marketing" and its use in preserving and optimizing revenue streams.

Chapter 7, "Virality," discusses the viral effects that freemium products can benefit from. The chapter starts with a definition of virality within the context of a software product, including an approach for calculating virality, and then discusses a detailed step-by-step guide to modeling virality in a spreadsheet. The chapter ends with a product-centric discussion of virality and the ways it should be considered (and intentionally engineered) in the product development process.

Chapter 8, "Growth," presents a framework for growing a freemium product's user base. The first focus is "strategic growth," which outlines the considerations to make before product launch, at the time of product launch, and after product launch to maximize the size of the product's user base. The chapter then discusses paid user acquisition, including a detailed overview of the networks and systems by which paid user acquisition is achieved, treating paid user acquisition on mobile as an independent topic. The chapter ends with a discussion of various alternative techniques for user acquisition.

The Freemium Business Model

Commerce at a price point of $0

All business models are malleable thought structures, meant to be adapted and decisively employed to best achieve a specific product's or service's goals. This being understood, and for the purposes of this book, a broad and basic formal definition of the *freemium business model* is described as follows:

The freemium business model stipulates that a product's basic functionality be given away for free, in an environment of very low or no marginal distribution and production costs that provides the potential for massive scale, with advanced functionality, premium access, and other product-specific benefits available for a fee.

The freemium business model is an adaptation of a fairly common distribution and monetization scheme used in software since the 1980s: the *feature-limited* software paradigm was when consumers saw most of the fundamental core components of a product released for free, with the product's remaining functionality (such as saving progress or printing) becoming available only upon purchase, either in a one-time payment or through recurring subscription payments.

The most basic point of difference between the freemium business model—*freemium* being a portmanteau of *free* and *premium*—and the feature-limited model is distribution: feature-limited software products were generally distributed on physical discs, whereas freemium products are almost exclusively distributed via the Internet. So the distribution speed and ultimate reach of feature-limited products were a function of the firm's capacity to produce and ship tangible goods; no such restrictions limit the distribution of freemium products.

A second distinction between the freemium and feature-limited business models is the scope of functionality of each: whereas feature-limited products often merely showcased the look and feel of the full product and could not be used to fulfill their primary use cases at the free price tier, with freemium products, payment restrictions generally do not limit access to basic functionality. Rather, freemium products exist as fully featured, wholly useful entities even at the free price tier; payment generally unlocks advanced functionality that appeals to the most engaged users.

The freemium model represents a fundamental evolution from the feature-limited model, given a new set of circumstances under which software is distributed and consumed: mobile devices give users access to products at a moment's notice and throughout the day, cloud storage services and digital distribution channels allow products to be discovered and purchased without the need for physical discs, and digital payment mechanisms render purchases nearly frictionless.

The pervasiveness and connectedness of software, then, represents a heightened state of awareness with respect to the demands made upon software by users. And it also presents a massive opportunity to quickly and almost effortlessly reach millions, if not billions, of potential consumers upon product launch. This is the reality of the modern software economy, and it is the backdrop against which the freemium business model has emerged.

Components of the freemium business model

The ultimate logistical purpose of the freemium business model—and the source of the advantages it affords over other business models—is the frictionless distribution of a product to as large a group of potential users as possible. This potential for massive scale accommodates three realities of the freemium model:

1. A price point of $0 renders the product accessible to the largest number of people.
2. Some users will not engage with the product beyond the free tier of functionality.
3. If the product is extremely appealing to a group of users, and the product presents the opportunity to make large or repeat purchases, a portion of the user base may spend more money in the product than they would have if the product had cost a set fee. Thus, the revenue fulcrum, or the crux of a product manager's decision to develop a freemium product, is the potential to maximize scale, paid engagement, and appeal to the extent that the total revenue the product generates exceeds what could be expected if the product cost money.

While the freemium business model is not governed by a rigid set of physical bounds, some patterns hold true across a large enough swath of the commercial freemium landscape to be interpreted as intellectual thresholds. The first pattern that emerges is that the broader the appeal of a product, the more potential users it can reach and the more widely it will be adopted. A broadly appealing product has a widely applicable *use case*, or purpose. Generally speaking, products that address a universal need, pain point, or genre of entertainment appeal to more people than do products that serve a specific niche. Broad applicability obviously has a direct impact on the number of users who adopt a product.

The second pattern is that very few users of freemium products ever *monetize*, or spend money on them. The low proportion of users who monetize in freemium products contributes to the necessity of large potential scale: a low percentage of monetizing users within a very large total user base might represent a respectable absolute number of people. This concept is referred to in this book as the *5% rule*, or the understanding that no more than 5 percent of a freemium product's user base can be expected to monetize prior to product launch.

The third observable trend with the freemium model is that the spectrum of total monetization levels—that is, the total amount of money users spend within the product—spans a wide range of values, with a very small minority of users spending very large amounts of money. The larger the minority of highly engaged users, the more revenue the product generates in aggregate; when the spectrum of monetization levels is broad, more users tend to monetize than when the spectrum is limited to fewer values.

The confluence of these three trends establishes a freemium development directive: the broader the appeal, the higher the level of engagement; and the more numerous the opportunities to engage that the product offers, the more revenue it will generate. At some optimized point, these forces can contribute to a more advantageous revenue dynamic than could be expected under paid adoption circumstances. If frictionless distribution is the logistical purpose of the freemium model, then its commercial purpose is to establish the product attributes necessary to achieve greater monetization and absolute revenue than would be possible using a paid adoption model.

Establishing the aforementioned product attributes to fully leverage the advantages of the freemium model is not achieved through a trivial set of design decisions. The decision to apply the freemium business model to a product is one of the most formative choices made during the development process; it must be made while establishing the product's fundamental use case, and it must inform every aspect of the development process that follows.

The reality of the freemium model is that it can very easily be misapplied. Thus, the decision to employ the freemium model or another commercial framework is first and foremost a function of ability—not whether the *product* should be freemium, but whether the *team* possesses the expertise and experience to produce a successful freemium product. If the answer to this question is yes, but a qualified, conditional, or equivocal yes, then the team is not well positioned for success. The product that emerges from the development process is an external expression of the freemium decision point, while answering the questions, "Can this product succeed as a freemium product?" and, "Is this team capable of implementing the freemium business model?" is a more introspective exercise.

Scale

The potential for scale is essentially the conceptual foundation of the freemium business model. This isn't to say that freemium products must achieve massive scale to succeed; freemium products can be profitable and considered successful at any number of user base sizes. But the characteristics of a product that facilitates massive scale must be in place for a freemium product to achieve the level of adoption required to generate more revenue than it would if it was executed with another business model. These characteristics are low marginal distribution and production costs.

A product's marginal cost of distribution is the cost incurred in delivering an additional purchased unit to a customer. For physical products, these costs are often realized through shipping, storage, licensing, and retail fees, and they tend to decrease with increased volume through economics of scale; that is, the more products shipped, the lower the cost of marginal distribution.

Digital products are distributed through different channels and thus face different distribution cost structures. Often, the only costs associated with distributing a digital product are hosting expenses and platform fees. In aggregate, these costs can be substantial; at the marginal level, however, they are effectively $0.

Production costs are also structured differently for digital and physical goods. Physical goods are composed of materials that must be purchased before the product can be created; likewise, the production process represents an expense, as either a human or a machine must piece the product together from its source materials. Digital products incur no such per-unit production costs; they can be replicated for effectively no cost.

Low marginal distribution and production costs create the opportunity for a product to be adopted by a large number of people, quickly, at little to no expense on the developer's part. This is a prerequisite condition for the freemium model; because its revenue stream is not necessarily contributed to by the entirety of the user base—that is, product use and payment for the product are not mutually inclusive—the product must have the potential to reach and be adopted by a larger number of people than if each user contributed revenue.

Freemium distribution is achieved most often through platforms, or commercial outlets that aggregate products and allow for their discovery through digital storefronts. Platforms provide value through retail functionality such as the ability to comment on products, rate them, and search for them based on keywords. Platforms generally charge a percentage of the revenue generated by the product; a common fee is 30 percent, meaning the platform takes 30 percent of all pre-tax product revenues.

Freemium products can also be distributed on the web with stand-alone websites. Obviously, such a distribution method incurs no platform fees—meaning the developer keeps all revenues it generates—but it also does not benefit from the infrastructure of a platform store (most notably, the ability to search). Web distribution may also be impractical or ineffective for some freemium products, especially mobile products for which installation from the web complicates the adoption process.

The freemium product development cycle may differ fundamentally from the development cycle for paid adoption products; freemium products are generally fluid and are therefore developed through an iterative method. Freemium products also often take the form of software-as-a-service or software-as-a-platform; as such, they evolve over time, based on user preferences and observable behaviors.

The costs incurred in continuous, post-launch development cycles do represent production costs: overhead expenses, such as employee salaries, are shouldered for as long as products are maintained and developed for, which may match the lifetime of the product. But, given low distribution costs and the freemium model's potential for very broad reach, these costs, when distributed over a very large user base, can normalize to a level approaching $0 per unit. In other words, while a given development cycle represents a real and potentially large cash expenditure for a freemium developer, the size of the potential user base that product is capable of being exposed to reduces the marginal cost of production to an immaterial amount.

This dynamic imposes requirements on the total cost of production, however. Freemium products with limited appeal yet high development costs may face more substantial obstacles in reaching profitability than do products with broad appeal. Thus, the scale and scope of production costs should be constrained by the total potential size of the user base; certain product use cases may have limited intrinsic appeal, and the higher their costs of development, the higher the marginal costs of production.

While a non-zero marginal production cost doesn't limit scale in the short term—products that can be distributed for free are still accessible by large numbers of people—it does limit scale in the long run by creating higher threshold requirements for product monetization. In other words, to fund its continued development, a product with niche appeal must capture higher levels of revenue per user than must a product with broad, universal appeal. If this revenue threshold can't be achieved, the product will be shuttered.

Note that massive scale itself is not a condition of the freemium business model; products need not be large to be successful, especially if success is measured in profit relative to what could be expected from the product under the conditions of a different business model. Niche freemium products experiencing high levels of monetization from passionate, dedicated users can achieve success with modestly sized user bases. Similarly, no law of physics restricts to 5 percent the proportion of a user base that monetizes in a freemium product; this number could theoretically reach 100 percent. In practice, the proportion of users monetizing in freemium products is low—often extremely low—and preparing for such an outcome during the development process allows a developer to construct a revenue strategy that more prudently accommodates the realities of freemium monetization.

Thus the 5% rule is not, in fact, a rule; it is a design decision through which the developer embraces the practicalities of the freemium business model, which suggest that a small, dedicated minority of users can monetize to greater aggregate effect than can a larger population of users that has monetized universally through paid access. This design decision is an outgrowth of the freemium model scale requirement: the larger the total user base, the more meaningful will be the minority proportion of users who monetize.

Insight

A second cardinal component of the freemium model is insight, or a methodical, quantitative understanding of user behavior within the context of the product. Insight is achieved through a battery of tools and procedures designed to track the ways users interact with the product, and it is implemented with the goal of optimizing the product's performance relative to some metric.

Insight is a broad term that roughly describes a freemium product's entire data supply chain, from collection to analysis. Freemium product usage is *instrumented* through the use of data collection mechanisms that track the interactions between users and the product; this collected data can be aggregated, audited, and parsed to glean a valuable understanding of what users like and what changes could be made to the product to better serve users' needs.

Insight is composed of two constituent parts that are equally integral to the entire process but require disparate skills to implement. The first part is data collection, or the means through which user interaction is tracked, stored, and made available to data consumers. (Data collection is typically done by the product's developer, but sometimes it is done by the product users themselves). The technical infrastructure—the software and hardware components that accommodate data retrieval, storage, and end-user access—is often encapsulated with the broad term *analytics*.

The second part of insight is the work undertaken to make sense of the data collected and stored in order to improve the product. This work might take the form of regular reporting of key metrics or an analysis of a specific process or product feature in an attempt to understand its performance. These report templates and processes are usually described with the term *business intelligence*.

An important and frequently recurring type of analysis undertaken on freemium products is *user segmentation*, which aims to draw fault lines between the naturally occurring archetypes in the user base and then map the commonalities among them. Such an analysis is especially important in the freemium model, as user archetype groups may exhibit similar payment behavior and thus bring to light meaningful opportunities to optimize revenues.

Because not every user of a freemium product can be expected to directly contribute revenue to the product, the needs of the users who will—the users for whom the product's core use case holds the most appeal—must be identified and catered to with the highest degree of expediency and zeal. Doing this requires understanding what those users pay for and some knowledge of when they pay for things and why. Insight is not mere record collection; it is the process of erecting a model of users' needs from user interaction histories in order to better meet those needs through further product development.

Freemium products encompass such broad and diverse user bases that mere developer intuition is not sufficient for tailoring the product to the desires of the most enthusiastic users. User feedback can take many forms, but perhaps the most salient of those forms is the monetary contribution. Relating that feedback to behavior requires a reasonably sophisticated framework for examining data both from a theoretical perspective and with practical granularity.

Insight into the user base—the ways users interact with the product, the impetuses on which users make purchases, and the factors that inspire users to abandon the product—is required in order to best leverage the advantages of the freemium model. The user base scale the freemium model provides has inherent value in the volume of data able to be mined for instructions on how to best serve the needs of the most enthusiastic users. Even when a user does not contribute monetarily to a product, the data artifacts that user produces can be used to draw conclusions about the product that may be useful in accommodating the users who can and do contribute monetarily.

Scale and insight are therefore complementary and mutually reinforcing: as a product scales in user base size, the data produced by the users and captured by the product confers on the developer additional knowledge about user behavior. This knowledge holds value even when it does not specifically relate to users who pay; all knowledge about user behavior can be used to optimize the product.

Data that is exclusively descriptive of users who don't contribute revenue—even if its only value is helping the developer to build better profiles of exactly that user archetype—establishes between the users and the developer a more robust, more refined channel of understanding, through which the users' needs and preferences can be communicated.

Monetization

Monetization is an obvious requirement of any business model. And despite the fact that the freemium model stipulates a price point of $0, monetization is not a secondary concern for freemium products; in fact, monetization is the nucleus of the freemium experience around which all product features are organized. The difference between monetization in the freemium business model and in the paid access business model is what a transaction delivers to the user. In the paid access model, a transaction delivers admission into a feature set environment that, depending on the amount of research the user conducts prior to purchase, may or may not capably fulfill user expectations. In the freemium model, a transaction delivers an enhanced experience.

The paid access model presents an inherent barrier to adoption with an upfront cost; the greater that cost, the smaller the potential user base. Under paid access conditions, eventual users of the product must meet two requirements: sufficient interest in the product generated by a perceived value equal to or higher than the product's cost, and sufficient disposable income equal to or higher than the product's cost. When these requirements are met for a potential user, that person purchases the product. But two other groups of potential users exist who will not purchase the product: the potential users who do not possess disposable income that matches the product's price, and the potential users who do not believe the product delivers value equal to its price.

The product may be significantly appealing to the first group of potential users; were the product priced lower, matching the lowest common denominator of what users in this group are equipped to pay for it, the product's use case would sufficiently meet those users' needs. To the second group, the product may hold limited appeal, and, likewise, if the price were decreased to match the lowest common denominator of what users in this group consider its value to be, the product's use case would sufficiently meet those users' needs. (See Figure 1.1.)

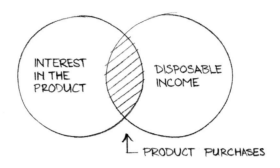

FIGURE 1.1

Purchases occur at the intersection between sufficient interest and sufficient disposable income.

In the abstract, the lowest common price denominator of both potential users groups—what users with low disposable incomes and what disinterested users are willing and prepared to pay for the product—is $0. In the paid access model, where the price of the product is paid up front, only the users with the greatest enthusiasm for the product and the means to purchase it are able to access its full feature set. But in the freemium model, all users in all three groups are given access to a limited feature set and invited to pay for additional functionality.

The advantages of the freemium business model are thus realized under two sets of circumstances. The first is when a subset of the group lacking disposable income, who otherwise would not have purchased the paid access product, experiences a fortuitous change in financial stature. These users, having adopted the freemium product upon discovery, are now able to spend money on additional functionality within a product they have already familiarized themselves with.

These same users, had they discovered only a paid access version of the same product, might not have purchased when their financial stature changed for any of several reasons: perhaps they forgot about the product, or perhaps they found a comparable freemium product, or perhaps they felt alienated by the product's price requirement. Whatever the case, and no matter how small this group of users might be, under these circumstances the freemium product would likely capture more total revenues from this group than would the paid access product.

The second, and more common, set of circumstances under which the freemium model boasts advantages over the paid access model is when some subset of users who can afford and want to purchase the paid access product are capable of extracting value from it in excess of its price—in other words, the product is worth more to the users than what the developer is charging for it. When a freemium product's revenue strategy provides a broad spectrum of levels across which users can potentially monetize, each user is given the agency to enjoy the product to whatever extent the user's disposable income provides for. A considerable amount of money may have been lost had the product been monetized exclusively through an upfront, singular price point.

The goal of the freemium model is to optimize for the second set of circumstances: to give those users who find the most value in the project the latitude to extract as much delight from it as possible. When this condition is met, the benefits of the freemium model are unlocked and can create a revenue dynamic that eclipses what would have been possible under paid access conditions. But the pricing model required to establish such a level of monetization is not inherent in every product with a price point of $0; rather, establishing such a pricing model requires significant effort and strategic consideration.

Optimization

As noted earlier, freemium products are generally developed under the auspices of the iterative method because of the aforementioned pillars of freemium design—scale, insight, and monetization—in that the developer must collect and parse data on the habits of its users before it can improve upon the product to an appreciable extent. The faster the developer implements these improvements, the faster the fruits of that labor are gained. Therefore, the iterative development mantra is to make decisions as fast as possible on sufficiently sized but not superfluous volumes of data.

Optimization is the process of converting data about user behavior into product improvements that increase some performance metric. These improvements are generally incremental and, individually, not wholly significant. The purpose of implementing them quickly, after studied and careful measurement, is that the improvements can compound each other and result in appreciable performance enhancements in a shorter amount of time than with the *waterfall model*, which consists of sequential, end-to-end development cycles punctuated by full product releases.

Optimization is a delicate process that can sometimes resemble a development tightrope walk. Too much emphasis on optimization can result in new product features or content being sidelined, and too little can leave potentially valuable performance improvements unexploited. Like any other element of software development, optimization incurs costs: direct costs in the form of developer time and focus, opportunity costs by not pursuing other development goals over the course of implementing optimizations, and hidden costs. The hidden costs of optimization are the hardest to measure, as they are usually the result of too narrow a focus on optimizing existing processes. In other words, when a developer's enthusiasm for optimization exceeds a certain threshold, the developer can lose sight of the product's long-term performance and instead pursue improvements to specific processes that render only short-term, incremental product gains.

The concept of product changes producing competing effects is predicated on the idea that optimization takes two forms: *local optimization* improves the performance of a process, while *global optimization* improves the overall performance of the product. Both forms of optimization are necessary, but global optimization is more abstruse and requires a broad understanding of the user experience and a definition of product success (usually related to revenue). Whereas local optimizations are easy to undertake and evaluate—a process either improves relative to its previous state or it doesn't—global optimization requires a much longer measurement scope and the organizational wherewithal to think about the product in the abstract. For these reasons, local optimizations are potentially easier to both execute and build design decisions around, but the gains made from local optimizations may be illusory if they haven't been thoughtfully considered as part of a global optimization strategy. In fact, local optimizations may produce negative long-term results when undertaken aggressively or without considering the secondary effects on other processes or performance metrics.

For instance, when monetization mechanics are rendered highly visible, many of them improve with respect to revenue performance, but they may also alienate users. When measuring the effect of the optimization on a specific process (local optimization), a product manager might consider the change a success; when measuring the effect of the optimization on the rate of satisfaction on the entire user base (global optimization), a product manager might consider the change a failure. Thus, a delicate balance must be struck between continually designing and implementing tests that bring real performance improvements to the product and ensuring that the net aggregate effects of these optimizations are positive at the product level. This dual focus can be achieved only through the aforementioned insight: systems that measure both short- and long-term impacts and can alert a product manager to negative trends as they emerge.

Freemium products are often designed as platforms that will evolve over years; short-term thinking with respect to process improvements is necessary, but it must also be tempered by the understanding that, to continue to serve the needs and tastes of its users, a product must evolve, not rapidly transform. Small, iterative process improvements over long time frames allow for slight but impactful changes to be quickly implemented (and potentially reversed) without taking for granted users' desires for stability and consistency.

Optimization allows the freemium model to flourish by adapting the product to the needs and tastes of its users, but it must be undertaken methodically. While it is important, optimization must be seen as a tool that can be utilized in the development process and not as a development strategy itself. As an application of data and quantitative methods, optimization should not be substituted for product development; rather, it should be used to heighten the effects of already-developed product features, with the goal of achieving long-term performance improvements.

Freemium economics

The freemium business model does not exist in an intellectual vacuum; a number of established, mainstream economic principles can be used to describe the dynamics of a freemium system at the levels of both the user and the product. Since the purpose of the freemium model is to allow for scale and optimize for monetization from the most engaged portion of the user base, the focal points of an academic analysis of the model are necessarily price and supply.

Academic models are generally drafted in the abstract; although the aim of this book is to establish a practical framework for the development of freemium products, an overview of the economic principles undergirding the business model is valuable because the freemium model is so broadly applicable. Freemium products exist across a wide range of software verticals, or categories of software products grouped around a specific purpose or theme; an overly specific prescription for freemium development would necessarily be restricted to a single vertical (or perhaps even a single product) and would therefore limit the applicability of the framework. Such an approach would do a disservice to the freemium model; as a flexible, dynamic, commercial structure, viable across a range of platforms and demographic profiles, it deserves the utmost conceptual consideration. A survey of the economic principles contributing to its expansive viability is therefore necessary in providing a complete yet pliable practical framework for developing freemium products.

Price elasticity of demand

In his book, *Principles of Economics*, originally published in 1890, the economist Alfred Marshall unified a number of the disparate and nascent economic theories of the time into a coherent intellectual tapestry oriented primarily around the price effects of supply and demand. One concept Marshall posited was that of the *price elasticity of demand*, which describes the degree to which changes in price affect the volume of demand for a good. Elasticity in this sense relates to consumer responsiveness to price changes. Marshall proposed that price changes generally correlate negatively with consumer demand; that is, as the price of a good increases, consumer demand for that good decreases. This is a direct application of the law of demand as Marshall defined, which describes the inverse relationship between the price of a good and the quantity demanded, all other characteristics of that product and external market forces remaining equal.

The law of demand is generally visually represented with a *demand curve*, as depicted in Figure 1.2. A typical demand curve is constructed with price (*P*) on the

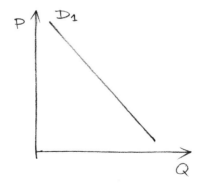

FIGURE 1.2

A linear demand curve.

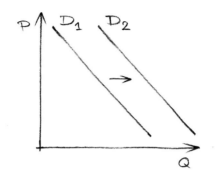

FIGURE 1.3

A demand curve shift to the right.

y-axis and quantity (Q) on the x-axis; the curve can be linear, indicating a constant relationship between the price of a good and quantity demanded, or nonlinear, indicating a changing relationship between price and quantity at various price points.

Movement along the curve happens when the price of a good changes but overall consumer sentiment and market conditions do not; a *demand curve shift* is said to take place when market dynamics change. A demand curve shift to the right is illustrated in Figure 1.3.

Broadly speaking, demand curve shifts for products are catalyzed by changes in consumers' abilities or desires to purchase a product, such as population migrations from rural to urban areas, worldwide economic recessions and recoveries, large-scale technological innovation, and other global or ultra-regional developments.

Within the context of market dynamics for software products, demand shifts are generally precipitated by either one or both of two factors:

- A change in the *total addressable market* for a product. In some cases this change is instituted through the increased adoption or deprecation of technology platforms (such as the increased demand for mobile applications brought about by the popularization of tablet computing), and in other cases is caused by changes in government regulations, decreased materials or production costs, etc.
- The evolution of tastes and expectations. As a product vertical matures, users become accustomed to a higher level of sophistication and functionality and develop increasingly demanding requirements on products in that vertical at a specific price point. This tends to gradually shift the demand curve for products in a vertical to the left, as rising levels of competition and consumer scrutiny reduce profit margins.

By definition, *normal goods* are those for which demand shifts in the same direction as changes to disposable income: as income increases, demand increases, and vice versa. This is at odds with the behavior of *inferior goods*, for which demand shifts in the opposite direction from that of changes to disposable income: as income increases, demand decreases, and vice versa. Inferior goods are more affordable

$$e_{(r)} = \frac{dQ}{dP}$$

FIGURE 1.4

The coefficient of price elasticity of demand.

relative to normal goods but are not necessarily of a lower quality; preference for normal goods relative to inferior goods could arise for any number of reasons.

Price elasticity of demand is measured in terms of movement along a demand curve. Marshall described this relationship as the coefficient of price elasticity of demand; this is illustrated in Figure 1.4, where dQ represents a percentage change in demand from one point on the demand curve to another, and dP represents a percentage change in price between those same two points.

When e is exactly -1, the product is considered to be *unit elastic*, meaning any change in price is met with an equal change in quantity demanded. When e falls between -1 and $-\infty$, meaning the percentage change in quantity demanded is greater than the causal change in price, the product is considered to be *relatively elastic*: small changes in price can cause large swings in demand. This is true of goods for which many *substitute goods*, or products that are considered effective alternatives and between which consumers are relatively indifferent, exist. When e falls between -1 and 0, meaning the percentage change in quantity demanded is less than the causal change in price, the product is considered to be *relatively inelastic*: large changes in price are met with relatively small changes in quantity demanded. This is true of goods that are considered *necessity goods*, or products for which few alternatives exist and without which consumers' lives would be adversely affected.

Two theoretical scenarios also exist: those of *perfect inelasticity* and *perfect elasticity*. A perfectly inelastic product—a product for which $e = 0$—incurs no change in demand due to any change in price. In other words, demand is constant across all price levels and is completely insensitive to price; this represents the theoretical scenario where a supplier has a total monopoly on the production of an absolute necessity good, and demand exists at a constant level.

A perfectly elastic product—a product for which $e = -\infty$—incurs absolute change in demand due to any change in price. This means that demand is infinitely sensitive to price, representing the theoretical scenario where a product could immediately be replaced with an infinite number of perfect substitutes. That is, an infinitesimally small increase in price reduces demand to zero, and an infinitesimally small decrease in price increases demand infinitely. (See Figure 1.5.)

The coefficient of price elasticity is only positive (i.e., price and quantity demanded move in the same direction) for two types of goods: *Veblen goods* and *Giffen goods*. Veblen goods, named after economist Thorstein Veblen, are luxury goods for which quality is considered a direct function of price. These goods are generally purchased in pursuit of status and therefore exhibit reverse demand sensitivity; as the price of a Veblen good decreases, demand for that good decreases as a result of a perceived decrease in status.

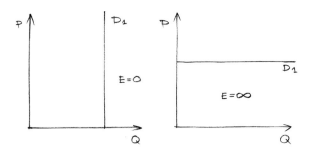

FIGURE 1.5

A perfectly inelastic product (*left*) and a perfectly elastic product (*right*).

Giffen goods, named after economist Sir Robert Giffen (although the concept was articulated by Alfred Marshall), are staple goods consumed as part of a basket of goods and for which no sufficient substitute exists. The quantity demanded of Giffen goods increases with price because, since no alternative for the Giffen good exists, the other goods in the basket are abandoned out of necessity. Giffen goods are generally inferior goods, and the phenomenon of Giffen goods usually takes place under circumstances of poverty. The prototypical example of a Giffen good is an inferior staple food item; as the price of that food item increases, consumers with constricted budgets are prevented from buying supplementary food items because they must apportion the remainder of their budgets to increased volumes of the inferior food item.

Price discrimination

The price elasticity of demand describes a dynamic where price sensitivity impacts the volume of goods sold at various price levels. But this concept is predicated on the assumption that only one price exists for any given product; that is, a supplier participating in a competitive marketplace uses only its marginal cost of production and the concept of price elasticity of demand to inform its pricing strategy and optimize total revenue.

In highly transparent markets with little barrier to entry, where a large number of suppliers produce near-perfect substitute goods, suppliers price their goods according to the intersection of the demand curve and their *supply curve*. A supply curve, like a demand curve, represents a series of points on the plane constructed with price (P) on the y-axis and quantity (Q) on the x-axis.

The supply curve slopes upward because, all other things equal, a supplier should be willing to produce more products at a higher sale price than at a lower sale price. The point at which the supply and demand curves meet is called the *equilibrium price*; this is the price P_1 at which the entire quantity Q_1 will be sold. Figure 1.6 illustrates a supply and demand curve meeting at equilibrium price *EP*.

While Q_1 units of the product are sold at the equilibrium price *EP*, the demand curve does not originate at this price point; it originates at the demand curve's intercept on the y-axis, P_0, which represents a price point at which no consumers would

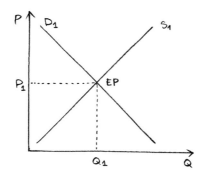

FIGURE 1.6

Consumer surplus is the area bounded by EP, P1, and the point at which the demand curve intercepts the y-axis (P0).

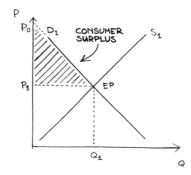

FIGURE 1.7

Consumer surplus, bounded by points *EP*, P_1 QUOTE and P_0.

be willing to purchase the product. Thus some units of the product could be sold at price levels between P_0 and Q_1; the total value of these units is the area of the polygon bounded by price points *EP*, P_1, and P_0.

This value is known as *consumer surplus*, and it represents a form of savings for consumers who were prepared to purchase the product at price points between P_0 and P_1 but were offered the product at the cheaper price of *EP*. Consumer surplus exists when a supplier imposes only one price point on its product, but the surplus can be captured by the supplier if the consumers willing to pay prices on the demand curve between P_0 and P_1 can be identified, segmented, and specifically marketed to. See Figure 1.7.

The process of offering different prices to different consumer segments, rather than pricing a product at its equilibrium price, is known as *price discrimination* (or *price differentiation*). The price point at which an individual consumer is willing to purchase a product is known as that consumer's *reserve price*; by charging consumers their individual reserve prices, down to the equilibrium price, a supplier maximizes its total potential revenue.

Price discrimination is generally considered to take three forms, as defined by economist Arthur Pigou in his book *Economics of Welfare*, first published in 1920. *First-degree price discrimination* occurs when a supplier charges consumers their individual reserve prices; this represents total consumer surplus capture by the supplier.

A few conditions must exist for first-degree price discrimination (sometimes called *perfect price discrimination*) to take place. First, the supplier must be a *price maker*; that is, the seller must exert sufficient control over the market of a good or service to be able to dictate prices. This is usually possible when the supplier is a monopoly or a member of an oligopoly participating in *collusion*, or organized price fixing. Under circumstances of perfect competition, first-degree price discrimination is difficult to achieve, as consumers being charged their higher relative reserve prices can migrate freely to suppliers charging equilibrium prices.

The second condition is the existence of a spectrum of reserve prices across a group of consumers. If all potential consumers have the same reserve price (which is usually the case in highly transparent markets, where consumers are aware of supplier profit margins and pricing schedules), then consumer surplus is 0.

The third condition is that consumer segments are isolated and cannot form secondary markets on which to sell the product. If secondary markets for the product emerge and consumers can resell the product between segments, then arbitrage opportunities will surface for consumers who were offered lower prices to sell to consumers who were offered higher prices, and the pricing systems will converge.

Second-degree price discrimination occurs when a supplier knows that multiple demand curves for its product exist but the supplier is not capable of identifying, prior to a sale, the level of each consumer's reserve price. In such a scenario, in order to increase total revenue, the supplier can establish different pricing tiers within its product without knowing about the consumers before they make purchases. A typical example of second-degree price discrimination is how tiered airline seating works: an airline knows that business travelers are willing to pay more for air travel than leisure travelers, but the airline cannot distinguish between the two groups before the travelers purchase tickets. By establishing both first class and economy seat tiers, the airline can capture additional revenues from business travelers based on their higher reserve prices by allowing them to self-select into the first class tier.

Third-degree price discrimination occurs when the supplier knows that multiple demand curves for its product exist across different groups of consumers and it can identify, prior to a sale, members of each group. In such a scenario, the supplier can establish price tiers valid only for specific groups and based on the principle of inverse elasticity, which posits that prices should be relatively high for consumers exhibiting demand curves with low price elasticity (i.e., consumers with little price sensitivity). This is known as *Ramsey pricing*, so named after economist Frank Ramsey, and is usually manifest when suppliers sell products to multiple markets, each with different levels of price elasticity. An oft-cited example of third-degree price discrimination is the relatively high price of food in airports; because airports represent a market where consumers' price elasticity is low (given the consumers' captive nature), food outlets can charge more for equivalent products inside airports than they can outside of airports.

Pareto efficiency

Pareto efficiency describes a state of resource allocation where no participant's situation can be improved upon without another participant's situation worsening. The concept is part of a broad body of work produced by economist Vilfredo Pareto in the late nineteenth and early twentieth centuries. Pareto efficiency represents a specific state of allocation that may not be equitable; that is, while no individual's situation can be improved upon without another's being impaired, a large disparity can exist between individuals' situations within the state of Pareto efficiency. The pursuit of Pareto efficiency—that is, making changes to the allocation of resources that improve the situation of one individual without worsening the situation of any other—are called *Pareto improvements*.

Pareto efficiency is measured in terms of *utility*, which is an abstract quantification of consumer satisfaction. Under conditions of finite resources, the best allocation of resources at the individual consumer level is that which maximizes that consumer's utility. This notion of maximized utility is often expressed as a curve with many points, with each point representing different combinations of goods, all of which produce the same value of utility. Such a curve is called an *indifference curve* (illustrated in Figure 1.8), so named because a consumer is indifferent to the various combinations of goods, given that they all produce the same amount of utility.

Because indifference curves describe a quantity of physical goods, they can be rendered only in the positive quadrant of a graph (i.e., the top right portion of a standard Cartesian plane, where both axes have positive values). Indifference curves

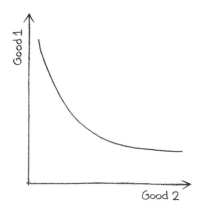

FIGURE 1.8

An indifference curve.

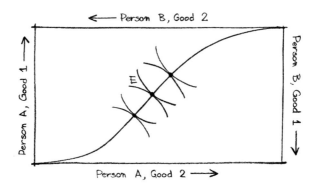

FIGURE 1.9

A contract curve.

are negatively sloped because resource constraints are considered concrete: the total frontier of allocation cannot extend beyond the real limitations of the consumer's ability to procure more goods. The bowed shape, or convexity toward the origin, of an indifference curve is a result of a concept called *diminishing marginal utility* (or Gossen's first law). Diminishing marginal utility describes the decreasing per-unit utility of a good that a consumer already has; because each additional unit of a good produces less utility than the unit acquired before it, the consumer is less willing to displace a unit of another good for it. The curvature of the indifference curve reflects this.

A *contract curve* is a set of points containing the intersections of all indifference curves between two parties, each trading one good, and produces a Pareto efficient outcome. A contract curve is constructed in what is known as an *Edgeworth box*: a four-axis graph on which individual parties are represented by origins at the bottom left and top right corners, with each commodity being put on an axis and running in the opposing direction to the axis across from it. Figure 1.9 depicts a contract curve between two individuals, A and B, who are trading in two goods, 1 and 2, with an equilibrium trade point of *E*.

Given that both individuals start with a discrete allocation of resources and are free to trade with each other, the contract curve evolves to represent the points at which both parties would stop trading, having reached Pareto efficiency. In game theory, the concept of *Pareto domination* is used to compare a set of points that are Pareto efficient: when one point P_1 is at least as beneficial for every individual as another point P_2, but at least one individual prefers P_2 to P_1, then P_2 is said to Pareto dominate P_1. And when a point P_X exists that no other point Pareto dominates, P_X is said to be *Pareto optimal*.

In 1950, two employees of the RAND corporation, Melvin Dresher and Merrill Flood, developed a game to illustrate the fact that a *non-zero-sum game*—that is, a set of transactions between two parties where each party's loss is not necessarily accounted for by an attendant gain by the other party—could produce a unique equilibrium outcome which is not Pareto optimal. The game became known as the

	CRIMINAL 2 CONFESS	CRIMINAL 2 NO CONFESS
CRIMINAL 1 CONFESS	(-3,-3)	(0,-5)
CRIMINAL 1 NO CONFESS	(-5,0)	(-1,-1)

FIGURE 1.10

Potential payoff options for a prisoner's dilemma.

Prisoner's Dilemma, and it serves as an example of the conflict between one individual's dominant strategy, absent knowledge of the actions of other individuals, and group rationality under non-zero-sum conditions.

The premise of the Prisoner's Dilemma, as defined in narrative form by mathematician Albert Tucker, is that two criminals have been arrested for committing a crime together and are being interrogated separately, in different rooms, by one district attorney. The district attorney realizes that he does not have enough evidence against the pair to convict them for the crime and admits as much to each one, although he notes that he has enough evidence to convict them on a lesser charge. The district attorney offers each criminal the following bargain:

- If one confesses and the other does not, the person who confessed goes free (payoff 0) and the other receives a heavy sentence (payoff −5).
- If both confess, each receives a medium sentence (payoff −3).
- If neither confesses, each receives a light sentence for the lesser charge (payoff −1).

The choices and outcomes facing the criminals are represented in Figure 1.10. The dominant strategy for both criminals, individually, is to confess; each criminal is better off confessing no matter what the other criminal does. But this outcome is non-Pareto optimal, as both players would be better off not confessing; if both criminals confess, they're both worse off than if neither had confessed.

The conceptual foundation of the Prisoner's Dilemma lies at the heart of many social phenomena and informs modern digital pricing strategy, given low or zero marginal distribution and production costs. When deciding whether or not to reduce the price of its products, a developer may reason that a price cut could attract a rival developer's customers to its own products, compensating for the loss of per-unit income with sales volume. Likewise, if the developer believes its rival will cut prices, it reasons that it must also cut prices to remain competitive. In either scenario, the developer's dominant strategy is to cut its prices; when the rival engages in the same logic, it also cuts prices. The end result is a loss for both developers, having forced prices down without capturing additional market share.

An eventual price floor emerges in such a scenario, usually representing the developers' marginal costs of production and distribution, around which the market converges. Once this price floor has been established as a standard, ascending above it is difficult, given consumer expectations and the fear of market share capture by rival developers.

Freemium product case studies

There is perhaps no better means of understanding the fundamental principles of the freemium model than by examining them through the lens of highly successful freemium products. Certainly there is no shortage of successful freemium products from which to draw case studies; an entire book could be written consisting of nothing but case studies.

The three products presented in these case studies were selected based on a specific set of criteria. The first criterion was that the product achieved scale in a relatively short amount of time through viral features. In considering only products that achieved appreciable virality, each case study provides a context against which the discussion in chapter 7 can be considered. This requirement dismisses products with user bases developed primarily through paid advertising (which is outside the reach of most small freemium developers).

The second criterion was that the product was available on multiple platforms, if not at the time of initial launch, then shortly thereafter. The goal of this book is to provide a framework for developing freemium products, irrespective of the platform on which the product is designed to operate. By choosing products that work across a broad range of platforms (and, with some products, a broad range of devices), the implementation of the freemium model, and not the idiosyncrasies of the product's platform, are isolated for examination.

The third criterion was that the product achieved considerable scale. As has been discussed, while the potential for massive scale is a hallmark of the freemium model, many freemium products have achieved success with modest user bases composed of zealous, enthusiastic users. But these products tend to appeal to a narrow demographic scope: users with generous amounts of both disposable time and income. In order for a freemium case study to be broadly applicable to a large number of product verticals, it needs to appeal to a diverse cross-section of potential users.

The case studies are presented at the beginning of the book to frame what follows and to add depth to the topics explored later in the book by way of example. While they are not exhaustive, these case studies do cover a wide range of use cases, geographic points of initial development, and company sizes. The cases were selected with care to serve as a practical introduction to the freemium business model.

Skype

Skype is a software application that facilitates Voice-over-Internet-Protocol (VoIP) calling functionality. In its initial incarnation, VoIP allowed users to speak to each other through the Skype application over the Internet; over time, the application evolved to provide a rich feature set such as video calls, file transfer, group calls, and chat. Skype eventually grew into a platform used by more than 600 million people and, after a tumultuous period (which included multiple complicated transactions that changed the ownership structure of its parent company, as well as a formal filing by its parent company for an initial public offering [IPO] and the subsequent retraction of that filing), Microsoft acquired Skype's parent company in 2011 for $8.5 billion.

The origins of Skype are inextricably linked with the origins of Kazaa, a peer-to-peer file sharing service developed by three Estonians, Jaan Tallinn, Ahti Heinla, and Priit Kasesalu, using their proprietary peer-to-peer technology framework, FastTrack P2P. Kazaa operated without the use of a central routing server; instead, users of the service formed a network across which files were transferred, with the speed of transfer dependent on the number of users online. While Kazaa was eventually shuttered, having faced a battery of legal issues related to the trade of pirated and otherwise illegal materials made possible by the program, the core technology powering the product lived on as the functional core of Skype.

Kazaa and its FastTrack P2P technology platform were purchased by entrepreneurs Niklas Zennström and Janus Friis (from Sweden and Denmark, respectively), who, in turn, sold Kazaa to Sharman Networks in 2002. Zennström and Friis, along with the Estonian developers of FastTrack P2P, began developing Skype soon afterward. The first beta version of Skype was released in August 2003; it was a free download exclusively for the Windows operating system. Using the software, two users could call each other using their computers' speakers and microphones.

Like Kazaa, Skype's network consisted of no central servers; calls were routed through the network established between users. As a result, the larger the network grew, the more stable and robust it became; similarly, Skype calls between users in sparsely populated areas were capable of higher fidelity than some cellular telephone network operators were able to provide, given that those regions are generally underserved by cellular coverage. In June 2004, Skype launched a beta version of its product on the Linux operating system, and in August 2004, Skype launched a beta version for Macintosh computers.

Skype eventually added chat functionality and video conferencing to its client (all of which was available for free) and introduced its initial monetization mechanic with paid calls to physical phones via traditional phone networks in what it called SkypeOut. Paid calls could be made from a Skype client to any phone number around the world; because the international rates Skype charged were often cheaper than those offered by telecommunications companies, Skype, over time, became a major carrier of international telephone volume. From 2005 to 2012, Skype's share of worldwide international telephone call traffic grew from 2.9 percent to 34 percent.

From its earliest days, Skype's user base growth was meteoric. By 2006, the service had grown to 100 million users; by the third quarter of 2009, that number had ballooned to 500 million. But while revenues grew with the user base, profit was elusive: in its filing for an initial public offering in August 2010, Skype's parent company noted that only 6 percent of Skype users contributed revenue (although average revenues for that user group sat at $96 per year) and that its net income for the first half of 2010 was a mere $13 million on revenues of $406 million.

Throughout its history, Skype had experimented with various revenue streams, including Skype-branded phones, but by the time it filed paperwork for an IPO (the last point at which public financial records for the company are available), the bulk of its revenue stream was represented by SkypeOut calls. In 2010, Skype's board appointed a new CEO: Tony Bates, a veteran of Cisco. Bates' ambition was to increase Skype's ability to monetize by increasing the scope of Skype's brand appeal from a purely consumer platform to a fully capable business telecommunications solution. This was achieved through a number of product initiatives, the most prominent of which was probably the paid Skype Premium account upgrade, which allowed a user to organize video conference calls between more than two participants, among other things. Before its acquisition by Microsoft, Skype also introduced advertising products that users saw during phone calls.

Skype's success materialized despite the difficulties it faced in generating revenue. because its user base grew at an impressive, continuous clip from inception. From the very beginning, Skype was an inherently viral product; it couldn't be used without adding contacts, and as the service became synonymous with free telephone functionality, it spread virally, primarily through word of mouth. In fact, the word Skype eventually evolved into a verb in colloquial use; to "Skype" someone means to call them via Skype.

This rapid adoption likely contributed to the challenges Skype faced in monetizing users; as the product became more and more commonplace, fewer users needed to use its paid SkypeOut functionality. In other words, the growth of its free product essentially cannibalized revenues from its paid product, as both products essentially served the same use case: voice communication between people. The proliferation of smartphones in Western markets most likely exacerbated this dynamic, because not only did many users carry a Skype-capable device with them everywhere, but that device allowed for free video calling, whereas SkypeOut calls to physical phones did not.

By the time Microsoft acquired it, Skype boasted incredible breadth: 600 million global users (100 million of them active each month) across a variety of devices ranging from desktop computers to mobile phones and tablets. Users were using Skype to make telephone calls, host video conference calls, and send SMS messages. Skype had grown to form a truly integral layer of the modern communications amalgam when it was purchased and had accomplished it all with a fairly humble number of employees (500 as of the time of its IPO filing) distributed throughout multiple offices around the world.

Spotify

Spotify is an application that allows a user to stream music over the Internet. The application initially launched with two tiers of functionality: free and premium. The free tier, which launched as invite-only, imposed limits on usage, exposed the user to advertising, and was only available on the desktop; the premium tier offered ad-free, unlimited usage across multiple devices. Spotify's parent company had negotiated licensing agreements with a broad range of record labels, both large and small, upon its initial launch, which ensured that all usage of the service complied with copyright restrictions.

Spotify's parent company, Spotify AB, was founded in Sweden in 2006 by Daniel Ek and Martin Lorentzon, who had worked together previously at a Swedish marketing company called Tradedoubler. The genesis of Spotify was precipitated by a discussion between Ek and Ludvig Strigeus, the Swedish developer behind uTorrent, one of the most popular clients for BitTorrent, the peer-to-peer file sharing protocol. Ek, who had been interested in pursuing a music streaming project, realized that Strigeus' peer-to-peer expertise was the key component to developing such a service, and, together with Lorentzon, purchased uTorrent from Strigeus, only to sell it to the company behind BitTorrent. Ek and Lorentzon subsequently retained Strigeus to develop the peer-to-peer framework that would later evolve into Spotify.

Spotify initially experienced impressive but measured growth: by the end of 2009, a little more than a year after its initial launch, the service had garnered 6.5 million registered users. The service's growth was limited by a number of factors, most of which are the result of the dynamics of a two-sided marketplace. Spotify is essentially a medium through which content consumers (the application's users) connect with content providers (music labels); in order to facilitate the provision of content from providers to consumers, Spotify must manage relationships with the legal entities that control how music labels engage with intermediaries.

Because of the labyrinthine legal and procedural morass through which Spotify must continually navigate, the service has been rolled out on a country-by-country basis (usually in groups of countries). This natural impediment to large-scale, universal adoption was unavoidable: users in countries where agreements had not yet been struck between Spotify and the commercial associations that dictate the terms of streaming and downloading music were simply not permitted to install the application.

Music labels, too, had to be courted. To accomplish this, Spotify enlisted the help of perhaps one of the most highly visible luminaries in the technology sector at the time: Sean Parker, one of the original founders of Napster and the founding president of Facebook. Parker actually approached Spotify first, professing his admiration for the service in a 1,700-word missive to Daniel Ek. Shortly after, Parker invested $15 million into Spotify through the Founder's Fund, a venture capital firm Parker was a partner in. The investment led to Parker assuming a board seat; it was in this capacity that Parker negotiated key agreements between Spotify and the Warner and Universal music labels.

But perhaps the biggest coup Parker engineered was a partnership between Spotify and Facebook. From its initial launch, Spotify facilitated social sharing through linking: users could link to a specific song or a playlist they had created, linking by email, in chat, or on social networks like Facebook. The inclusion of these initial social features helped propel Spotify's growth, but the company's partnership with Facebook took that virality channel a step further: at Facebook's annual f8 conference in 2011, Sean Parker announced that Facebook and Spotify had come to an agreement to more deeply integrate Spotify into Facebook's "open graph," the data interface that facilitates sharing on Facebook.

Spotify's partnership with Facebook, which came mere months after the service launched in the United States, contributed to an intense surge in growth that year. From September 15th, 2011 (a few days before the Facebook partnership was launched) through December 2012, Spotify's user base doubled, from 10 million to 20 million users. Even more impressive was Spotify's rate of conversion; on December 6th, 2012, Spotify announced that 5 million of its 20 million active users, or 25 percent, were paying subscribers. A month earlier, Spotify raised approximately $100 million on a valuation of $3 billion from investors including Goldman Sachs and Coca-Cola.

Spotify's remarkable percentage of paying users was likely the result of its product strategy; in October 2009, Spotify offered an "offline mode" for its premium product tier, allowing users to download songs to their devices for non-streaming listening as long as their subscriptions were valid. And in May 2010, Spotify expanded its product portfolio to include an "unlimited" option, which provided the same feature set as the premium option but was limited to desktop clients, and an "open" option, which provided a reduced-functionality version of the free tier (with the free tier remaining invite-only). The free account types were combined into one in April 2011, with the amount of music accessible to free-tier users limited to 10 hours per month. New users, however, were not subject to this limitation for their first six months of product use.

Spotify's success as a freemium product can be attributed to the breadth and ingenuity of its product portfolio and the virality it experienced from its social features. Upon its initial launch, Spotify's product strategy involved engaging with the user on an unpaid basis, establishing regular use patterns, and then enticing the user to upgrade to a paid account tier. And once users had upgraded, they were incentivized to keep their subscriptions current through Spotify's offline mode, which only allows a user access to their downloaded songs while their subscription is active (the downloaded songs are deleted upon subscription lapse). By bundling cross-device functionality based on payment—paid accounts provide access through an unlimited number of the user's devices—the most engaged users are prompted to upgrade in order to access their music whenever they want. Aligning monetization with enthusiasm allows Spotify's premium users to feel that they are not only unlocking additional functionality with their payments, they are also unlocking omnipresence.

In terms of distribution, Spotify's viral, social strategy served as the engine of its initial growth. The ability to link to objects within the application allows users to simultaneously share the efforts of their playlist creation and incite new users to adopt the product. And through its partnership with Facebook, Spotify allows its viral dispatches to be associated with the feel-good sentiment of new artist discovery: what are essentially advertisements for the service on Facebook can be interpreted by their recipients as a courtesy by Spotify. This passive viral strategy was extremely effective in instilling initial growth in Spotify's user base, and by incorporating social features into the product, Spotify ensured that its growth would experience compounding effects.

Candy Crush Saga

Candy Crush Saga is a puzzle game published by King, the London-based social game developer. The game was released on Facebook in April 2012 and experienced considerable success on that platform, claiming the top position (in terms of daily active users, or DAU) from Zynga, which Zynga had held non-stop for years, in January 2013. The game soared on mobile, where it was released for both the iOS and Android platforms in November 2012; in December 2012 alone, the game was downloaded more than 10 million times. Candy Crush Saga breached the Top 10 Grossing list, overall, for the iPhone in the United States—a considerable feat— on December 4th, 2012, and reached the number 1 position on March 11th, 2013. Such positions on the Top 10 Grossing list, which sorts applications by revenue, are indicative of substantial daily revenue generation, usually in the range of hundreds of thousands to millions of dollars.

King was founded in 2003 as Midasplayer International Holding Co. with the intention of developing web-based games, primarily for Yahoo! but also for its own website and other portals. The company was founded by Riccardo Zacconi, Patrik Stymne, Lars Markgren, Toby Rowland, Sebastian Knutsson, and Thomas Hartwig, six former employees of a company called Spray. Spray had ambitions of launching an initial public offering in March 2000, but those plans were sidelined when the market for stock listings soured in the face of the burst of the dotcom bubble, and the company was sold. Three years after the sale, the six co-founders, with Zacconi at the helm as CEO, formed Midasplayer International Holdings Co., and in 2005, the company raised nearly $50 million from investors Apax Partners and Index Ventures. Shortly after the investment, the company rebranded as King.com.

King.com published a wide variety of games on its own website and across a number of partner websites and portals. The company specialized in what it called "skill games"—primarily puzzle, strategy, and board games—and built a competitive social platform on its site where members could participate in tournaments and compare their performances against each other through leaderboards. The impetus for the change in brand name was a player ranking system that bestows titles onto users, ranging from "Peasant" to "King," based on the users' achievements in the company's portfolio of casual games.

The rise of Facebook as a gaming platform provided King.com with an additional medium on which to market and distribute its games, and the company quickly emerged as one of the social network's top gaming providers. In July 2012, King.com boasted 11 million DAU on Facebook, behind Zynga (at 48 million) but ahead of Electronic Arts (at 9.5 million). At that time, King.com's largest game, measured by DAU, was Bubble Witch Saga, a witch-themed bubble shooter puzzle game first launched on Facebook in September 2011. Bubble Witch Saga was King. com's first foray into mobile: the game was released for iOS in July 2012.

Candy Crush Saga's release on Facebook in April 2012 catalyzed a sea change on Facebook's gaming platform; less than one year after release, in March 2013, King.com's Candy Crush Saga took the number 1 position from Zynga's FarmVille 2. And a month later, in April 2013, the company, which had rebranded itself simply as King on its tenth anniversary in late March 2013, announced that it had surpassed Zynga in terms of DAU on Facebook, with 66 million daily users to Zynga's 52 million.

Candy Crush Saga was a major contributor to King's ascension up the Facebook charts. The game belongs to the "match 3" puzzle family, which describes a game board filled with shapes of varying colors; the positions of any two of the shapes can be swapped to create either a vertical or horizontal line of three or more similarly colored shapes. When those shapes are matched, they disappear from the board, and the shapes above the void created by their absence drop, with new shapes appearing at the top of the board. Each match earns the player points, and various combinations, special shape matches, and lengths of matches can engage point multipliers that increase the player's total score.

In Candy Crush Saga, the shapes are candies, and the game progresses through levels separated into episodes. Levels are completed by satisfying either a points requirement or a predetermined objective (such as clearing all candies of a specific type). Players in Candy Crush Saga are given a set of five lives, which regenerate every 30 minutes; a life is consumed each time a player attempts a level but either does not meet the objective or does not meet the minimum score required to obtain at least one star. (Based on performance, a player can earn up to three stars on any given level.) When a player's lives are depleted, three options are presented to the player: (1) wait for a new life to regenerate, (2) ask an in-game friend to provide the player with a life, or (3) purchase a life from the in-game store.

This set of options represents one of two "choice gates" at the heart of Candy Crush Saga's success. Because the game was initially developed for Facebook, it is inherently social; players can view and connect with their friends on the network by default. As the difficulty of the game increases (and, despite its youthful aesthetic, the game becomes challenging quite early on), the importance of being connected to friends in-game becomes paramount. In fact, borrowing lives from friends (and gifting them in turn) is a core component of the game; rather than detracting from the experience, the interactions between friends enhance it. This core social communication mechanism is an effortless and organic source of significant virality for Candy Crush Saga.

The second "choice gate" in Candy Crush Saga occurs at the end of certain episodes, when players are required to either invite friends to the game or pay money to progress to the next set of levels. This gate sets a hard, decisive contribution condition on each player reaching that point in the game, through either virality or direct monetization. These choice gates and gifting opportunities dovetail with a competitive element to the game; players are shown their performance on a per-level basis relative to their friends' performances, and players can see their friends' progressions through the game.

Candy Crush Saga is uniquely monetized compared to other popular freemium social games; the product catalogue is limited and is priced directly in platform currency as opposed to being priced in an in-game hard currency. With a product catalogue consisting only of one-time-use gate advancements and boosts—which improve the player's performance in a single level—and a small number of permanent performance-enhancing accessories called charms, Candy Crush Saga focuses on long-term retention and user base scale, as opposed to product catalogue depth, to deliver revenue.

Retention and scale certainly haven't escaped the game. In May 2013, Zacconi announced that Candy Crush Saga was generating 500 million gameplay sessions per day on mobile devices alone. That level of engagement is likely due in part to the massive amount of content available in Candy Crush Saga; since its launch, King has released a new episode for Candy Crush Saga every few weeks, each one consisting of 15 levels. Upon launch of the game, the player is shown the vastness of the map over which levels are dispersed; the volume of levels and potential for gameplay hours is obvious from the first session of play.

As a game, Candy Crush Saga's combination of a proven entertainment archetype with social and competitive features contributes significantly to retention, and its gifting and gate mechanics inspire substantial virality. But in terms of engagement, King's decision to develop the game as truly persistent across all platforms—meaning a user's progress is tracked across all devices the game is played on—probably had the most profound effect on its staying power with highly engaged users. Because game progress is never lost from one device to another, the most engaged players can advance in the game on their phones, tablets, or desktop computers whenever they have the time to play it.

Candy Crush Saga is perhaps one of the most iconic games of the mobile era, given its inherent social functionality and its cross-platform support. The game proved that casual games can generate massive volumes of revenue, given a large enough user base and a compelling enough social infrastructure. And the game also proved that a developer with an employee count in the hundreds—not thousands—can develop a hit mobile franchise and maintain a competitive chart position for months on end.

Analytics and Freemium Products

Insight as the foundation of freemium product development

Since only 5 percent or less of a freemium product's users can be expected to generate revenue through direct purchases, a freemium product requires the potential for massive scale to produce meaningful returns.

But the freemium model doesn't operate under "low margin, high volume" conditions; the scale of a freemium product doesn't necessarily produce massive revenues with a linear relationship to the user base. A large user base merely increases the *odds* that users matching the profile of those most likely to engage with the product to the greatest extent are exposed to it.

In this sense, the freemium model is the opposite of "low margin, high volume"; in fact, the freemium model is "high margin, low volume" because the users who will eventually pay (the members of the 5 percent) must be given the opportunity to glean enjoyment from the product to the greatest extent possible in exchange for an exceptionally personal, exceptionally enjoyable experience. The massive scale of a freemium product's user base is only a prerequisite for the model's success because it is very difficult to identify the 5 percent of people who will make direct purchases through the product before they begin using it. The more users recruited into the product, the more data the user base produces, and very large data sets facilitate insight.

Analytics

Building a freemium product is like hunting in a large river for a very rare fish that is physically indistinguishable from other, less valuable fish, with the expectation that the rare fish will reveal itself once it is caught. An extremely wide net is cast to attempt to catch *everything*; once the caught fish have been brought on board the boat, the rare target reveals itself.

But how would the rare fish reveal itself to the fisherman if it looks the same as the other fish? Presumably, by its behavior. The same is true of highly engaged users in freemium products: they are indistinguishable from other users at the time of product initiation, but they use the product differently than do other users and exhibit patterns that can sometimes be identifiable before they even spend money.

The dynamic between scale and the 5% rule raises an interesting question about the required general appeal of a product in determining whether the freemium model is an appropriate business model choice for it. Specifically, how large must the potential user base be in order to justify building a product with the freemium model? There is no definitive answer to this question. The problem with a small potential user base is of course that 5 percent won't represent a meaningful number of users and thus cannot produce a meaningful amount of revenue. But if that small group of users is more passionate for that niche product than, say, a more generic product that appeals to a larger group of people, users in the small group might spend more money and close the revenue gap.

Market size is a crucial consideration when making the decision to build a product using the freemium model, which is why holding the 5% rule as a given assists in making a realistic determination about which business model best suits a given product. A common pitfall when evaluating the freemium model's appropriateness for a product is to assume that the product in question will collect revenues from an unprecedented number of users.

Product teams are inherently optimistic when launching new products; after all, they wouldn't be attempting to build something if they didn't think it was going to introduce an innovation to an existing paradigm. But very few products disprove the 5% rule, and those that do usually accomplish that feat only after many product iterations. Assuming that any freemium product will convert users to payers at a level consistent with the freemium model on aggregate is sound business model design; it ensures that lofty expectations and overly optimistic revenue estimates don't prevail over historical norms.

With the 5% rule taken as fact, the product team is forced to design the freemium product around either one or both of two requirements: extracting large amounts of revenue from the users who do pay and increasing the product's scale by expanding its universal appeal. Both of these initiatives are accomplished by measuring user behaviors and identifying patterns within them that can be used to iterate on the product. This measurement method is known as *analytics*.

What is analytics?

Analytics is a fairly broad term that can mean different things in different industries. In the abstract, *analytics* describes a measurement system that produces auditable records of events across a period of time that can then be used to develop insight about a product. For freemium products, analytics is used to record the actions of users, store the records, and communicate the information in them, mostly visually graphical depictions (or, to product executives and statisticians in order to facilitate analysis.

Analytics is the heart, the foundation, of the freemium model because analytics is the only means through which highly engaged users can be identified early and accommodated for. And analytics is the only means of determining how a freemium product can best be improved in order to enhance the experience for highly engaged users.

Analytics has been a cornerstone of web development for years—the largest web applications record every click, every page view, and every followed link to better understand how their products are being used. Many desktop software products instrument use to a high degree, recording interactions between the user and the software in an attempt to improve the user's experience.

Analytics for a freemium product is necessarily more complex than analytics implemented for most other web products because improving a freemium product user's experience, as a general concept, doesn't necessarily increase revenues. While averages can certainly be measured in the freemium model, they don't convey meaningful information when aggregated over the entirety of a user base; users are segmented into non-paying and paying groups, and those groups have different needs, desires, and proclivities. Exposing these fundamentally different user types to the same product experience would only serve to alienate one group or the other.

Analytics is a somewhat abstract concept because it doesn't exist as a singular function point; it can be implemented in any number of myriad ways, and what most people associate with analytics is merely its output. Analytics should be thought of as a system, an entire chain of features and independent products that collects, stores, processes, and outputs data.

The highest purpose of an analytics system is to provide insight on product performance to product teams. In freemium development, analytics is a paramount concern because, without insight, a product team is left with aggregated information that doesn't help drive product improvement. Global averages from freemium data are very rarely useful and can, in some cases, be misleading; the important metrics in freemium products are those that identify and quantify the behavior of specific user groups. When a maximum of 5 percent of total users will ever contribute revenue through direct purchases, of what use is a global average in determining how a product feature should be improved?

To that end, analytics must be flexible and granular. The ability for a product team to group users by specific behaviors or demographic characteristics, or to limit a view of data by date, is an absolute necessity, and this functionality must be provided for throughout the entire *analytics stack*, the collection of software products that comprises the freemium product's analysis capability.

The analytics stack can be broken down into three component pieces: the *back-end*, the *events library*, and the *front-end*. An analytics back-end is a storage mechanism that collects data; it can be implemented in any number of ways using any number of technologies, some of which will be outlined later in the chapter. Although the market dynamic in analytics is shifting toward what is known as *Big Data*, most freemium products still rely on a *relational back-end* (such as MySQL or PostgreSQL) that stores data in relational database tables.

An events library is a protocol for recording and transmitting data to the back-end. It usually takes the form of a discrete list of events—important data points that, when collected, can be used to glean insight about a product—that are meant to be tracked. Events libraries are generally integrated into software clients, meaning that an update to the library will be adopted only through an update to the user's client. As Big Data systems move further into the mainstream, events libraries are being jettisoned in favor of logs that keep track of literally everything that happens in a product. But for the foreseeable future, events libraries will likely remain relevant, as developers must choose which data points they wish to collect for storage concerns.

An analytics front-end is any software that retrieves and processes the data stored in the back-end. Third-party solutions are generally used to fulfill this function; products such as *Tableau*, *QlikView*, and *Greenplum* allow product teams to connect to a data set and almost instantly use it to build graphs and charts, segment data, and spot patterns. Some analytics stacks rely on ad-hoc querying and analysis in lieu of a front-end; an analyst will query data directly from the database and manipulate it using a statistical interface or desktop spreadsheet software. In other cases, a bespoke front-end is developed from scratch to fit the specific needs of product teams.

Taken together, the back-end, events library, and front-end form the complete and fully functional analytics stack (illustrated in Figure 2.1), although most product teams only ever interact with the front-end. How these component pieces are developed and maintained can have a significant impact on how well they function; distributing each component across three functional teams within an organization might disrupt the extent to which each piece communicates with the others. Additionally, changes to the events library must be communicated clearly to the team maintaining the back-end, and front-end requirements must similarly be made known to the team maintaining the events library.

The best-functioning analytics stacks are those that are developed by a cohesive analytics group dedicated exclusively to analytics. Systems distributed across functional groups within an organization have a tendency to break or, worse yet, function poorly and produce inaccurate metrics. Keeping an analytics stack entirely within the purview of one organizational group ameliorates the risk of this happening.

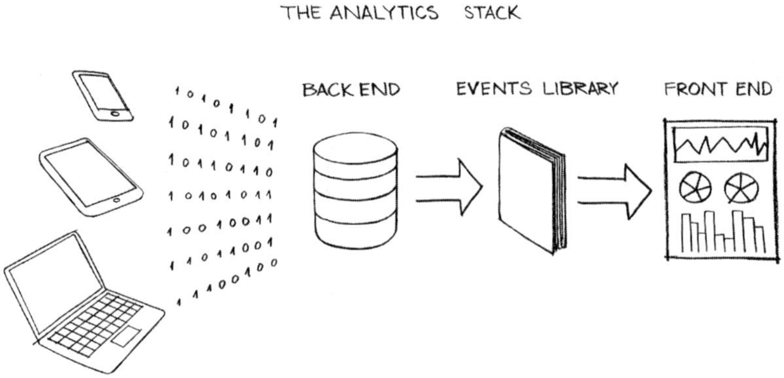

THE ANALYTICS STACK

FIGURE 2.1

The analytics stack.

What is big data?

The term "Big Data" is generally over-used and poorly understood, especially by non-technical professionals. And Big Data is often mistakenly viewed as a panacea to fix product problems that would be better addressed not with more data but with more *insight*. In fact, Big Data describes both a storage trend and an analysis trend. The storage trend is straightforward: the price of storing data has declined as storage technologies have improved. Combined with innovative storage solutions from companies like Rackspace and Amazon, storing huge volumes (terabytes and petabytes) of data is cost-effective and manageable for companies without dedicated hardware infrastructure teams. The term "Big Data" reflects the contemporary capability of storing and accessing massive amounts of data; when a product team so chooses, it can store literally every interaction users have with the product.

The analysis trend behind Big Data is more nuanced. The massive data sets that resulted from decreasing storage prices presented a problem to analysts: large volumes of data cannot easily be parsed and processed, and most statistical software products are not capable of working with data that is too large to store in memory. A process was needed to build manageable data sets out of the cumbersome, distributed, unwieldy caches of unstructured data (usually in the form of server logs) created by Big Data frameworks. The most prominent solution to this dilemma was developed by Google and is called *MapReduce*; it is a routine for parsing massive, distributed datasets (the map) and building a set of aggregate statistics from them (the reduce).

MapReduce allows data distributed across a cluster of cheap commodity servers to be parsed and analyzed as a monolith; in other words, MapReduce glues together disparate, independent data sets and allows them to be analyzed as a cohesive whole. Although many implementations of MapReduce exist, the most popular is a free framework from Apache called *Hadoop*.

The innovation of MapReduce over traditional data storage techniques, namely, relational databases, is programmatic. Relational database systems, such as those mentioned earlier, suffer performance burdens as they increase in size. A traditional solution to this problem is database *sharding*, or separating large data sets into smaller, independent segments based on some characteristic, usually time. These database shards are not easily unified and can lead to analysis blind spots.

MapReduce routines, on the other hand, can quickly and easily be "spun up" (executed) across a large number of commodity servers. This means that, as long as it isn't deleted, data that is stored can be processed and analyzed persistently into the future; it's always available. And the execution time of MapReduce routines can be reduced by distributing the routines across more commodity servers; using services like Amazon's Elastic MapReduce (EMR), a large number of commodity servers can be quickly appropriated for a MapReduce routine.

Big Data is important because it accommodates complete instrumentation; literally every interaction a user has with a product can be stored, analyzed, and used to influence future product iterations. This information is priceless to quantitatively oriented product teams that, armed with an adequate understanding of statistics and the tools to process and render data, can make highly informed design decisions when implementing new features or adjusting old ones.

Big Data also alleviates the need for product teams to attempt to conceive of all possible relevant metrics and data points before the product is released; because all product usage data is stored under Big Data conditions, metrics that were not considered upon launch can be retroactively aggregated. This is generally not possible in relational database systems, where data is collected only as warranted by existing groups of metrics.

But Big Data can also be a burden: data overload can muddy a product team's understanding of a feature's use, and without proper statistical training, product teams can misinterpret trends or jump to spurious conclusions about what exactly is happening within the very complex system of their product. Big Data requires real expertise in statistical analysis in order to provide value; without the ability to properly and accurately interpret data, more information simply produces more noise.

That said, Big Data is an important topic for any product team to understand and is a precursor to full comprehension of the freemium model. While this book is not a technical guide, it would be remiss in not addressing Big Data as a freemium concern; the massive scale required by the freemium model is a product asset precisely because it produces massive volumes of data. Those massive volumes of data are at their most helpful when analyzed in their entirety, which can only be done with modern Big Data solutions.

A Big Data approach to product development allows the freemium product team to iterate faster, execute deeper analysis of feature performance, and draw sounder conclusions about how users are interacting with the product than through traditional, relational database-oriented analytics. When properly resourced and utilized, Big Data analytics systems provide the capacity for the kinds of incremental performance improvements needed in a freemium product: small, consistent, and predictable metrics enhancement based on behavioral user data.

Designing an analytics platform for freemium product development

The first step in building an analytics stack is determining what data should and can be tracked. Collecting data isn't necessarily as straightforward as it may seem at first, and the format of tracked data must be carefully considered; once an event takes place, recording it from a different perspective, or with more attributes, is impossible. Excess data can always be disposed of in the future if its storage is deemed unnecessary, but unrecorded data is surrendered to the ether.

The best way to build an events library is to work backward from a set of questions that the data should be able to answer. Use cases can be hard to predict (and it should be understood that data will reveal patterns that hadn't been considered during

FIGURE 2.2

An events hierarchy structure for the "Social" event group.

the product's design phase, thus spawning the need for further metrics), but a set of operating questions such as, "For how long do highly engaged users remain with the product?" can generate a reasonable set of baseline metrics ahead of a product's launch.

Once a set of baseline events has been catalogued, some sort of reporting structure should be considered around which events can be organized. The organization applies a hierarchy to the events so that reporting systems can easily aggregate metrics under different filters. An example of a hierarchical structure is *Group–Category–Label*, where group represents a high-level description of the type of event (e.g., Social), category represents a class of this group (e.g., Friend List Change), and label describes the event in fine detail (e.g., Add Friend), as illustrated in Figure 2.2. Group may have several categories, and category may have several labels; all events given a specific label can be easily aggregated (or disaggregated) by their group and category designations.

Applying hierarchical structure to events data makes reporting much easier, as it installs fault lines throughout the stored data around which aggregations can be made. This exercise also forces order onto a process that can very easily become chaotic; when events fit into predefined groups, they're less likely to record the same thematic data from differing angles, thereby avoiding confusion.

Once event hierarchies have been catalogued, a structure for event storage must be devised. This involves considering which attributes of the data will be required for reporting purposes: in essence, what filters must be applied to the data when analysis is conducted. Date of occurrence is the first attribute that should be associated with a given event; without date information, almost no insight can be gleaned. Other attributes that are almost universally necessary are:

- User ID. The identification of the user executing the event.
- User state. This isn't necessarily one attribute; user state could represent a group of attributes describing the user's state at the time the event was executed. Some examples of state attributes are session ID, device type (if the product is accessible on multiple platforms), social connections within the product, etc. These attributes should reflect the user's state at the precise moment the event was recorded.
- Event state. Specific attributes of the event that may not apply universally to all events, or attributes that could change based on other factors for different instances of this event.

Attaching attributes to events allows those events to be audited in the future in case values associated with those events change as the product evolves. Figure 2.3 illustrates a sample events table column list with user state and event state attributes.

In the figure, the row labeled *CUMULATIVE_TOTAL_SESSIONS* relates the number of sessions a user has completed up to the recorded event, and the row labeled *FRIENDS_IN_APP* relates the number of friends the user has in the app at the time of the event. These attributes describe the user state because they are unique to that particular user at a specific point in time and provide context around the ways the user's previous interactions with the product may have influenced the event in question.

The row labeled *USERS_ONLINE* relates the number of users online in the app at the time of the event, and the row labeled *PROMOTIONS_LIVE* relates the promotions (discounts, purchase bundles, special offers, etc.) live in the app at the time of the event. These attributes describe the event state because these product-level factors may have influenced the user's behavior (and thus the fact that the event took place) independent of the user's usage of the product.

Events are not the only data that should be collected; information about users and product feature values (such as pricing information, access, etc.) must be stored, not only for the functionality of the product but for future reference and analysis. This data is generally less dynamic than events data, and its structure is less important to get right prior to product launch. A user's location, for instance, can always be gleaned based on use, but events data is lost forever if it is not tracked at the time the event is executed. A users table holds data about individual users such as email address, location, first and last name, date of registration, and source of acquisition (e.g., this user was introduced to the product through paid search, from a link on a partner website, from an organic search, etc.).

The events library holds an auditable behavioral records—trails of data artifacts—that are used to improve the product. The time spent constructing a

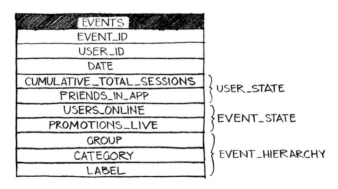

FIGURE 2.3

A sample events table column list.

thorough, instructive events library prior to launch is equivalent to a fraction of the time needed when implementing the same library post-launch. Data that isn't stored can't be recovered, and neither can the insight that said data might produce.

Storing data for a freemium product

Once an events library has been constructed, organizing the product's data artifacts must be considered. While the implementation of a database schema is a technical task, the product team should provide input into how the tables that will be used for analysis—especially *derived tables*, which store aggregates based on nightly batch processing of metrics calculations—are designed. (See Figure 2.4.) Analysis is as much an element of product development as is user experience design, and therefore the product team should play a role in determining how the data used for analysis is organized.

Whether or not an analytics stack is built as a Big Data system, some layer of relational data should exist for analysis purposes, for two reasons:

- Aggregated data stored in a relational database is easily accessed. Unstructured, distributed data can be queried through Big Data tools, but these techniques still

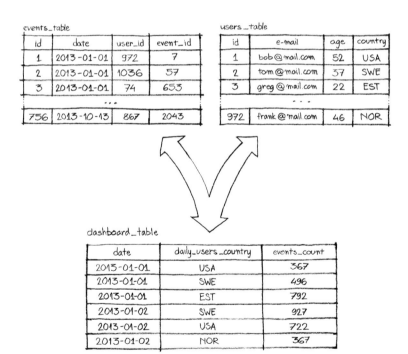

FIGURE 2.4

A derived dashboard table formed from normalized events and users tables.

require running MapReduce routines and, in most cases, are much slower than SQL queries.

- SQL is much older than the tools that allow for querying Big Data. As a result, hiring analysts familiar with SQL is much easier than hiring analysts who can query from Big Data systems. Likewise, the tools that cater to SQL-based systems are far more numerous than those that provide for Big Data querying.

The relational database tables that hold event data should be *normalized*, that is, optimized to reduce storage redundancy. Database normalization simply means that no column in a table has a partial dependency on another column and that the items stored in any given table are only stored once. Normalization is the optimal way to store raw data, but it isn't ideal for tables that are used primarily for analysis, as normalization segments data in a way that almost always requires tables to be *joined*, which is the process of unifying data across tables based on a common characteristic.

To that end, tables holding data inserted into the database by the events library for the explicit purposes of storage should be normalized; tables derived from that data should not be normalized. At a minimum, the product, via the events library, should maintain raw data storage in an *events* table in a database. For the purposes of normalization, that events table should be able to reconcile user information with a *users* table via the user ID. Likewise, the events table should reconcile with tables that hold product information relevant to events. The number and character of tables holding raw data is entirely dependent on the technical (and not design) requirements of the product, however, and these decisions are not likely to be made by a product team. Derived tables, on the other hand, are driven entirely by product design requirements. Derived tables hold aggregated metrics about product performance and are used exclusively for reporting and analysis; these tables will power design decisions by storing actionable metrics specifically defined by the product team and thus require active participation from product stakeholders when being designed.

Two very useful derived table templates are the *user state* table and the *dashboard* table. A user state table stores a snapshot of every user's state for each day users engage with the product; the table is composed of running totals for many metrics up to a given point. This table creates an easily auditable record of activity on a per-user basis and alleviates the need to calculate the data-intensive metrics that are the precursors to most analysis initiatives. In other words, the user state table eases the analysis process by making the most common metrics readily available.

The dashboard table is composed of aggregate metrics for the product's entire user base, broken down by day, that are directly used in populating a product dashboard: a succinct collection of graphs, charts, and data points that provides broad insight into a product's use and growth. The dashboard table contains aggregated information about product usage and revenue that can be used to assess the general health of a product. Product dashboards don't facilitate analysis per se; they're designed to give product teams and corporate management an all-encompassing view of a product's health over time.

As the name implies, a derived table is calculated based on data in other tables. This is accomplished through a process known as *extract, transform, load (ETL)*. This process produces aggregated metrics from raw data, usually in a nightly, automated routine, by applying business logic to unprocessed records of activity. An example of a function of the ETL process is storing a count of daily active users in the dashboard table. The process queries the number of session start events from the events table (extract); counts them, potentially removing duplicates and accounting for dropped sessions (transform); and stores that aggregation in the row of the dashboard table containing metrics for that day (load).

While a product team shouldn't be actively involved in deploying an ETL process, understanding the fundamentals of data warehousing—the process through which raw data is stored, processed, and aggregated—is a critical component of design-driven development. The data available for analysis directly affects the pace and quality of product iterations; if a product team isn't abreast of how and when a product's data artifacts will be converted into actionable metrics, the reliability of insight is called into question. Proper, consistent data administration is an essential component of the product management life cycle in a freemium product.

Reporting data for a freemium product

Reports comprise the portion of the analytics stack visible to the organization and thus receive the most scrutiny. Reporting is essentially the collection of tools that product teams and other employees interact with to retrieve, manipulate, and depict data. Depending on the organization's size and priorities, reporting, might be centralized internally or it might be distributed across all product groups; that is, product groups may be charged with handling their own reporting tools. Each approach has its unique benefits.

Centralized reporting—wherein one group, usually called the analytics or business intelligence group—maintains the organization's data warehouse and provides a set of unified reporting tools and interfaces to all product teams. The benefit of this is consistency and transparency: the calculation of all metrics is standardized because the reporting group defines metrics, and the tools (and thus the output of those tools) used for reporting are the same across all product groups. This consistency provides convenience: metrics from one product can easily be compared with those from another product because the two products are calculated and communicated similarly.

Embedded reporting, where an analyst sits in a product team and handles reporting exclusively for that team's products, provides the benefit of flexibility: tools can be calibrated to fit the specific needs of the products being covered, and calculations can be tailored to the intricacies of the product's user base behavior. Embedded, dedicated analysts can generally turn analysis requests around more quickly than can centralized reporting teams, as they have the benefit of familiarity with the product's data set and peculiarities. Analysis from internal, team-specific reporting analysts may not be consistent with that from other groups, however, and the inconsistency could hinder management's ability to compare product performance or to set a baseline standard for certain metrics.

A hybrid model between the two options exists wherein an organization-wide reporting team maintains the organization's data and standards for calculating metrics, and embedded product analysts conduct analysis independently under those parameters. This model works well when a company has a large yet fairly homogenous product catalogue that lends itself to metrics comparison.

The tools used in reporting are myriad and serve a number of purposes and tastes. The most popular class of reporting tool, and by far the easiest to become proficient in, is desktop spreadsheet software. Spreadsheets can usually store a fairly large amount of data in memory, are capable of performing reasonably sophisticated calculations, and quickly create visuals such as charts and graphs.

Other desktop-based analysis tools (i.e., tools that are not hosted on a server but reside on a user's computer) range in sophistication from command-line statistical packages such as R to extremely powerful yet user-friendly solutions such as Tableau. The philosophical current unifying all desktop solutions is that the end user can define metrics and can save analysis output as local files capable of being physically or electronically distributed. The converse of this philosophy is the hosted analysis tool, an authenticated (i.e., password-requiring) Internet-based tool that predefines all metrics and allows analysis output to be shared only via an auditable link.

Desktop analysis software suffers a few critical drawbacks; for example, persistent database connections are not easily accommodated, meaning data must be actively pulled from the data warehouse each time it needs to be refreshed. This poses data consistency risks: a user could base an analysis on an outdated data set. Likewise, placing the responsibility of defining metrics calculation in the hands of report stakeholders could result in a situation where consumers of the report have defined the same metrics differently in their own analyses, which can lead to decisions being made with conflicting information. But the largest drawback is access; once a file has been saved, the organization that owns the data the analysis was based on no longer controls access to that data. By preventing data from being copied from the source (the data warehouse), an organization ensures that only approved employees will ever have access to it. This is only possible when an analysis tool is hosted.

Hosted analysis solutions have increased with popularity alongside the data-driven product development movement as product teams demand higher accessibility from their reporting software. Hosted analysis solutions boast the benefit of being generally platform-neutral: when an analysis is hosted on the web, the only requirement for viewing it is a web browser, which almost all smartphones and tablets have by default. Additionally, hosted analysis solutions maintain a persistent connection to the data warehouse (when an Internet connection is present), meaning that the report consumer can always assume the data being presented is current.

The downside of hosted analysis solutions is that they may not provide for data to be accessed offline. They're also generally not very flexible; working with the data in a hosted solution is limited to whatever filtering options are provided by the software. Many product teams require the ability to manipulate data sets based on assumptions about changes to certain metrics—for instance, that one metric will shift in a certain way if the value of another increases by a known amount—which isn't always possible with a hosted solution. Instead, hosted solutions may be incapable of doing more than communicating information through fixed-format dashboards.

Data-driven design

The benefit of the massive volumes of data provided by the freemium model's scale is that products can be designed around user behavior. Users emit innumerable preference signals when they use products; by collecting and measuring those signals, the product team can ensure that the 5 percent receive the best possible experience from the product.

This feedback loop—develop- release- measure-iterate—is known as data-driven design. (See Figure 2.5.) The ubiquity of instrumentation in products provides for a rich bank of data about the performance of product features to be available very quickly after launch. Those features can thus be improved on as quickly as that data can be parsed and analyzed; what drives product development, then, is not only the intuition of the product team but the use patterns of users. And since those patterns can be quickly synthesized and acted upon, product development can be done continuously, in small increments, as opposed to being done in large batches.

This concept is called *continuous improvement*—small, incremental product *improvements* are continuous implemented based on behavioral user data. Continuous improvement is the only effective means of implementing the freemium model: since only 5 percent of the user base contributes all product revenues, and that specific 5 percent of users is unrecognizable before it begins generating behavioral data, the product must be flexible upon launch and capable of being rapidly improved on to optimize the experience for that user segment. Long product

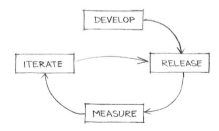

FIGURE 2.5

The develop-release-measure-iterate feedback loop.

improvement cycles reduce the number of hypotheses that can be tested in a given period of time and thus delay the eventual arrival of revenue-producing product enhancements.

Continuous improvement is facilitated by a product development methodology dominated by an emphasis on return on investment: product features and changes are prioritized based on the revenue they are expected to produce. Those revenue assumptions can be made only with a robust analytics infrastructure capable of processing the behavioral data of the very small proportion of the total user base that contributes revenue, which is likewise identified using that robust analytics infrastructure. In the freemium model, data drives development—it sets the standard by which features are prioritized and implemented.

The length of a product iteration cycle is generally left to the discretion of the product team; cycles can range from as short as one day, especially for web products, to as long as two weeks. The purpose of a post-launch product iteration cycle is threefold: to implement features that were conceived of prior to launch but deprioritized; to fix bugs that were discovered post-launch; and to implement new features at users' requests. A list of features intended to be added to the product is known as a *product backlog*, elements of which should be prioritized in descending order by a mixture of projected return on investment and estimated time required to implement.

Methodologies differ on how the product backlog should be constructed, but the team should estimate the development length of each backlog item and take only those that can feasibly be accomplished within the predetermined iteration cycle, with the understanding that some very large features will be implemented across multiple cycles through multiple component backlog items.

Product teams are incentivized to keep iteration cycles short because the develop-release-measure-iterate feedback loop is more difficult to interpret when multiple features are launched at once. If two features produce conflicting results— say, one produces an increase in revenue and the other produces a simultaneous decrease in revenue—the effects of each feature may be difficult to measure. The fewer changes implemented at once, the clearer the effects of those changes on revenue and the faster those effects can be extrapolated to existing assumptions about which features best serve the interests of the 5 percent (potentially changing the priority of the product backlog).

Data-driven design is an operational pillar of the freemium model, a fundamental component of its proper and successful implementation. The dynamics of the freemium model don't support assumptions about user behavior, and they don't support non-optimized experiences for the 5 percent. Data-driven design allows the most engaged users to be given the best possible experience by appraising their tastes and preferences through behavioral signaling. Building products on assumptions is antithetical to the freemium mindset, which accepts a very small percentage of revenue-generating users on the premise that those users will generate more revenue, through personalization and optimization, than all users in total would have in a paid access scenario. Data-driven design is the means through which this mentality manifests, but development before product launch is driven by a different concept: the minimum viable product.

The minimum viable product

The concept of the minimum viable product (MVP) was popularized by author and entrepreneur Eric Ries in his book, *The Lean Startup* (2011). Ries argues that startup companies, owing to a lack of funding with which to build products solely around assumptions, must directly address customer needs very early in their product life cycles. Reconciling a product's features with the real needs of end users— as opposed to assuming what their needs are during prelaunch—is known as achieving *product-market fit*.

Ries contends that a startup should endeavor to launch a product as soon as it can capably address its core use case (i.e., as soon as the product is viable) and thus enter into the develop-release-measure-iterate feedback loop as quickly as possible. His point is that any development beyond what is needed for a minimum release is, by definition, based on assumptions and thus is not optimized for user taste. By releasing the MVP and orienting future development around customer behavior, the product team reduces the amount of development that isn't driven directly by use patterns.

Given the freemium model's fundamental dependence on data-driven design, the MVP methodology holds heightened significance for it. For most products, the needs of the user can be approximated fairly accurately through market surveys, focus groups, and user testing; because monetization is oriented toward average behavior in non-freemium products, a substantial amount of data, while helpful, isn't necessary before understanding product–market fit. But monetization in the freemium model is driven by anomalies—by the 5 percent. As a result, a small sample of user data for a freemium product is useless: any valuable sample must be large enough to include, with confidence, a meaningful number of the 5 percent. And since the 5 percent isn't identifiable within a freemium product before behavioral data has been collected, the only way to engender such a large sample is to release the freemium product.

The minimum viable product methodology is the cornerstone of the freemium model, not only because it prevents assumptions that may alienate the 5 percent at launch, but also because it represents a philosophical adherence to data as a significant (but not exclusive) influence on product design decisions. Releasing an MVP as a freemium product sets the tone for a product's development pace and method of prioritization and is an excellent means of unifying the product team's development ethos.

The economic justification of using the MVP methodology in the freemium model relates to the time value of money and the degree to which user behavior can be estimated in the specific product vertical. A complete product, built around perfect assumptions of how users will engage with it (especially the 5 percent), will monetize to a theoretically infinite maximum degree upon launch; it's the perfect product. But that complete product will have taken longer to develop than the MVP. For example, assume the MVP is ready six months before the launch of the final product. In the six months between MVP launch and launch of the completed product, the MVP is monetizing to some lower extent than the complete product will. And all the while during that intervening period, development is being driven by data (not assumptions), although no changes are made to feature prioritization in this case because the product team's assumptions from the start were perfect.

So, even under circumstances when the product team's assumptions about user behavior are perfect, the MVP methodology still produces more aggregate revenue than a model for which the product is not released until it is complete. And no product team's assumptions can ever reliably be considered perfect; markets are dynamic, and user tastes change as a reaction to new products launching. Assumptions should be kept to an absolute minimum, especially with freemium products, where the users whose behaviors relate to revenue are a small fraction of the total user base. The only way to minimize assumptions is to release the MVP and drive development with the develop-release-measure-iterate feedback loop as early as possible.

Because the feedback loop is necessarily driven by data, the MVP includes not only a minimum product feature set but also a minimum level of analytics capability. Launching a freemium product without an analytics infrastructure renders irrelevant the freemium model's principle benefit, which is behavioral data. A freemium product must, at MVP launch, provide granular data about user behavior that can be used to pump the feedback loop. Without that data, development decisions will be assumptions-based; the complete product will be no more tailored to user tastes than it would have been had the MVP not been launched.

Methodologies like MVP are designed to help product teams produce better products. Releasing an MVP shouldn't be a product team's goal in itself—rather, it should be a means to an end that culminates in a higher-quality, better-performing, and more satisfying product.

Data-driven design versus data-prejudiced design

The importance of tracking multiple metrics under the minimum viable product model relates to gaining insight from product iterations: any iteration containing more than one significant change might introduce conflicts of effect, and those conflicts are impossible to identify without tracking multiple metrics. For instance, a change to a product's registration flow might increase retention, but a change to its product catalogue might decrease retention to an even greater extent. If these changes are implemented in one iteration, with the net effect being negative, the entire iteration might be withdrawn without the registration flow change being retained. A broad portfolio of metrics could potentially catch this conflict; a single-metric focus (presumably on retention) would not.

The MVP model is an implementation of the data-driven design paradigm: data should be descriptive of the product, not of a single feature or outcome. Tracking only one metric doesn't assist with product development, it merely describes the state of a product as it exists at that moment. Focusing on a single metric when developing a product is *data-prejudiced design*: it utilizes things that are already known to justify decisions that have already been made.

Prejudice in this sense refers to product decisions made based on intuition rather than behavioral data, with assumptions stemming from past observations that may or may not apply directly to the product being developed. The problem with resurrecting design decisions from past products is that user tastes and expectations change as markets evolve; an innovation to product design may produce a broadly cascading change in overall market behavior. In other words, innovations can cause extensive market disruption in a shorter amount of time than the average freemium product's development cycle, so decisions made from even the immediately preceding product cycle may already be dated.

The point of using data to inform product decisions is to replace preconceived notions about development priorities with information about user behavior, so resources can be allocated to develop the highest-return features. Improving retention, when possible, should always be a goal of a product team; but in all circumstances, is *any* incremental improvement to retention the highest-return allocation of time? Most likely not, but if retention is the only metric being tracked, it is impossible to make an informed decision about prioritization.

Tracking only one metric introduces prejudices into the design process: prejudices about which outcomes are most ROI efficacious and prejudices about how those outcomes should be achieved. Very few experienced product teams would be unable to achieve *some* progress toward a discrete outcome (say, improving conversion) in a development sprint. And, in most cases, strong, surefire precedents exist for improving any given metric. But the purpose of data-driven product development is not to achieve just any outcome; it is to achieve the most beneficial possible outcome under existing resource constraints.

Data-prejudiced development is facilitated through a myopic focus on an immutable set of metrics that has been subjectively selected based on past product experience. Product development experience is obviously not a bad thing, but it can introduce baggage that is difficult to jettison, especially when that baggage was accumulated on a different platform than what the current product is being developed for. Data-driven product development requires three things:

1. A quantitative understanding of how a product produces revenue in order to facilitate prioritizing feature development. Efficient resource allocation requires knowing where resources do the most good, which is impossible to determine without a model of revenues that takes into account the dynamics of a product's use.
2. A high level of instrumentation and robust analytics for identifying the exact causes of changes in product metrics. The net effects of product iterations on multiple metrics can be assessed only when those mechanics are thoroughly measured. Broad, nebulous metrics are not enough: a full tracking library,

capable of recording the individual actions of each user, needs to produce an auditable historical record of behavior.

3. The capacity to conduct analysis. Large volumes of data are impossible to parse with dashboards: an analysis group must have the analytical expertise to perform statistically authoritative investigations into product usage.

Data-driven product development is easiest in an environment that places a premium on data-driven decision-making; the hardest part of avoiding data-prejudiced design may be escaping an organization's over-reliance on intuition. Product teams may likewise bristle at the notion that their experience and insight should be cast aside during the product development cycle in favor of usage metrics. But when considering the vast extent to which intuition influences product development—in deciding which products to develop, which platforms to develop for, and which people to staff on a project—data-driven design can be seen as, among other things, a hedge against poor judgment. And data-driven design is not implemented through broad, extensive feature deployment but through incremental development and metrics-based testing.

Quantitative Methods for Product Management

3

Data analysis

The large volumes of data generated by freemium products can't be used in a product development feedback loop without being analyzed; analysis is the medium through which data informs iterations. And while many products are attended to by well-trained and highly skilled analysts whose sole job it is to parse insight out of data sets, product teams should understand the basic concepts of data analysis in order to effectively communicate in the vernacular of data.

Data analysis is usually discussed in terms of *variables*, or dimensions by which data is collected and calculated. Variables fall into two broad categories: *independent variables*, which are observed as model inputs and, for the sake of analysis, are considered to be unaffected by other variables in a model, and *dependent variables*, which are calculated as model outputs and derived with respect to a potential relationship with independent variables.

A variable can exist as one of a number of different *data types*, depending on the range of values the variable encompasses. *Binary variables* take the form of one of two possible values: most commonly, true (1) and false (0). *Categorical variables* take the form of one of a limited number of specific values; country of origin, day of week, and month of year are examples. *Count variables* are non-negative numbers that span the scale from 0 to infinity and represent the frequency with which a specific value exists over an arbitrarily defined interval. Finally, *ordinal variables* are numeric variables used to provide rank to a set of values; the value of the variable itself is generally irrelevant and is used solely for the sake of sorting objects.

In order to glean meaningful insight from a data set, a basic set of characteristics that describe that data set must be known. These characteristics are known as *descriptive statistics*—summary attributes about a *sample* of data that don't rely on any probabilistic methods to draw conclusions about the broader *population* from which the sample came. Descriptive statistics of user behavior help a product team understand, at the highest conceptual level, fundamental truths about the way users interact with a product.

Descriptive statistics

A small sample data set is shown in Figure 3.1. The data set is depicted with a horizontal bar graph; below the graph is a table containing the set's data points (with x

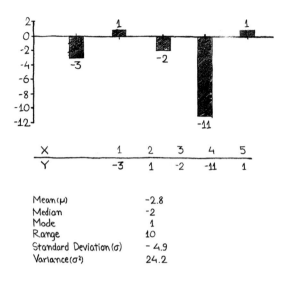

X		1	2	3	4	5
Y		-3	1	-2	-11	1

Mean (μ)	-2.8
Median	-2
Mode	1
Range	10
Standard Deviation (σ)	- 4.9
Variance (σ²)	24.2

FIGURE 3.1

A five-point sample data set with descriptive statistics.

values on the top and y values on the bottom). The data set's basic descriptive statistics are below the data table.

The word "sample" is used deliberately to describe a subset of a larger data set because the data was sampled, or selected, from a larger source of data. When a data set represents a sample of the broader scope of data (the population), the size of the set is designated by *n*; when a data set represents the entire population, the size of the set is represented by *N*.

Given the degree to which freemium data is collected, sampling is often necessary; conducting basic analyses on data sets consisting of millions or tens of millions of data points requires significant infrastructure overhead and reduces the speed with which conclusions can be drawn. The most common method of selecting a sample from a larger population is known as *simple random sampling*, and it is undertaken by defining a size for the sample and then selecting data points from the population at random, with no given data point in the population having a greater probability of being selected than any other.

The most common descriptive statistic is the *mean*, or average (usually represented as μ when describing a population and $\bar{x}$ when describing a sample). Note that, while in common usage the terms "mean" and "average" almost always refer to *arithmetic mean*, other flavors of the mean statistic, such as the geometric and harmonic means, do exist. For the sake of simplicity, the term "mean" in this text always refers to the arithmetic mean, which describes the central tendency of a group of numbers.

The mean of a data set is calculated by summing the values of the data points and then dividing that sum by the number of data points in the set. The calculation

$$\text{Sample Mean } (\bar{x}) = \frac{-3+1+-2+-11+1}{5}$$

FIGURE 3.2

The calculation of the mean of the sample data set.

$$\text{Median} = -11, -3, \boxed{-2}, 1, 1$$

FIGURE 3.3

Identifying the median value from the sample data set in Figure 3.1.

of the mean from the data set in Figure 3.1 is defined in Figure 3.2. The mean is a useful statistic when comparing trends between groups such as mean revenue or mean session length. But the mean is susceptible to influence from anomalous data points; in statistical parlance, these are called *outliers*. Outliers are data points that represent extremes on a distribution of expected values.

The *median* can be used to contextualize the mean and act as a safeguard against drawing spurious conclusions against a data set populated with extreme outliers. The median of a data set is the value that separates the bottom half of the set from the top half when the set is sorted by value. In other words, the median is the middle value. When a data set contains an even number of data points, the median is the mean of the middlemost two values.

The median provides depth to the mean statistic by highlighting influence from outliers; the larger the difference between the mean and the median, the greater the influence on the mean from outlier values. Figure 3.3 illustrates the process of identifying the median value from the example data set defined in Figure 3.1.

One example of the median's usefulness in making product is demonstrated when user session lengths are evaluated; a very large difference between the median session length and the mean session length, where the mean is greater than the median, might point to the presence of a few very long sessions relative to a majority of very short sessions. In most cases the median and mean should be presented together to add clarity to the data set.

The *mode* and *range* of a data set describe the set's numerical properties. Mode is the value occurring most often in the data set, and range is the difference between the highest and lowest values in a data set. While these descriptive statistics aren't often used in product management analysis, they can be helpful in gaining a deeper understanding of the structure of a data set.

A data set's *variance* (usually represented as σ^2 when describing a population and s^2 when describing a sample) is a measure of its "spread," or the degree to which its data points differ in value from the mean. The variance of a sample is measured by taking the squared sum of distances of the data points from the sample mean and dividing that sum by one less than the number of values in the sample (called the *unbiased sample variance*). A high level of variance within

$$\text{Sample variance } (s^2) = \sum_{i=1}^{m} (x_i - \bar{x})^2 \cdot \frac{1}{(m-1)}$$

$$\text{Sample variance } (s^2) = \frac{\begin{array}{c}(-3-(-2.8))^2 + (1-(-2.8))^2 + (-2-(-2.8))^2 \\ + (-11-(-2.8))^2 + (1-(-2.8))^2\end{array}}{(5-1)}$$

$$= \frac{0.04 + 14.44 + 0.64 + 67.24 + 14.44}{4}$$

FIGURE 3.4

The calculation of variance from the sample data set in Figure 3.1.

a data set means that values don't generally cluster around the mean but rather fall across a wide range of values. In such a case, the mean value doesn't provide much help in terms of predicting future or unknown values based on the properties of the data set. The equation used to calculate variance from the data set in Figure 3.1 is defined in Figure 3.4.

A data set's *standard deviation* is the square root of its variance (and is thus represented as σ when describing a population and s when describing a sample). Standard deviation is a helpful descriptive statistic because it communicates the same general concept as variance (average dispersion from the mean value, or "spread") but is in the same unit of measurement that the data set is represented in (variance is squared). Therefore, standard deviation corresponds to distance from the mean.

A common way to distribute descriptive statistics is with a *key performance indicator* (KPI) report, which may take the form of a dashboard or a regularly distributed spreadsheet file. The KPI report contains a set of descriptive statistics that are usually disaggregated by filters such demographic or behavioral characteristics and presented as a time series.

Insight from descriptive statistics is usually delivered as change over time; for instance, it is hard to take action on knowledge of a specific value for the running total average session length for a specific product, but it is instructive to know that the average session length dropped by a specific value over the past week. For that reason, descriptive statistics in KPI reports usually take the form of bar charts or line charts, with the x-axis representing dates and the y-axis representing values on those dates.

Descriptive statistics can be calculated on any sample size at any level of granularity. Generally speaking, descriptive statistics benefit from specificity: broadstroke characteristics of an entire population don't provide much depth to product design decisions at the feature level. Some filtering is usually necessary before a given descriptive statistic can be used in the design process; this is especially true for descriptive statistics describing revenue metrics for freemium products. Given the 5% rule, most descriptive statistics about revenue—especially averages over the entire population—are useless unless segmented by behavior.

Removing outliers from a data set before calculating descriptive statistics is a controversial practice in product management for a number of reasons, the most important of which is that outliers represent the behaviors of real people and aren't necessarily statistical noise. Extreme values, especially in revenue and engagement metrics, should be taken into account when evaluating the performance of a product feature. In freemium analyses, outliers generally represent the behaviors that a product team endeavors to optimize for: outliers in terms of spending, engagement, and virality are often the lifeblood of a freemium product. Removing those values to deliver a clearer mean value for a metric might remove a valuable data point that could better inform a decision.

There is another reason the practice of removing outliers from data is controversial—it generally leads to misrepresentation of a data set. The manipulation of a data set prior to calculating metrics from it generally comes as a surprise, even when the manipulation is clearly stated in a report. Providing broad context through a collection of descriptive statistics is more sensible than changing a data set. The insight gleaned from differences in descriptive statistics—such as the spread between median and mean—is a form of meta data that can be as helpful in facilitating decision-making as the descriptive statistics themselves.

Exploratory data analysis

Exploratory data analysis refers to an *ex ante* investigation of a data set that is conducted to build informal assumptions and hypotheses about the data set before undertaking more rigorous analysis. Exploratory data analysis is an important component of the develop-release-measure-iterate feedback loop; it allows for drawing general conclusions without committing to exhaustive analysis. It also helps to provide structure and focus to subsequent analyses so that effort is expended only on the most fruitful analytical pursuits. Exploratory data analysis serves as an introduction to a data set and is an important part of the resource allocation strategy in freemium product development.

When exploratory data analysis is informing the product development cycle, it generally takes one of two forms: as an initial interpretation of data generated by a newly launched feature to gauge the feature's effectiveness, or as the precursor to a larger analysis when considering the development of a new feature. Both of these points in the product's life cycle should be inflective based on performance. If a new product feature isn't meeting expectations, it should be either iterated upon or shut down. If a new product feature concept is being vetted, the decision must be made as to whether it should be built. In either case, exploratory data analysis is not meant to fully explore an issue but rather to provide some context so that further analysis is focused specifically on the trends that will facilitate a decision.

Exploratory data analysis is not exhaustive; it is usually conducted with desktop spreadsheet software and consists primarily of high-level descriptive statistics and visuals. Since the point of exploratory data analysis is to provide guidelines for future analysis, it should paint in broad strokes a picture of the product being analyzed and focus on the key metrics (such as revenue and engagement) that evaluate the feature's success.

In exploratory data analysis, descriptive statistics should inspect the data set from as many perspectives as possible. Aggregation by relevant demographic and behavioral attributes, such as user location or total revenue generated, can provide insight into how successful a product feature is among broadly defined user segments, while, descriptive statistics help set the tone for future analysis.

Mean and median metric values may not provide adequate context for making optimization decisions, but at the product cycle inflection points—build or don't build, iterate or shut down—these statistics provide a starting point for framing a discussion. Exploratory data analysis doesn't necessarily need to address specific questions; that can be done in further stages of analysis. Exploratory analysis is meant for gaining familiarity with a data set so that the most productive analysis themes can be pursued first.

Probability distributions

A *probability distribution* ascribes a probability to each value in a range of potential outcomes from a random experiment. It is usually represented as a graph, depicting a set of values on the x-axis and the result of the experiment, or the probability of those specific values occurring, on the y-axis.

Probability distributions take two forms, depending on whether the random variable under consideration is *continuous* or *discrete*. A continuous random variable is a variable for which values are not *countable*, or for which an infinite number of partial values can exist (e.g., the length of a user's first session, given that time can be measured to a theoretically infinite number of decimal places). A discrete random variable is a variable for which values are countable, or for which values must be whole numbers (e.g., the number of friends a user invites to the product in the user's first session; friends can be invited in whole numbers only).

A function describing the probabilities at various values of a continuous random variable is called a *probability density function*, although the probability for a specific point on the density function is never referenced. This is because the probability of an experiment resulting in any one specific value, given an infinitely large number of potential result values, is 0. To illustrate this paradox, consider the probability that the length of a user's first session will be exactly 60.12345 seconds; given an infinite number of decimal places by which to measure seconds, it must be 0.

Instead, probabilities for continuous random variables are always discussed relative to ranges of values, for example, "The probability that the length of a user's first session falls between 60 seconds and 120 seconds is .80." The area under the curve formed by a probability density function always sums to one, representing a 100 percent probability that the result of the experiment will be of some value within that range.

For discrete random variables, a *probability mass function* is used in lieu of a probability density function. The probability mass function represents the

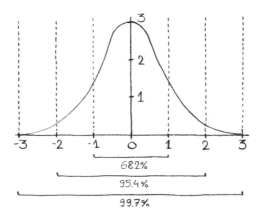

FIGURE 3.5

A bell curve with $\mu = 1$ and $\sigma^2 = 1$.

probability that a given value included in the discrete set of possible values is the result of an experiment. Probabilities that correspond to precise points on a probability mass function curve can be determined because a discrete random variable can take only a countable number of values, for example, "The probability that a user will invite five friends into the product in the user's first session is .10." Similar to a probability density function, the values of all discrete probabilities on a probability mass function sum to 1.

The concept of the probability distribution is important to understand when undertaking any form of analysis; any sample data set's underlying probability distribution affects the applicability of assumptions drawn from it. The most widely recognized probability distribution is the Gaussian, or normal, distribution. This is the standard "bell curve," which is symmetrical and densest around the mean, as shown in Figure 3.5. One useful property of the bell curve is that it abides by what is known as the 68-95-99.7 (or the three-sigma) rule: 68 percent of the points on the probability distribution function lie within one sndard deviation of the mean, 95 percent lie within two standard deviations, and 99.7 percent (or nearly all of them) lie within three standard deviations of the mean.

One common concern when interpreting a data set is *skew*, the effect of a cluster of values on the symmetry of the probability distribution relative to the mean. In a normal distribution, the probability distribution function is symmetrical around the mean; in a skewed probability distribution function, a mass of values on one side of the mean shifts the distribution in that direction, causing the tail on the other end to be thinned. *Negative skew* exists when this mass exists on the right side of the mean, shifting the probability distribution curve to the right (i.e., to higher values) and creating a thin tail on the left (i.e., to lower values); *positive skew* exists when the opposite is true. (See Figure 3.6.) In some cases, positive skew can shift the mean below the median and negative skew can shift the mean above the median, but this isn't always true.

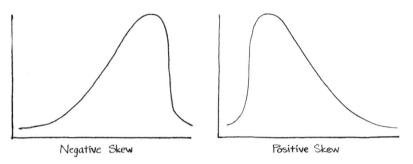

FIGURE 3.6

Two skewed probability distributions.

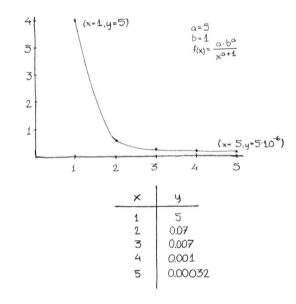

FIGURE 3.7

The probability density function for a Pareto distribution with shape parameter $a = 5$ and scale parameter $b = 1$.

While normal distribution is present in many natural phenomena such as biology and demography, it isn't broadly applicable in product management. A far more common distribution for freemium data is the Pareto distribution, which is a power law probability distribution often used in social sciences and finance. The Pareto distribution describes a system in which the majority of values are clustered at the lowest end of the distribution with a long tail that accommodates extreme values at the highest end of the scale, as shown in Figure 3.7. The Pareto distribution is often used in the insurance industry to calculate premiums for incidents where catastrophic damages are improbable but the incidents have a non-zero probability of happening.

The Pareto distribution describes many aspects of the freemium model well because the model is viable only under the premise of the existence of extreme values (in terms of revenue, user base size, user lifetime, etc.). The Pareto distribution provides a more appropriate framework for making freemium product decisions than the normal distribution does; behavioral data rarely cluster around mean values, and outliers generally represent desirable behavior.

Freemium products should be built to entice behavior that falls on a Pareto distribution and to exaggerate to the greatest degree possible the low-probability, long-tail events. When a massive user base is driven through a product producing Pareto-distributed behavioral data, the long-tail events can occur with enough frequency to meaningfully influence the metrics they are designed to impact.

The utility of knowing a data set's probability distribution within the context of freemium product management is that user behavior won't always fit the normal distribution—in fact, it very rarely does—and thus assumptions about a data set's distribution can lead to reports containing inaccurate descriptive statistics for a product feature. For instance, when the vast majority of users spend nothing, the mean for revenue data can often sit above the median in a Pareto model with a long right tail. While it almost always makes sense to report a mean value, that value must be contextualized with other descriptive statistics relevant to the distribution, such as standard deviation and variance. For data to drive beneficial product decisions, that data must be capably interpreted; in the freemium model, evaluating a data set within the context of its probability distribution is a cornerstone of prudent data analysis.

Basic data visuals

When exploring a data set for the first time, creating visual depictions of various aspects of the data may provide a greater depth of understanding of the underlying dynamics of the system than merely computing descriptive statistics. Most statistical packages have simple commands that allow for quickly rendered visuals from a data set; creating visuals of a data set's elements is therefore a common component of early exploratory analysis.

Charting data is an easy way to spot blatant trends or relationships. The type of chart used to depict the data depends on the types of dependent and independent variables. When the independent variable is categorical—that is, it is represented by a limited range of discrete values—then bar charts are often the best way of describing the data set. An example of a data set conducive to a bar chart, depicted in Figure 3.8, is a count of individuals by geography: the x-axis represents a selection of countries, and the y-axis represents counts of users in those countries. The height of each bar is determined by the proportion of the group's value to the scale of the y-axis.

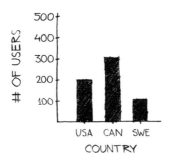

FIGURE 3.8

A bar chart depicting counts of users by country.

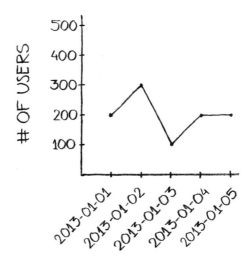

FIGURE 3.9

A time series of user counts measured by day.

When a data set's independent variable is represented by progression values—values that increase or decrease by a regular interval, such as time—then it is best illustrated with a line chart, with the dependent variable plotted on the y-axis. An example is a *time series*, or a set of data points measured at regular intervals across a period of time. A common time series used in freemium analytics is the count of users measured by day, where the x-axis tracks days and the y-axis tracks user counts. This example is depicted in Figure 3.9.

When both the independent and dependent variables of a data set are continuous—that is, when the values of both variables are numeric and fall across a continuous range—then the data can be instructively depicted with a *scatter plot*.

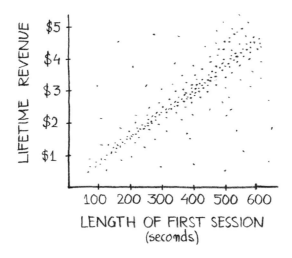

FIGURE 3.10

A scatter plot capturing total lifetime revenue spent by length of the first session.

A scatter plot places a point on the graph for each point in the data set with the x-axis labeled as the independent variable and the y-axis labeled as the dependent variable.

Scatter plots are useful in identifying clusters of commonality and trends in relationships. A common example of two freemium variables well-suited to depiction in a scatter plot is the total amount of revenue a user spends (the dependent variable) and the length of the user's first session (the independent variable). This example is depicted in Figure 3.10.

A *histogram* is a type of bar chart that plots the frequency of values for a continuous variable and can be rendered to visually approximate its probability density function. Generally, when a histogram is invoked by a statistical package, the program determines the appropriate size of each range of values for the independent variable over which frequency counts will be calculated; these ranges of values are known as *bins*. Put another way, a bin establishes a range of values for the independent variable, and the frequencies (or counts) of values within each bin are calculated as values for a dependent variable. Bins are generally grouped in equivalent ranges; that is, the range of each bin is the same size. An example of a histogram for a freemium product is the count of users by the range of the first session length, as illustrated in Figure 3.11.

The shape of a histogram provides basic insight into a data set's probability distribution. A cursory glance at Figure 3.11 reveals that the data is not normally distributed; rather, it follows a negative exponential distribution, with the value at each bin decreasing non-linearly from the bin before it.

A *box plot* (sometimes called a box-and-whisker plot) is a graph used to illustrate the dispersion, or "spread," of a one-variable data set. A box plot segments a

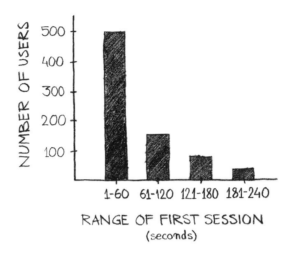

FIGURE 3.11

A histogram of user counts by first session length.

data set into quartiles and graphs the median for each quartile within a box; additionally, the plot graphs the minimum and maximum values for the entire data set, as well as the data set's median. In order to graph a box plot, five metrics must be calculated: the median of the highest and lowest quartiles, the median of the entire data set, and the minimum and maximum values of the data set. These are calculated for a sample data set of users' first session lengths and shown in Figure 3.12.

In order to calculate the median and quartiles, the data set must first be arranged in numerical order. Once sorted, the upper quartile is calculated as the median of the higher half of the range, and the lower quartile is calculated as the median of the lower half. The median of the data set in Figure 3.12 is 66, or the midpoint of the third (60) and fourth (72) sequential values. Once these values are calculated, they can be plotted on a graph as a box containing the quartiles with "whiskers" representing the overall median, minimum, and maximum values. A box plot for the data in Figure 3.12 is depicted in Figure 3.13.

Data visuals are not themselves analyses; rather, they should be used to develop a basic understanding of a data set's structure in order to preempt analysis. Visuals may provide better guidance than do numerical descriptive statistics for the transformations that must be executed on a data set before proper analysis can be undertaken, especially as related to a data set's distribution. Likewise, visuals can highlight relationships between two variables that would otherwise require iterative guess-and-check testing to spot numerically. For these reasons, the construction of visuals is often the starting point of an analysis.

USER ID	FIRST SESSION LENGTH
1	60
2	27
3	96
4	55
5	72
6	80

MEDIAN	66
MINIMUM	27
MAXIMUM	96
UPPER QUARTILE	55
LOWER QUARTILE	80

FIGURE 3.12

The calculated components for a box plot from a sample data set of user first session lengths.

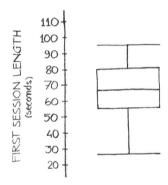

FIGURE 3.13

A box plot for a sample data set of first session lengths.

Confidence intervals

The descriptive statistics introduced thus far are used to describe a sample, or a sub-set of a larger data set collected from the entire population. This is often done to avoid engaging with the processes needed to parse very large freemium data sets (which often add a significant layer of complexity to the analysis process, delaying the delivery of results). But the values of descriptive statistics derived from sample data sets must be tempered with some measurement of how well they reflect

$$P(L \leq \theta \leq H) = C$$

FIGURE 3.14

The general expression for a confidence interval.

the properties of the entire population; without knowing how representative of the population a sample is, conclusions drawn from analyses conducted on sample data sets can't be applied to the product without imposing significant risk.

In order to contextualize a descriptive statistic (or any other statistic, usually referred to in this context as a *parameter*) derived from a sample data set, a range of values can be provided that are likely to include the population parameter. This range is called the *confidence interval*, denoted by *CI*; a confidence interval is always given with the probability that the interval contains the true value of the parameter from the population. This probability is called the *confidence level* and is denoted by *C*. For instance, the mean value of a sample parameter, such as mean first session length, can be more instructive when communicated alongside a range of values where the broader population's mean first session length is likely to sit. This is the value of the confidence interval: it describes how well the mean first session length per user, as measured from the sample, matches the actual mean first session length per user for the broader population of users.

The use of the word "confidence" in naming this convention is a bit peculiar; the word is not used in other areas of the statistical discipline. This is because the confidence interval concept comes from the frequentist school of statistics, which stipulates that probability be employed to describe the methods used to build samples from populations and not to describe the experimenter's sense of certainty for a result, which would be subjective. The confidence interval, then, is a means of reconciling the need to attach a level of probability to a statistic derived from a sample data set and an adherence to reporting only objective metrics.

A confidence interval contains four elements: the two values that define the range within which the population parameter is likely to be found (*L* and *H*), the population parameter (θ), and the attendant level of confidence for the interval (*C*). These elements are combined to form the expression shown in Figure 3.14.

For frequentist statisticians, this expression is valid in the abstract. The expression becomes invalid, however, when real values are inserted into the expression because, in frequentist statistics, probabilities are objective, and thus there is no need to attach a probability to a value existing between a range of two other values; the statement is either objectively true (the population parameter falls between the two endpoints) or not true (the population parameter does not fall between the two endpoints).

Thus, the interpretation of the confidence interval expression has nothing to do with the population parameter; rather, the probabilistic sampling method (*SM*) by which the sample is drawn is what produces the interval bounded by *L* and *H*. Thus, when a confidence interval is derived and values are placed into the expression

$$SE = \frac{s}{\sqrt{n}}$$

FIGURE 3.15

Standard error calculation.

from Figure 3.14, the correct interpretation of the expression is, "The true value of the population parameter θ will sit between L and H for C percent of the time that a sample is taken using sampling method SM." As stated earlier, a common sampling method in freemium data analysis is the simple random sampling approach.

Confidence intervals are generally constructed with standard levels of confidence of 90 percent, 95 percent, and 99 percent, with the higher levels of confidence corresponding to smaller value intervals. The level of confidence of the interval relates a range across the normal distribution within which one can expect to find the true value of the population parameter. Because the normal distribution is symmetric, the area of the curve considered is centered around the mean.

Following from the earlier discussion of normal distribution, estimating a range of probabilities for a given distribution requires knowing the distribution's mean and its standard deviation. But the calculation of a confidence interval assumes only knowledge of the sample, not the population. However, these components of the population's distribution can be estimated using what is known as the *sampling distribution of sample means*.

The sampling distribution of sample means is a theoretical distribution of all possible samples that could have been taken from a population. The mean of the sampling distribution of sample means can be substituted for the unknown mean of the population as an application of the *central limit theorem*, which states that the recorded mean values of a sufficiently large number of samples taken from a population will be normally distributed around the mean of the population.

The standard deviation of the population can be approximated by the standard deviation of the sampling distribution of sample means—known as the *standard error* (SE)—which is calculated by dividing the sample's standard deviation by the square root of the sample size, as defined in Figure 3.15.

A *z-score* (represented by Z) corresponding to the required level of confidence must also be known; z-scores represent the number of signed (positive or negative) standard deviations at which a value sits from the mean on a normal distribution. The z-scores for levels of confidence at 99 percent, 95 percent, and 90 percent are listed in Figure 3.16. (These z-scores are the basis of the 68-95-99.7 rule, as described earlier).

Given that a z-score describes the distance from a specific value to the mean, the z-score for a level of confidence value can be multiplied by the standard error of the sample distribution to determine an endpoint for the interval. This logical reversal is true as a result of the properties of a normal distribution, which the sample distribution of sample means always assumes: if 95 percent of the sample means lie within 1.96 standard errors of the true population mean, then it follows that the true

Level of Confidence	Z-Score
99%	2.577
95%	1.96
90%	1.645

FIGURE 3.16

A table of selected z-scores.

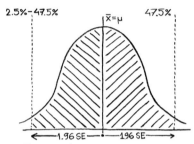

FIGURE 3.17

The sample distribution of sample means, with 95 percent (1.96 standard errors) of the distribution shaded in around the mean.

population mean has a 95 percent chance of being within 1.96 standard errors of any given sample mean. This is illustrated in Figure 3.17.

Calculating a confidence interval for a given level of confidence simply involves multiplying the z-score by the standard error of the sample distribution. Take, for example, an analysis of first session lengths (assuming first session lengths are normally distributed) on a sample of 2,500 users. The average first session length of the sample is 100 seconds with a standard deviation of 25 seconds. The endpoints of the confidence interval for the population mean can be calculated as [99.02, 100.98] with a 95 percent confidence level (corresponding to a z-score of 1.96), as shown in Figure 3.18.

Note that decreasing the confidence level decreases the range of values produced for the confidence interval. Using the same example, calculating a confidence interval for a confidence level of 90 percent produces endpoints of [99.17, 100.82], as illustrated in Figure 3.19.

The results of the second confidence interval could be interpreted as "The true population mean of first session lengths will sit between 99.17 seconds and 100.82 seconds 90 percent of the time that a sample is taken when using the same sampling method as the one used in this experiment."

$$\text{CI Endpoints}_{95\%} = \bar{x} \pm Z \cdot SE$$

$$= \bar{x} \pm Z \cdot \left(\frac{s}{\sqrt{n}} \right)$$

$$= 100 \pm 1.96 \cdot \left(\frac{25}{\sqrt{2500}} \right)$$

$$= 100 \pm 0.98$$

$$= (99.02 \leq \mu \leq 100.98)$$

FIGURE 3.18

The calculation of a confidence interval at a 95 percent level of confidence.

$$\text{CI Endpoints}_{90\%} = \bar{x} \pm Z \cdot SE$$

$$= \bar{x} \pm Z \cdot \left(\frac{s}{\sqrt{n}} \right)$$

$$= 100 \pm 1.645 \cdot \left(\frac{25}{\sqrt{2500}} \right)$$

$$= 100 \pm 0.82$$

$$= (99.17 \leq \mu \leq 100.82)$$

FIGURE 3.19

The calculation of a confidence interval at a 90 percent level of confidence.

A/B testing

The term *behavioral data* is used specifically when describing data-driven design because it adds nuance to the concept of user data, which can be gleaned qualitatively. Behavioral data is objective: it represents users' reactions to various feature implementations, ranging from core mechanics to design. While qualitative user data is valuable, behavioral data is better suited to the MVP development mindset; quantitative, objective data points allow a product team to easily make a binary decision about retaining a specific feature.

What is an A/B test?

Behavioral data is collected and most effectively interpreted via tests—limited feature implementations that produce data points about how users interact with those features. For the freemium model, and for most digital consumer products acquired via the Internet, the most popular form of testing is called the *A/B test*. The term

"A/B test" is so named because it represents making a decision between two variants, A and B. The process involves selecting a group of users, based on a set of criteria, splitting them into sub-groups, and then simultaneously exposing each group to a different variant of a feature.

The number of groups in an A/B test isn't necessarily restricted to two; any number of variants can be tested. An example of an A/B/C test would be a test where data is collected from three variants, although tests composed of more than two variants are more popularly called multivariate tests. For the sake of simplicity, A/B testing as discussed in this book refers to a test comparing two groups.

The key to performing an A/B test and generating an actionable result is gathering enough data to be confident that the differences in the performances of the groups are due to the differences in the variants and not due to chance. This confidence is known as *statistical significance*. The larger the number of people in each group, the easier statistical significance is to determine, which is why testing more than two variants is reasonable only when the group sizes are very large.

An alternative to simultaneous A/B testing is A/B testing over time—that is, comparing the effects of different features in successive implementations and not concurrently. In general, simultaneous A/B testing is preferable to A/B testing conducted over time, because it avoids cyclicality and exogenous factors that can't be controlled. For instance, measuring one group in December and another in January for a feature that impacts revenue might skew the data in favor of December, owing almost completely to holiday shopping and not to a difference in the feature variants.

Time-based testing may be the only option for feature testing when just a small number of users can be reached at once. Since A/B tests become more reliable at larger sample sizes, simultaneous A/B testing results can be less actionable than those from time-based tests when sample sizes are restricted. The type of test chosen depends on data availability and the impact of time-based effects on the behavior of users, but generally speaking, A/B testing over time should be undertaken only when simultaneous A/B testing is not viable.

To produce actionable, interpretable results, an A/B test should be isolated; that is, it shouldn't be run in conjunction with another A/B test. Mixing A/B tests can muddy the effects of each test, rendering them difficult to act on. The benefit of running different A/B tests sequentially and not in unison is that each test receives a maximum proportion of the total available user base; the downside of testing sequentially is that it requires an extended period of time over which to execute all tests. But this isn't necessarily a bad thing; as a product evolves based on testing, certain product features in the development pipeline may become irrelevant. Sequential testing provides for a more flexible and reactive—as opposed to deterministic—product backlog.

Ultimately, A/B testing should provide a clear result of the supremacy of one feature implementation over another. The granularity of feature differences isn't prescribed as a rule, but when feature variants differ significantly from one another, it becomes more difficult to ascribe the difference in user behavior to a specific aspect of the better-performing feature. Ideally, the feature variants compared in an A/B test would be identical save for one key difference.

Designing an A/B test

Designing an A/B test and an A/B testing schedule requires forethought and consideration. As discussed earlier, A/B tests shouldn't conflict; users should see only one A/B test in a given session and, preferably, with enough infrequency so as to produce credibly independent results.

A filter should determine which users are exposed to an A/B test; for instance, a change to user registration flow necessarily involves only new users, whereas a change to a feature that only long-time users find relevant should be restricted to that user group. A/B tests must also be designed with consideration given to sample size. But demographics and past behavior may influence which users a given feature variant should involve; for instance, testing the effects of advertising positioning on users' propensities to click on those ads might be appropriate only for users who have not previously made direct purchases, limiting the total number of users available for the test. In such a case, consideration must be made for further restrictions on sample size; excluding users from a certain geography or age bracket might reduce the sample size to an unacceptable level. As the sample size of a test decreases, its results become less clear.

The logic that selects which users are exposed to a given test must be implementable in the product; this means that a mechanism for A/B testing needs to be developed and integrated into the product. Depending on how robust the product's framework for grouping users is, the logic might be limited to specific predefined attributes, which could ultimately determine which A/B tests are feasible. In general, A/B testing infrastructure is complicated to implement and requires extensive upkeep as products develop; more often than not, the limitations of the A/B testing mechanism define the parameters of an A/B test, rather than the other way around.

The length of time over which an A/B test runs will contribute to the overall sample size of the test, given that a longer test will apply to more users. The sample size needed to produce confidence in the test results isn't set in stone; sample size depends on the difference between the results of each variant. A large difference in variant results requires a smaller sample size to produce statistical significance; thus, establishing a time limit for the test is less effective than establishing a minimum user threshold. Unless user exposure can be predicted with reasonable certainty, the test should run until it has reached some minimum level of exposure, at which point it can be tested for significance.

As with product development, testing should be managed through iterations; the best-performing variant of one test is not necessarily the best functional variant possible. Tests can be continually executed on a product feature to ensure optimal performance, but testing should be regarded as a means to an end and not an end of itself. In other words, testing for the sake of testing is a distraction that can potentially divert resources from their best possible applications. Multiple iterations of the same thematic test (e.g., the background color of a landing page or the text on a registration form's submit button) will, at some point, experience a diminishing rate of return; when that rate of return drops below the 1 percent threshold, testing resources may be better allocated to new thematic tests (or moved away from testing altogether).

A/B testing is a product development tool, and like all such tools, it can help improve existing product features but it can't manifest new features out of the ether. Testing accommodates the iterative, data-driven design process by providing an avenue through which design decisions can be quickly audited for effectiveness. Testing provides data; the burden of utilizing that data to the greatest possible effect falls upon the product team.

Interpreting A/B test results

The purpose of an A/B test is to determine the superiority of one feature variant over another. If each variant is exposed to the same number of people, and the behavior of one user group is clearly preferable to the behavior of the other, then determining the better variant is straightforward: choose the variant that produced the best results. But this approach is overly simplistic, as the differences in those results could potentially be due entirely to chance. If the number of users exposed to each variant was low—say, less than 100—the results from either group could be skewed by outliers or coincidence and not by genuine, fundamental differences between the variants.

To safeguard against skewed results polluting an experiment's data sample, the product team must validate the results. This can be done in a number of ways: the first is to continue to run the test, exposing more users to it and collecting additional data points. With enough data, the product team can be confident that the sample that the test produces approximates the distribution of expected values—that is, that the sample of users being tested resembles the greater population of users and thus the results from the test represent the anticipated behavior from the entire user base. This approach necessarily requires a longer timeline than simply acting on an initial result set; in entrepreneurial environments, this extended time horizon may not be acceptable.

A second method of ensuring that test results are actionable and representative of the broader behavioral predilections of the user base is to run the test again. If the results of subsequent tests fall within an acceptable margin of the original results, then those results can be considered reliable. The problem posed by this approach is the same as that presented when staggering tests: exogenous, time-related factors (such as intra-week cyclicality or seasonal effects on user behavior) might significantly influence the results of any one test, making it incomparable to tests conducted at other times.

A third approach to validating test result reliability is a statistical method called the *t-test*, which gauges whether the difference in the average values of two groups (specifically two groups; measuring the differences across more than two groups is done with a different statistical method) is due to chance or to reliable differences in the behavior of those two groups. The t-test produces what is known as an *inferential statistic*, a generalization for the population from which a specific sample was taken.

For a t-test to produce valid results, three assumptions about the data sample must be true. The first assumption is that the groups being tested contain roughly the same number of data points. The second is that the underlying distributions of the two groups being tested exhibit the same degree of variance; this simply means that the values in each group are spread out around the average value to the same degree. The third assumption is that the samples taken from the population are normally distributed for small sample sizes, where "small" is defined somewhat loosely as fewer than 30. (Note that, when using the t-test, one does not assume that the population is normally distributed but assumes that the samples are). When the experiment samples are not normally distributed, the *Wilcoxon signed-rank test* can be used as an alternative to the t-test. If any of these assumptions are violated, the t-test will require some adjustment before producing trustworthy results. If all three of these assumptions hold, however, then the t-test, known in this case as the *independent, two-sample t-test*, can be executed on the groups.

To undertake a t-test, a *null hypothesis* must first be formulated. A null hypothesis is any statement that corresponds to a default position regarding the two test groups: the null hypothesis should represent a situation in which the test results promote that no concrete action be taken. For instance, when a test is run on the effect of a change to the background color of a registration process on two variants, a possible null hypothesis would be that a blue background versus a red background for the registration process screen produces no meaningful increase in the number of successful registrations. If accepted, neither variant would be preferred over the other, and the null hypothesis would be true. If rejected—that is, a blue background *does* result in a meaningful increase in the number of successful registrations versus a red background—then the blue background would be accepted and the null hypothesis would be rejected. The t-test produces a t-statistic, as expressed in Figure 3.20.

In the numerator, $\bar{x}_1$ represents the mean value of group one and $\bar{x}_2$ represents the mean value of group two. In the denominator, *SE* represents *standard error*, described earlier as a measure of the level of variance within the sample distribution of sample means. Standard error in the context of the t-statistic is calculated differently than within the context of confidence intervals because the t-statistic encompasses multiple samples, A and B. When calculated across more than one sample,

$$t = \frac{\bar{x}_1 - \bar{x}_2}{SE}$$

FIGURE 3.20

The t-statistic calculation.

$$SE = SP \cdot \sqrt{\frac{1}{n_1} + \frac{1}{n_2}}$$

FIGURE 3.21

Standard error calculation for the t-statistic.

$$SP = \sqrt{\frac{s_1^2 \cdot (n_1 - 1) + s_2^2 \cdot (n_2 - 1)}{(n_1 - 1) + (n_2 - 1)}}$$

FIGURE 3.22

Pooled standard deviation equation.

standard error must be adjusted by *pooled standard deviation (SP)*, as expressed in Figure 3.21.

Pooled standard deviation serves as a mean value of variance for both sample groups. Pooled standard deviation is multiplied by the square root of the sum of n_1 and n_2 to produce standard error. The symbols n_1 and n_2 represent the sizes of group one and group two, respectively and, in a two-sample t-test, they should be the same value. The equation to calculate pooled standard deviation is defined in Figure 3.22.

In the equation for pooled standard deviation, s_1^2 represents the variance of group one and s_2^2 represents the variance of group two. Likewise, n_1 and n_2 represent the sample sizes of groups one and two, respectively.

When combined, the factors defined in Figure 3.20, Figure 3.21, and Figure 3.22 form the t-statistic, which represents the ratio of the difference between the groups to the difference within the groups. The t-statistic is paired with a corresponding *p-value*, which can be referenced from any standard p-value chart. A p-value represents the probability that a result is at least as extreme as what could be expected in a subsequent test given that the null hypothesis is actually true; in other words, the p-value doesn't produce a binary decision about the result but rather a probability that the result was achieved by chance.

As with confidence intervals, standard p-values used in accepting and rejecting hypotheses, and that correspond to ranges on the normal distribution, are 10 percent (or 100 percent minus 90 percent), 5 percent (or 100 percent minus 95 percent), and 1 percent (or 100 percent minus 99 percent); in academia, a p-value less than 0.05 (5 percent) is generally required to reject the null hypothesis. The product team must determine an acceptable p-value for a given test; a lower p-value corresponds to a stricter interpretation of the test results in rejecting the null hypothesis.

Whatever the method used to validate the results of an A/B test, the general principle underlying the testing methodology should be to acquire as much data as possible. No statistical acrobatics can substitute for a robust data set; data affords confidence, and product decisions made confidently are more authoritative and, ultimately, more gratifying for the product's users.

Regression analysis

Building products that cater to (and are optimized for) observable patterns of user behavior is a necessity in the freemium model because of the revenue dynamics presented by the 5% rule. But perhaps more important than accommodating existing user patterns is predicting future behavior; since product development is iterative and data-driven in the freemium model, the trajectory of various user profiles is constantly changing. In order to gauge the effect of product changes or new features on the overall performance of the product, some predictive statistical methods must be utilized at the product management level.

One such method, and perhaps the most popular, is the regression method. It quantifies the relationship between a set of variables; a regression model produces a framework for predicting an outcome based on observable patterns in a given set of data.

What is regression?

Regression models are built using a data set of historical values. They are used to evaluate the relationship between independent and dependent variables in an existing data set and produce a mathematical framework that can be extrapolated to values of the independent variables not present in the data set. A diverse range of regression models exists, and the appropriate model to employ for a given task depends on the nature of the dependent variable being predicted. In some cases, an explicit value must be predicted—say, the total amount of revenue a new user will spend over the user's lifetime.

In other cases, the value predicted by the regression model is not numeric but categorical; following from the example above, if, instead of the total revenue a new user will spend over the user's lifetime, a model was constructed to predict whether or not the user would ever contribute revenue, the model would be predicting for a categorical (in this case, binary) variable: revenue or no revenue.

Regression models for prediction face two basic limitations. The first is that, in complex systems, the number of independent variables that affect the value of the dependent variables may be too numerous to accommodate. Following the revenue example, consider a model designed to predict the exact numerical revenue contributed by a user on a given day. Such a model might take as inputs (independent variables) various aspects of the user's behavior on the day prior to the day being predicted for: amount of contributed revenue, total sessions, total session length, etc. But a given user's predilection to contribute revenue on a specific day can be affected by events and conditions simply beyond the scope of what the product can observe: job stability, major life events, weather, etc. Any such model of per-day revenue contributions is therefore fundamentally inadequate; its output data can never be trusted as accurate, given an incomplete set of inputs.

The second limitation of regression models is that predicting future results is dependent on historical data. This problem isn't unique to regression, but regression models in product management can sometimes be interpreted as unimpeachably accurate—analytical solutions to creative problems—which, by definition, they are not. User behavior can change over time for any number of reasons, in aggregate and at the individual level.

As discussed earlier, any competent product released into a market changes the dynamics of that market and the demands that users make of products in that vertical. Since these changes take place over time, regression models must adapt to new behaviors, and behavioral transition phases—where new behavioral data conflicts with old—wreak havoc on regression results. For these reasons, regression models must be tempered with seasoned product management intuition and market insight. No market is static, and neither is user behavior.

With these limitations considered, regression models can provide valuable guidance in predicting user behavior. Regression models are commonly used in freemium product management to put users into segments that predict their "end states"— descriptions of how the users interacted with the product over their lifetimes of use—starting as early as possible. This predictive segmentation allows broad product decisions to be made from a limited set of data on a restricted timeline.

In order to make decisions from actual end state data, the product team must collect data points over many users' entire lifetimes; the behavior most important to analyze with a regression model is that of the most highly engaged users, who are in an extreme minority and can use a product for months or even years. Collecting enough real data points on highly engaged users' behavior isn't practical; instead, users must be predictively segmented from an early stage, using their behaviors throughout their lifetimes to improve the segmentation routine. The downside of this approach is lack of accuracy, but the benefits are an increased speed at which decisions can be made and an increased volume of decision-making data (since every product user, by definition, creates behavioral data artifacts in their first product session, but fewer users create data artifacts weeks later).

The regression model in product development

The process of influencing product development decisions using regression models fits nicely into the develop-release-measure-iterate feedback loop. Regression models are always built on a set of historical data in a procedure known as *training*. Training a regression model involves iteratively adding and modifying parameters to the base model until the model reaches an acceptable level of error. Once the model has been trained, it is run on a second set of data to ensure that it is predictive; in this stage, a different set of historical data is fed into the model and the model output is compared to actual independent variable values.

The definition of an acceptable level of error in a regression model's output depends on a product team's tolerance for inaccuracy, how important the metric being predicted is to the organization, and the significance of the product decision being made. If the model's output can be useful and can provide value in being merely directionally accurate or accurate in magnitude, then the precise value of the output isn't necessarily important as long as the model produces a reasonable result. If, instead, absolute precision is required, then regression modeling should be allocated an appropriate level of resources to fulfill that requirement (or a more intensive machine-learning technique should be employed).

In order to build a training set, a *feature space*—a set of independent variables that could potentially affect the value of the dependent variable or variables—must be selected. If this feature space isn't available in its entirety in the existing events library, the missing features should be added and tracked to accumulate a historical data set. Often in regression modeling, categorical (usually binary, taking a value of 1 or 0) variables that indicate the absence or presence of a user's behavior or characteristic (called *dummy variables*), are included in the feature space.

An example of a dummy variable is a 1 or 0 value corresponding to whether or not a user provided a valid email address upon registration or has ever contacted customer support. These behaviors, while not measured as continuous variables, could potentially have an effect on the independent variable, especially when the behaviors are directly related to some consequence of the independent variable.

The analyst should take care to not include too many parameters, dummy or otherwise, into a regression model in an attempt to perfectly match training data. In any model (and indeed, any system), randomness contributes to whatever outcome or pattern is being observed. No model can be totally, unfailingly accurate; the more parameters that are added to a model to attempt to perfectly match the training data, the more the model is susceptible to *overfitting*. This term describes a model that puts undue emphasis on randomness, thereby sacrificing an accurate measurement of the underlying relationship between the variables. There may not be a relationship between two variables; common sense necessarily plays a role in discerning viable candidates for regression models, lest spurious relationships be overfitted and used to make important product decisions.

Meaningfully extracting value from a regression model can take a number of forms. If the purpose of the regression model is to predict long-term behavior given some nascent product change—perhaps a change implemented through an A/B test—then the regression output itself is the value; the output dictates whether or not the change should be retained (given a minimum success threshold for the change, e.g., 50 percent increase in revenue). Often, however, a regression model may test the long-term impact of assumed changes to various metrics in an attempt to prioritize feature development. In these cases, regressions may fill no other purpose than to add analytics depth by providing several "what if" scenarios to what will essentially be an exercise in intuition.

Regression can be programmatically implemented into products to automate certain features, especially as it relates to classification; for instance, users put into certain revenue groups via real-time regression modeling may dynamically experience a change to the product interface. This happens often with advertising; as users are classified as likely to make purchases in the future, advertising features

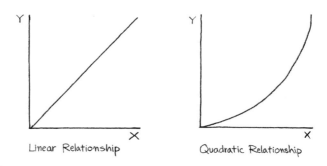

FIGURE 3.23

Graphs depicting linear (*left*) and quadratic (*right*) relationships.

are dynamically turned off to avoid alienating them. These regression classifiers tend to not be accurate unless they are trained on a voluminous set of data, however, and manual testing should reveal some level of accuracy before these are deployed in an automated fashion.

Linear regression

Linear regression is a type of regression model where a set of data points is entered into a scatter plot and a straight line is fitted to the data as well as possible. The line indicates a directional trend resulting from the relationship between the independent and dependent variables. A linear regression model works on the assumption that the relationship between the variables is linear; that is, the relationship's intensity and direction are constant over the range being examined. The purpose of linear regression is to quantify how the dependent variable changes, given a change in the independent variables.

Before a linear regression model can be constructed, some assumptions about the data set must be validated. The first assumption is that the variables indeed share a linear relationship; that is, on a per-unit basis, a change to the independent variable will always result in the same change in the value of the dependent variable. This doesn't hold true in a quadratic relationship, which is illustrated by a curvature in the data points. See Figure 3.23.

The second assumption is what is known as *homoskedasticity*, which relates to the vertical distance between the straight line drawn through the data points on the scatter plot and the data points in the sample. The vertical distance between a given data point and the line drawn through the plot is called a *residual*, and homoskedasticity means that the residuals over the range of the line are consistently spread out. This is easy to see with the scatter plot: if the data around the line grows more or less scattered at any segment, the data is not homoskedastic but *heteroskedastic*, and thus a simple linear regression model cannot be built on the data set. See Figure 3.24.

The third assumption is of *residual independence*, meaning the residuals at any point on the graph are not influenced by the residuals at the preceding point on

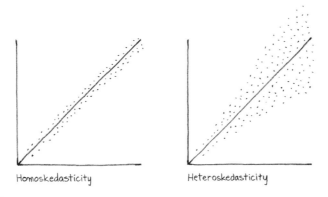

FIGURE 3.24

Regression graphs exhibiting homoskedasticity (*left*) and heteroskedasticity (*right*).

the graph. This assumption is more difficult to rigorously test for; it requires either plotting the residual values on a separate graph and looking for a pattern (which indicates that the residuals are *not* independent of each other) or calculating what is known as the *Durbin-Watson statistic*. A less scientific test for this assumption is to look for randomness in the residuals on the original graph; in other words, if a pattern is apparent within the residuals over the course of the graph, it probably indicates dependence and thus means a linear model is not appropriate for this data. If this assumption doesn't hold true, then it means the residuals are *autocorrelated*.

The fourth assumption is not a strict requirement but makes interpreting regression results easier: the residuals should be *normally distributed* around the line. Essentially, this means that a normal probability distribution function should apply vertically at each point along the line, with the bulk of the residuals falling within one standard deviation of the mean (which is a residual of 0, or the line itself) and very few falling outside of three standard deviations. This is difficult to test for and, in most cases, is not a significant concern.

The most practical approach to building a linear regression model is known as the ordinary least squares (OLS) method, which is used to minimize the sum of the squared vertical distances between the data points in the sample and the line drawn through them. The OLS method minimizes the residuals in order to build a model of the relationship between the independent and dependent variables. Thus, the model output produces a set of equation variables that can be applied to independent variables not present in the data set to produce *predicted* values of the dependent variable (given that the assumptions detailed above can be expected to hold true for data outside the original set).

The OLS method produces an equation in the form of $y = mx + b$, where y is the value of the dependent variable, m is the slope of the linear regression line (in other words, the quantified relationship between the variables), x is the value of the independent variable, and b is the value at which the line intercepts with the y-axis.

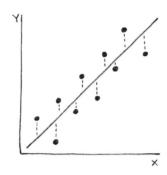

FIGURE 3.25

An ordinary least squares regression line.

Running an OLS regression by hand is impractical and unnecessary; most desktop spreadsheet software can automatically execute an OLS regression even on a fairly large data set, and statistical software packages can handle OLS regression with data points numbering in the millions. The inputs for any OLS calculation are the dependent variables (x values) and the independent variables (y values).

The important output values from the OLS function are the values for the slope of the line, the y-intercept, and the *coefficient of determination*, which is almost always represented as R^2 in statistical packages. The coefficient of determination measures the strength of the linear relationship between the variables on a scale from 0 to 1; 0 indicates no explanatory relationship between the variables and 1 indicates a perfect explanatory fit between the variables. The more robust a relationship is between the variables, the closer the R^2 statistic will be to 1.

Once the output from the OLS regression is available, values of the independent variable outside of the range provided in the data set can be substituted into the equation $y = mx + b$ to predict values of the dependent variable. These substitutions, especially when being made to predict user behavior such as revenue generated or user engagement, are usually graphed out, either in spreadsheet software or in a report.

When using only one independent variable in constructing a linear regression model, the approach is known as *simple linear regression*. When using more than one independent variable, the approach is known as *multiple linear regression*. Other models exist, too, many of which address cases wherein the assumptions outlined above are invalidated, such as those of heteroskedasticity or of non-normality of residuals.

As new test data is available, the regression model should be updated, especially if the model is not being used to make a singular decision about a product feature but rather for forecasting a metric, such as revenue. When implemented programmatically, regression models can be automated to accommodate a steady stream of new user data.

Logistic regression

Logistic regression is an extremely robust and flexible method for dichotomous classification prediction; that is, it is used to predict for a binary outcome or state, such as *yes/no*, *success/failure*, and *will occur/won't occur*. Logistic regression solves many problems faced in freemium product development that linear regression can't, because rather than predicting a numerical value (e.g., a user's total lifetime revenue), it predicts a discrete, dichotomous value (e.g., the user will spend money or not spend money on the product). For this reason, logistic regression might more accurately be called logistic classification.

Problems around health issues are often given as examples for which logistic regression is appropriate, such as whether or not a person has a specific disease or ailment, given a set of symptoms. But the examples of logistic regression's applicability for freemium product development are abundant and obvious because user segmentation is such an important part of the successful implementation of the freemium model. In order to optimize the user experience within the context of the freemium model, a user's tastes and behavioral peculiarities must be accommodated, and doing so early in the product's use allows for the greatest degree of optimization. Logistic regression is perhaps one of the best ways of undertaking such classification.

Similar to linear regression, logistic regression produces a model of the relationship between multiple variables. Logistic regression is suitable when the variable being predicted for is a probability on a binary range from 0 to 1.

Linear regression wouldn't be appropriate in such cases because the independent variable values are constrained by 0 and 1; movement beyond the dependent values provided in the sample data set could produce impossible results (below 0 or above 1). A probability curve on a binary scale must therefore be sigmoid shaped (s-shaped) and mathematically constrained between 0 and 1, which the logistic regression model provides. See Figure 3.26.

A perfectly shaped S on the probability curve in a logistic regression corresponds to a perfectly straight line in linear regression; in order to test the residual distance from the curve in the logistic regression to assess the fit of the model, the data must be transformed. This is done by converting the probabilities to *odds*, creating a logistic function from the odds and, instead of fitting the curve using the lowest value of the residuals, iteratively testing different parameters until a best fit for the log odds is found (called the maximum-likelihood method).

The maximum-likelihood method is computationally intensive and, although it can be performed in desktop spreadsheet software, it is best suited for statistical software packages. The output of logistical regression is reported in terms of *odds ratios*, which is the numerical odds (bounded by 0 and infinity) of the binary, dependent variable being true, given a one-unit increase in the independent variable.

Compared to the results of a linear regression, which might read, "A one-unit increase in day 1 user retention correlates with a 10-unit increase in lifetime user revenue," the results of a logistic regression would read, "A one-unit increase in

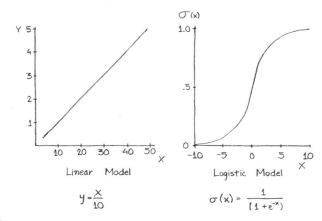

FIGURE 3.26

A linear regression equation on a linear scale (*left*) and a logistic regression equation on a probability scale (*right*).

day 1 user retention correlates with an increase by a factor of 10 in the odds that the user will eventually spend money in the product (versus not spend money)."

Because logistic models are inherently heteroskedastic, and thus the maximum-likelihood method does not seek to minimize variance in the model, there exists no measure of fit in logistic regression analogous to the R^2 statistic in linear regression. There do exist, however, several *pseudo-R^2* statistics that convey the same basic information—goodness of fit—as does R^2 and are formulated along the same scale of 0 to 1 (although in some cases, exact values of 0 or 1 may not be possible). Some common pseudo-R^2 statistics reported by statistical packages include *McFadden's R^2*, *McFadden's Adjusted R^2*, *Efron's R^2*, and the *Cox-Snell R^2*. As with the OLS R^2 statistic, the closer a pseudo-R^2 value is to 1, the better the model fits the data.

User segmentation

User segmentation is a technique used to personalize and optimize the product experience for different use cases and tastes; it involves separating users into groups based on predefined characteristics and exposing each group to the product experience that most strongly resonates with the group. User segmentation is one of the primary means by which freemium products optimize the user experience at the level of the individual user, and it is an important strategy for effectively monetizing a product within the constraints of the 5% rule.

User segmentation can be undertaken in myriad ways. One approach is to apply a semi-permanent "tag" to a user, usually within the analytics infrastructure, which adjusts the user's experience according to an optimized rule set associated with that tag. The most common such tags are related to the user's geography (such as country) and device; an obvious and straightforward example of user segmentation to optimize the user experience is localization, whereby all text in a product is automatically displayed in the official language of the user's country.

Another approach is to segment users based on past interactions with the product in order to conform the product's content and design to the user's tastes. For instance, a news reader might arrange stories based on a user's specific browsing habits. Behavioral segmentation is the most sophisticated and data-intensive implementation of the method, but it also has the potential to optimize the user experience to the greatest degree by utilizing data at the granularity of the individual user.

Data plays a central role in user segmentation: segments are built using models that gauge how different groups can best be catered to and what metric thresholds should define those groups. As a product evolves, so should user segments; product use cases can change over time, and static user segments are generally useful only for reporting or when those user segments represent demographic characteristics that are unlikely to ever change.

As new data becomes available, the models that define user segments must reassess their prior determinations to ensure that relevant optimization takes place. The need for timely data must be balanced against resource limitations and the pace of the product development schedule, but models that determine user segments—especially if those user segments have a meaningful impact on the user experience—should be revisited as often as is practical to ensure that they haven't fallen out of date.

Behavioral data

Behavioral data is the richest form of insight a product team can utilize to optimize the experience at the individual's level. Qualitative, explicit feedback from users is helpful in the product development process, and users can often articulate the shortcomings of a product very eloquently, but behavioral data communicates a more sincere truth about users' needs that aren't being fully satisfied.

Behavioral data fits nicely into user segmentation models because user segments are meant to facilitate behavior. A common user segment class is engagement. Users may be divided into groups ranging from those representing very highly engaged users to those representing users considered highly likely to abandon the product (*churn*) in the near term. With such a segment class, user behavior is the only valid means of defining the group a user belongs to, usually through number and length of product sessions. A product team might use such a segment class to dynamically reintroduce various product features to lightly engaged users or to prompt highly engaged users to invite their friends into the service. Whatever the decision, a user segment defined by engagement—a fundamental behavioral measure of delight—can only be accomplished using behavioral data.

A user segmentation model built around behavioral data likely uses a predetermined set of requirements to establish the different groups into which users are funneled. Such a requirements set should be the product of an analysis on product use and an acknowledgement of the organic way that use cases have emerged. An exploratory data analysis of, say, a new product feature might involve looking for breaking points between patterns of use and then using those breaking points to define a set of user groups. Once those user groups are defined, the breaking points are set as thresholds for grouping users and users are segmented accordingly.

The purpose of behavioral user segmentation is to influence future behavior, which can best be done with a granular, individual approach (rather than a broad, one-size-fits-all approach). Continuing from the engagement example, a product team might look at how patterns of use have naturally evolved in a product and create a set of groups (based on a combination of engagement, revenue, and usage metrics) that acknowledges those patterns, such as *highly engaged*, *mildly engaged*, and *likely to churn*. Users would then be organized into those groups based on the defined usage thresholds, and the product team's agenda would include initiatives to influence the behaviors of each group into a desired result.

Inflection metrics are very helpful in setting goals for behavioral influence and defining user segments. An inflection metric is a measure of the point at which a user is considered likely to achieve a desired later result—convert, retain, invite a friend into the product, etc. An example of an inflection metric in a freemium news reader might be *number of feeds subscribed to*, where the product team has observed that users who subscribe to at least 10 feeds become far more likely to purchase a premium subscription to the service than do users at engagement levels below 10 feeds. In other words, the tenth news feed represents a threshold at which conversion becomes probable. This threshold represents an inflection point on the user's trajectory toward conversion.

Inflection metrics are not absolutes. In the case above, the inflection metric doesn't mean that a user will convert on the tenth RSS news feed subscription, or that all users with 10 RSS news feed subscriptions ultimately convert. The metric simply represents a strong indication that a user will convert; the purpose of such an indication is to provide a concrete, easily articulated goal for the product team, in terms of influencing product behavior.

If the tenth RSS news feed subscription is seen as a goal, the product team can endeavor to influence every user to subscribe to at least 10 news feeds. This creates an obvious line about which users can be organized into groups: users who have subscribed to at least 10 news feeds and users who have not. The users who have not yet subscribed to 10 news feeds will likely be exposed to a different product experience than those who have, with the experience featuring vigorous inducements to subscribe to additional news feeds until they reach their tenth subscription.

Inflection metrics provide clear guidelines for testing and updating behavioral models. An inflection metric might represent the basis over which a product feature is prioritized, given that feature's impact on progress toward the inflection metric. When inflection metrics can be established as critical goals, prioritizing a product feature backlog becomes a quantitative and objective, rather than an intuitive, process: whichever features best position the product to achieve the inflection metric are of the highest priority.

Behavioral objectives, especially inflection metrics, must be revisited as the product evolves and its feature set grows. New users across long time horizons bear little relation to each other in freemium products; an inflection metric for early adopters doesn't necessarily hold true for users who adopt the product in a more mature state. The models that define inflection points and user segments don't need to be dynamic and automated, but they should be timely enough for product teams to feel comfortable that they're striving to achieve ambitious yet achievable goals.

Demographic data

Demographic data plays an important role in user segmentation strategy, but it is not nearly as valuable as behavioral data. Behavioral data provides richer, more individualized insight into how a specific user interacts with a product from a perspective more conducive to increased monetization. Demographic data points are broad and difficult to infer specific conclusions from and demographic data tends to not shift over time with the evolution of the product. Whereas behavioral data adapts to new product features being introduced, demographic data say, a user's country of origin—remains constant.

That said, demographic data used in conjunction with behavioral data can contribute new dimensions to analysis initiatives and therefore provide value. What's more, demographic data is available as soon as a user interacts with a product for the first time, whereas meaningful behavioral data must accumulate through product use. As a set of first-pass regression points, demographic data allows for determining an initial segmentation of a user, which can be revisited once behavioral data related specifically to that user's tastes is collected. The timeliness and immediacy of demographic data in itself is of value; the sooner a user can be profiled, the sooner the user's experience can be optimized.

Additionally, while behavioral data provides context around intent (especially with regard to monetization), demographic data provides context around ability. And though optimizing a product for user tastes has more potential in terms of personalizing the product experience and optimizing for revenue, understanding a user group's ability to make purchases can help in making prioritization decisions.

Certain geographies don't monetize well in freemium products, especially when those freemium products haven't been localized for those regions. Likewise, monetization patterns between various devices and product platforms differ. A user's demographic profile can contribute useful insight into the user's propensity to monetize. Location is the most basic and generic user demographic information available and should be accessible on almost any platform. Location can be used to estimate disposable income and linguistic and cultural norms that can affect how the product is used. Localization is a particular concern with respect to freemium products, given concerns over scale: the amount of text present in a product's user interface can significantly impact how well it is received in markets for which it has not been localized.

Localization is a time-consuming and, in some cases, expensive endeavor that must be undertaken with a full understanding of the potential return on investment.

Such an expense should be assumed only when the size of the applicable segment is known, which is possible only through tracking geographic user data and researching the product's potential addressable market in a given region.

Device data can be very instructive when segmenting users, especially on stratified platforms like mobile, where the quality of devices spans a broad range. Device data should inform product feature launch decisions—specifically, which user segments to launch for—because compatibility and general performance problems can have a negative impact on the reception and growth of a product. This impact is most notable in highly social products with active communities and in products launched on platforms for which user reviews affect discoverability. The quality of a user's device can also serve as an indicator for disposable income and thus the propensity (and ability) to spend money in a freemium product, although it is a weaker signal than some behavioral indicators.

Demographic data can become more useful when it is available at a deeper level, such as when a user has connected to a product through a social network's API and the user's behavioral data from that network is accessible. This level of granularity of demographic data—age, gender, education level, employment, general interests, etc. —can be used to emulate behavioral data, which combines the benefits of user tastes with the immediacy of demographic data.

Better still, social networking connectivity also provides information about a user's friends and whether or not they are also using the product. Friends' use of a freemium product can be a potent leading indicator of a propensity to make purchases in the product, especially if those friends have made purchases in the past. Social networking data can represent a goldmine of demographic information (albeit unverifiable) about a user that can add nuance to segmentation filters.

All told, while it is valuable in its own right, demographic user data is put to best use when combined with behavioral data. Broad-stroke generalizations about users from a specific geography or who use a specific device aren't independently actionable; they merely describe the state of the user base. Information about how a user interacts with a product is far more valuable than information about the user in a real-world context, especially in freemium products where monetization and engagement are driven by personal delight.

Predicting user segments

User segmentation based on the current state of users is valuable for the purposes of reporting, where it can be used to gauge, over time, the success of new product features in engaging and monetizing users. But current state user segmentation can't help in the feature pipeline prioritization process, and it can't help determine how features should be implemented. To assist in these initiatives, segments must be based on predictions for a future state, most often the end state.

An example of an end state, predictive user segment is the total revenue segment class, where users are grouped based on how much total revenue they are expected to spend in the product over their lifetimes. Such a prediction, if accurate, could help in optimizing the experiences of the users predicted to contribute the most revenue, as well as helping the product team provide a better product experience to all users by using monetization as a proxy for delight. In short, current state user segmentation, while immediately accurate (because it merely articulates the narrative captured by the product's data infrastructure), can do little to direct the future of the product toward an optimized user experience.

Predicting a user's future state requires knowledge about their current state. Demographic and behavioral data can be used to build a profile of the user in the user's current state, and certain aspects of the user's behavioral history might be able to be extrapolated into the future. But the best way to predict a user's future behavior (and thus the user's future state) is to understand how similar users behaved. This is how regression models are implemented: historical data is used to estimate the relationship between variables, and that relationship is applied to the user's current state to project a future state.

Freemium products are designed for longevity; a long lifespan goes hand-in-hand with long-tail monetization. Current state user segments are most useful for the purpose of reporting and as inputs to models that facilitate estimating end state segmentation; in turn, end state segments are only useful if user behavior can be influenced. Every user interacts with a freemium product for the first time as a non-engaged, non-paying user, someone touring the product but not yet committed to using it with any enthusiasm. Some product teams neglect to address the malleability of that user's trajectory through the product; they consider a first-time user's relationship with the product as predestined and immutable. But users do respond to personalized, optimized experiences, and a user's future state in a product can be molded in a way that benefits both parties. Users provide a vast amount of information to product teams about what they want, but they will only do so if they believe that information is being acknowledged. Churn is the result of product teams ignoring what users tell them, through the users' own behaviors, about how they want the product to be developed.

User segmentation prediction models need not be tightly integrated into the analytics system; if enough demographic and behavioral data about current user state is available, then models can be built independently and the results can exist separately from the ever-growing product data set. More important than current data in user segmentation prediction models are relationships that are abstract enough to be generally true, short of drastic changes in the product or the user base. If, for instance, monetization patterns in the earliest sessions of product use are strong determinants of end revenue state, then constantly measuring the degree of that relationship is a less impactful use of resources than is using that data to influence early monetization behavior.

Flexibility is an important characteristic of user segmentation models. If models cannot be easily updated with new assumptions or historical data, they aren't likely to be revisited once new information becomes available. The best models are built as frameworks that can adapt to new parameters without being programmatically reconstructed. And as end state data accumulates—that is, as users churn out—the model should be tested against not only current state inputs but also end state outputs. Users abandoning the product leave a trail of data artifacts as they do so; these artifacts can be used to help hone the product team's understanding of the relationship between current state and end state. Such artifacts are perhaps more valuable than timely current state data, if only for being more scarce.

Actual end state data is the only standard against which the accuracy of predictive user segmentation models can be judged. But numeric accuracy isn't necessarily the highest concern with predicting a user end state; if models are directionally accurate and accurately assess the magnitude of a relationship between variables, they can be used to prioritize feature development.

Only a wizard could predict a user's end state in terms of revenue to the penny, and the pursuit of wizardry through programmatic statistical prediction faces rapidly diminishing returns. An understanding of the dynamics of a product is enough to make decisions not for the sake of matching reality to predictions but for enhancing the user's experience to the utmost degree.

Freemium Metrics

4

Instrumenting freemium products

The minimum viable product (MVP) model has data at its functional core: the develop-release-measure-iterate feedback loop drives the product, from its earliest state through to release, based on behavioral data harvested from users, not product team intuition. But the need for data—actionable, reliable data—is greater within the context of the freemium business model than perhaps any other commercial configuration because only a very small fraction of the user base can ever be expected to contribute revenue. In the freemium model, a second-order requirement is imposed on the data the MVP produces: it must provide for identifying the 5 percent.

Minimum viable metrics

Without robust behavioral data, a freemium MVP cannot effectively undergo the iterative metamorphosis process that results in a finished product. This reality places a requirement on the freemium development process: the necessity of tracking a minimum set of metrics needed to optimize development in pursuit of greater user engagement. This set is known as the *minimum viable metrics* (MVM).

In non-freemium business models, almost all data produced by the MVP is actionable because the average use case, and thus, high-level aggregate data, provides valuable, revenue-relevant insight into product usage. But in the freemium model, only data generated by the users who will eventually pay can be used to make product decisions that lead to increased revenue. The difficulty presented by this model dynamic is that the MVP requires a data sample large enough to ensure that revenue predictions are possible; such a data sample can be collected only from a user base so large that a company can assume that a meaningfully sized contingent of highly engaged users is present.

Minimum viable metrics are necessarily more extensive in the freemium model than in other business models because freemium behavioral data must provide enough volume and enough diversity to make informed product development decisions that drive revenue. Minimum viable metrics cover a broad range of product characteristics, which can be broken down into four high-level categories: retention, engagement, monetization, and virality. While each metric category contributes to the picture of a product's overall health, the retention metrics are considerably more decisive than the others are; user retention is the principal measure of freemium product performance.

Since analytics are largely invisible to users, minimum viable metrics might seem to be incompatible with the concept of an MVP. But a traditional MVP release simply doesn't work under freemium conditions; the business model requires a minimum level of user insight that is an order of magnitude greater than what is needed in other models. Since business models fund development methodologies—not the other way around—an MVP must first and foremost facilitate the generation of revenue. In freemium product development, that is accomplished through minimum viable metrics.

Working with metrics in the freemium model

The core requirement of robust freemium analytics blurs and complicates the traditional professional designations within the realm of business intelligence. In non-freemium businesses, analytics infrastructure development and maintenance can be accomplished almost entirely independent of analysis; production programming is required only of database administrators, and analysis can be conducted capably with knowledge of only SQL and, in extreme cases, a scripting language. Generally speaking, outside of the freemium model, analysts conduct analysis and database administrators maintain the data warehouses from which data is extracted.

Analysis in a freemium context is contingent on the existence of very large data sets, and these can be accessed and analyzed only programmatically. If analysts lack proficiency in a programming language, large data sets are inaccessible to them without complete reliance on a database administrator or software engineer. Perhaps more importantly, large data sets are practically useless without some knowledge of programming, because the true value in massive volumes of data can be extracted only through statistical techniques that are too sophisticated to be implemented non-programmatically.

The challenges posed by the size and character of the data sets produced by freemium products (and data-intensive products from traditional business models) have spawned a new class of analyst: the *data scientist*. A data scientist employs predictive statistical techniques to large volumes of data to produce granular insight into behavioral patterns. With a background in a quantitative field such as statistics, economics, mathematics, or computer science, a data scientist can utilize large volumes of data to the fullest extent possible by employing what are known as *machine learning* techniques: pattern-based predictive algorithms that become more accurate with increased exposure to data.

In a freemium data environment, the data scientist sits somewhere between the product and the back-end, training and implementing algorithms that optimize the user experience using data collected either directly from raw data dumps (usually in the form of server logs) or from the data warehouse. The data scientist's principal role is to glean insight from the data that can be used directly to improve the product; rather than analyze data sets and make product recommendations,

ANALYTICS ROLES

DATA SCIENTIST   ANALYST   DATA ENGINEER

CREATES & IMPLEMENTS   CONVERTS DATA   MAINTAINS DATA
OPTIMIZATION ALGORITHMS INTO ACTIONABLE   INFRASTRUCTURE
                        INSIGHT

FIGURE 4.1

The roles comprising an analytics team.

the data scientist builds automated mechanisms for optimizing product features dynamically.

Given the data scientist's focus on product feature optimization, the *analyst* in the freemium environment is freed to focus purely on revenue optimization through a broader managerial lens. In freemium product development, the locus of the analyst's focus shifts away from product feature optimization and toward product prioritization and general management insight. The analyst's data is provided primarily in aggregated format by the data warehouse and need not be precisely current—a lag time of a few hours or even a day is acceptable. The analyst leads reporting efforts, builds dashboards, and circulates key performance indicator reports.

The raw and aggregated data in the freemium environment is the purview of the *data engineer*, whose principal duties include maintaining the back-end and the events library to ensure data consistency and availability. The data engineer also manages the product's data warehouse infrastructure, ensuring that data is consistent, accurate, and aggregated according to business logic determined by the analyst. The data engineer doesn't interface directly with the product except to make changes to the events library for tracking purposes.

The titles mentioned here, illustrated in Figure 4.1, are less important than the separation of roles implicitly dictated by the freemium focus on revenue maximization. The data scientist handles all aspects of product optimization through deep statistical analysis of the large data sets afforded by freemium data. Data scientists may even develop what are known as *data products*—meta products within the product that are built entirely algorithmically (these are discussed in Chapter 6)—to enhance the performance of various product features. The analyst complements this product optimization effort with a singular focus on product revenue. The data engineer provides operational support by unifying the data available to the data scientist with that which is available to the analyst so that reporting and product initiatives can reconcile.

Retention

Retention is a retroactive, time-based measure of product use. Retention is generally calculated and presented for a specific day and is aggregated over a segment of the user base in terms of days since those users first interacted with the product. A retention dashboard might display values for a product's day 1, day 3, day 7, and day 14 retention metrics, which respectively communicate the percentage of users returning to the product one, three, seven, and fourteen days after interacting with it for the first time.

At the user level, retention metrics are binary indications (true/false) of whether or not a user returned to the product some specific number of days after first using it. For example, if a user first interacted with a product on a Monday and returned to it the next day, then that user's day 1 retention value would be true (or 1). If the user didn't return on Wednesday but did return on Thursday, then the day 2 retention value would be false (or 0) and the day 3 retention value would be true (or 1).

At the product level, retention metrics are aggregated across the user base; the values for all users' retention metrics are summed for each metric, then each value is divided by the number of users who first interacted with the product on the day being consider for analysis, in order to produce a percentage. For instance, to calculate a product's day 1 retention for yesterday, the number of users who first used the product yesterday and returned to it today would be summed and then divided by the total number of users who first used the product yesterday, regardless of whether they used it again today. A retention metric should be attributed to the day on which users first interacted with the product.

The retention profile

The purpose of retention metrics is to track the frequency and longevity of product use; through a portfolio of retention metrics, a product team can track the length of time, in days, over which users generally interact with a product before churning out of the user base. Retention metrics, when graphed, provide a valuable visual "funnel" that describes the timeline of the average use case for the product. Retention metrics can likewise be aggregated by any number of dimensions to provide granular analysis of use patterns.

Conceptually, retention is most beneficial to the product development process when thought of as a profile as opposed to a collection of disparate, independent metrics. The *retention profile* is the measurable, quantifiable curve that can be constructed by unifying the retention metrics into a singular property of product use. (See Figure 4.2.) In practice, the shape of this curve provides high-level visual cues about when, relative to first use, users generally abandon the product.

The retention profile is a useful measure of user behavior for another reason: it provides the product team with a quantitative basis for estimating user lifetime through a set of metrics that can be aggregated around any number of dimensions. In other words, the retention profile provides insight into how specific user

FIGURE 4.2

A freemium product's retention curve, with percentage of returning users on the y-axis and days since registration on the x-axis.

segments interact with the product and can be used to estimate how long they will use the product.

As a general rule, the retention profile decays in a pattern such that day 7 retention is 50 percent of day 1 retention, and day 30 retention is 50 percent of day 7 retention. For example, in a product in which 80 percent of new users return the next day, 40 percent of new users can be expected to return seven days after first use, and 20 percent can be expected to return 30 days later.

The area under the retention profile curve represents total likely lifetime, given that each point on the curve serves as a probability of a user returning to the product a corresponding number of days after first using it. Because the area under the curve extends theoretically indefinitely along the x-axis, calculating *terminal retention*—the point at which the curve descends to 0, or the point at which no users are expected to be retained—is impractical. In modeling the retention profile, a useful rule of thumb is to set day 365 retention to some terminal value (for example, 1 percent). Constraining the retention curve to a finite space allows for a more constructive calculation of total user lifetime.

The nature of the retention profile curve provides some guidance in the product development process when designing features to boost retention. The area of the curve (and, by proxy, total user lifetime) increases most when the entire curve is shifted up. But absent the possibility of a universal shift—which is generally implemented through fundamental product improvement and not at the individual feature level—increases to early-stage retention have a greater effect on total lifetime than increases to late-stage retention, assuming the decay pattern holds constant.

As stated earlier, retention is the most significant metrics category that a product team must address in the freemium development process, as retention metrics communicate *delight*: the extent to which a product meets users' needs. Higher retention corresponds to a better product experience, greater personal investment, and a

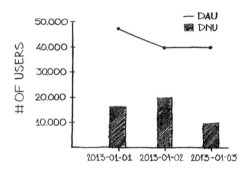

FIGURE 4.3

DNU and DAU graphed on the same chart.

higher level of fulfillment in the product's fundamental use case. Without a strong retention profile, no other metrics group is worth addressing; the retention profile measures the usefulness of a product, and a basic lack of usefulness cascades across monetization, engagement, and virality to broadcast poor performance.

Retention metrics

The most basic metrics related to retention are *daily new users* (*DNU*) and *daily active users* (*DAU*), which are simply counts of activity. A new user is generally defined as a user interacting with the product for the first time. The level of activity that represents an interaction is left intentionally ambiguous, as it can vary between platforms; for instance, for a mobile application, the point of first interaction could be defined as the initial application download, but for a web application, first inter-action might be defined as a specific event that takes place after registration.

DAU is defined as the number of users who interact with the product on a given day; as with DNU, the definition of an interaction is left to the discretion of the product team. DAU and DNU can be rendered on a daily basis as bar or line graphs. Since DNU is typically significantly lower than DAU, the metrics should either be rendered on different charts or on one chart with two y-axes, as in Figure 4.3.

In practice, daily retention metrics are tracked individually for days 1 through 7, day 14, day 28, and then intermittently, based on the age of the product and the product team's development agenda. (See Figure 4.4.) The purpose of tracking day 28 retention as opposed to that of day 30 is that, in multiples of seven, weekly cyclicality can be captured; if there is a pattern of product use on a specific day of the week, the pattern will be visible when retention metrics are tracked in seven-day intervals.

Retention is best calculated retrospectively, which means that the values of retention metrics are calculated for previous days, given activity on the current day. In other words, users returning to a product don't affect the current day's reten-tion metrics but affect the retention metrics for the various days on which those

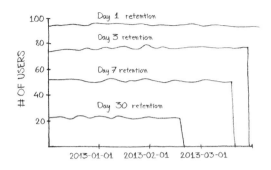

FIGURE 4.4

A retention chart tracking day 1, day 3, day 7, and day 30 retention over time.

users first interacted with the product. This type of grouping is an implementation of *cohort analysis*, a topic explored in more detail in Chapter 7.

Associating retention metrics with the days on which users first interact with a product allows retention changes to be tracked with product changes. For instance, in the retrospective model, a user who joins today and will return tomorrow is associated with today's day 1 retention metric (which is calculated retrospectively, tomorrow). If a change to the product is integrated today, all of today's retention metrics will reflect that change, making it easy to identify the effects of that change on the entire portfolio of retention metrics.

When retention metrics are not tracked retrospectively but are tracked as a function of the current day, the retention metrics relevant to a product change—especially long-term metrics like day 28 retention—are distributed across an extended reporting timeline and are more difficult to associate with any given product change.

Retention metrics are best depicted as individual line graphs on one time series chart. This allows for seeing changes in retention over time while still providing for broad trends to be understood. Since retention metrics depicted this way displays specific values for each day (as opposed to averages over a period of time), small data sets can produce results that may not make sense, giving, for instance, a day 1 retention that is below day 4 retention for a given day. With a large enough data set, these irregularities, which arise out of users returning to a product after a period of inactivity, generally correct themselves, and retention metrics converge to consistency.

When retention values are charted over a trailing period—that is, the graph depicts a time range up through the most recent date—the values for each individual retention graph will drop to zero for days not far back enough to calculate values for (since retention is attributed to the date of registration). For example, on a chart tracking retention values for the previous 90 days, day 30 retention values will be available only for dates at least 30 days in the past. Dates more recent than that—yesterday, for example—will exhibit day 30 retention values of zero. See Figure 4.4.

Churn can be an interesting metric to track alongside retention metrics, but its definition is subjective and prone to error. When churn is defined as a user who has left the product and is not expected to return, then, like retention metrics, it is most usefully tracked retroactively. The problem with calculating churned users is defining the threshold for likelihood to not return. If the threshold for likelihood to not return is determined to be the minimum point, measured in days since last interaction with the product, past which the majority of users do not return, then the metric will almost certainly overestimate churn. But if churn is determined to be the point past which no user has ever returned, churn will likely be underestimated. A happy medium exists between these two extremes, but the nature of the user base and the product dictate where that point lies. A good compromise might be defining churn as the point past which 80 percent of users do not return.

Variable historical metrics—metrics for which historical values can change—are generally considered to run counter to best practices because they obstruct the decision-making process. Therefore, churn is best defined in the abstract, as a measure of disengagement, or *likelihood* to abandon the product, and reported consistently, with exceptions not accommodated for. Bar or line graphs, reported daily, work well to represent churn.

Tracking retention

The calculation of retention metrics is highly dependent on how a product interaction is defined, which is a decision that should be made by the product team early in the development process. If an interaction is defined as the start of any use session, no matter the length or quality of the session, then interaction is simple. But if a minimum threshold is required in order for a session to count as an interaction, such as a login or progress past some point in the user interface, then that threshold should be precisely defined, documented, and rendered auditable in the events library.

Once a product interaction has been defined, tracking the retention metrics is fairly straightforward. DAU is a count of all users who interact with the product on a given day; DNU is a count of all users who interact with the product for the first time on a given day.

The calculation of daily retention metrics is more complex. For any given daily retention metric, the analytics system must calculate the day of product use for each user and group users accordingly. These values—the number of users who registered a given number of days ago and interacted with the product on that day—are then divided by the DNU from the given number of days ago and attributed to that date. For these values to be calculated, the analytics system must track the date of first use for each user. Once a given retention metric is calculated retroactively, its value should be recorded in the analytics system for that day and made available for reporting. See Figure 4.5.

Churn should be defined with precision before it is reported, as a product interaction is. Once the threshold for churn has been set (in terms of number of days),

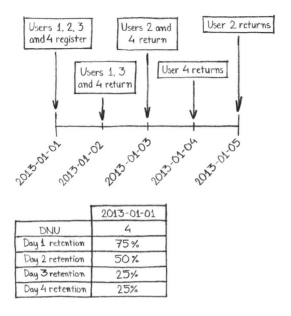

FIGURE 4.5

A data table with calculated retention metrics for a given day.

the churn metric can be calculated by counting the number of users from the entire user base that, as of today, have not interacted with the product in exactly that number of days. That value of churn can be stored in the analytics system. As with retention, this calculation delay creates an effect in which churn is not available for any trailing days, relative to today, below the defined threshold (e.g., if the threshold for churn is three days without product interaction, then churn metrics won't be available for yesterday or the day before).

Accurately tracking retention is eminently important. The events library should be designed to accommodate the idiosyncrasies of the product with respect to defining churn and product interactions; these are significant strategic determinations that should receive adequate consideration in the earliest stage of the development process. Conceptual ambiguity or insufficiently rigorous case consideration could result in a situation, after product launch, where retention metrics must be retroactively updated, or worse, where multiple versions of the retention metrics must be tracked to accommodate a use case that wasn't predicted at the design stage.

Monetization

Tracking monetization at a reasonable level of granularity is an important component of revenue optimization. Given the primacy of revenue concerns in the freemium development process, the fact that monetization metrics are relegated to a less decisive position than are retention metrics may seem counterintuitive. But strong user retention sets the premise for monetization (and other user behavior); a product that doesn't retain users to an acceptable degree will likewise not monetize to a degree that utilizes the advantages presented by the freemium model. Strong retention is a prerequisite in the freemium model, and retention metrics are therefore of the highest priority in scheduling the development pipeline.

That said, monetization metrics are a critical focal point in the product team's reporting regimen. Monetization metrics communicate not only volume of revenue but also crucial shifts in spending patterns over time and the degree to which the freemium model is being leveraged to produce highly monetizing users. Perhaps most crucially, monetization metrics elucidate the highly influential *conversion rate*, which is the percentage of users who convert to revenue producers through direct purchases. This number, tracked over time, provides valuable insight into how well the value proposition of paid features has been communicated to users.

Conversion

Conversion is a measure of monetization relative to the entire size of the user base. It is usually presented as a percentage of users who have made a purchase either on a specific day or over the lifetime of a product. Under freemium circumstances, conversion rates are usually extremely low; under the 5% rule, this book posits the percentage of users likely to ever directly contribute revenue through purchases in a freemium product at a universal value of 5 percent or less. Members of the 5 percent are considered as "converted users."

Conversion is not as straightforward a metric as it might seem. This is because many freemium products draw revenue from two sources: advertising and the purchase of premium functionality. Advertising revenue muddies the definition of a converted user; if conversion is considered simply the process of contributing revenue to the freemium product, then viewing advertising is a means of converting. But the act of showing advertising to a user can have a significant negative impact on that user's likelihood of contributing revenue to the freemium product through a direct purchase of premium functionality, which is the more traditional definition of conversion.

Some freemium products refrain from showing ads to users until those users have been deemed unlikely to convert in the traditional sense, meaning advertising is a form of anti-conversion; it is a method of monetizing users who will not otherwise convert. Pursuing this strategy, classifying the viewing of an ad as a form of conversion would result in an artificially high conversion rate (in some cases, 100 percent), since any user who made it past a behavioral threshold for purchase prediction would either be shown advertising or convert with a high probability. Artificially high metrics aren't useful; they are noisy distractions from true signal.

Viewing advertising shouldn't be considered a form of conversion in freemium metrics. The crux of the freemium product is that, through building massive scale with a price point of $0, the loss of upfront revenue can be compensated for and eclipsed by rigorous monetization of highly engaged users. This principle should inform the development and monetization strategy of a freemium product from the earliest stage of development.

Advertising and high engagement are, at a conceptual level, mutually exclusive: the purpose of advertising is to encourage a user to consider another product, whereas the purpose of the freemium model is to cater to the needs of the most highly engaged users. By definition, exposing a user to an ad could potentially discourage that user from engaging with the product to the greatest extent possible. Since conversion is a proxy measure of engagement, viewing advertising cannot be considered a form of conversion.

This doesn't mean advertising has no place in freemium products; when advertising represents a stream of revenue that in no way affects a freemium product's ability to monetize highly engaged users, then it effectively is a revenue optimization technique. The problem with implementing advertising into a freemium product is determining when that advertising negatively affects monetizing highly engaged users, which it can do in myriad indirect ways. The most obvious way is by alienating users who have not yet made a purchase but would otherwise become highly engaged users; unless a product's predictive models for purchase behavior are irreproachably accurate, any advertising shown to users will likely have a negative impact on future monetization. Calculating the impact of the advertising revenue versus the lost revenue by alienated potential purchasers is time-consuming and prone to erroneous results. The second way advertising can have a negative impact on the monetization behavior of highly engaged users is not intuitive; advertising can turn away users who will never pay. Passion for a product can't be completely captured through monetization; a user's enthusiasm for a product may not be reflected in the amount of disposable income that user has available to spend on it. Product advocacy can happen serendipitously and independent of spending patterns; this effect is amplified by the viral properties of modern social networks and social media channels, where an influential user's testimony might contribute far more aggregate revenue than any set of purchases that user could make directly in the product.

Users who will never make a direct purchase in a product, or *non-paying users* (NPUs), should be celebrated by a freemium product, as they not only represent a portion of the scale that freemium products so desperately need to achieve full business model optimization, but they can also serve as product ambassadors, recruiting through social or physical channels the future highly engaged users who contribute to the product's revenue streams. Advertising can estrange NPUs as easily as it can highly engaged users.

A product's *conversion rate*, therefore, should be calculated as the number of users who make direct in-product payments divided by the total number of users. Conversion rate is valuable when calculated over the lifetime of a product but also should be reported on a daily basis to highlight changes over time. When depicted in a report, conversion rate can take the form of a bar or line graph over time, as shown in Figure 4.6.

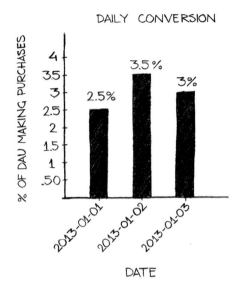

FIGURE 4.6

A daily conversion bar chart.

Revenue metrics

Revenue metrics should communicate the extent to which money is being spent through direct purchases in the product. This is best articulated through average revenue per user (ARPU) and average revenue per paying user (ARPPU).

ARPU is an average measure of revenue contribution on a per-user basis. The obvious value of this metric is, when calculated over the lifetime of the product, as an indicator of how much any individual user is worth. Lifetime ARPU, or the average revenue contributed per user over the lifetime of a product, can provide some insight into the habits of a large group of users within the product. But as stated earlier, the concept of an average user in freemium products is specious; when implemented properly, the freemium model produces a stratified distribution of behavioral profiles. Given the Pareto distribution, the word "average" is of little substance in analyzing a freemium product at the level of the entire population.

Lifetime ARPU, then, is not instructive when considered for the entire user base, but daily ARPU is. Daily ARPU communicates the average revenue contributed per user on a daily basis, or the total revenue from direct purchases divided by the number of users who interact with the product on any given day. Daily ARPU can be used to gauge the effectiveness of the product catalogue or the quality of users entering the product's user base; a declining daily ARPU value over time can point to a fading value proposition for the product's premium features. Daily ARPU is sometimes referred to as average revenue per daily active user, or ARPDAU.

Note that lifetime ARPU can be a valuable metric when considered for a specific, well-defined user segment, especially at the high end of the monetization scale. But lifetime ARPU is also susceptible to being rendered obsolete over an extended timeline; as a product evolves, the spending patterns of users from weeks or months in the past may not serve as valid indicators of how new users will behave with the improved product. When a product has undergone rapid, significant iteration, a user whose engagement is 180 days old likely had a completely different experience in the first week of use than a user registering today. Thus, lifetime ARPU, while important in ascribing value to user segments, can be difficult to interpret at later stages of product use.

Lifetime ARPPU is a bit more instructive with respect to the entire user base than is lifetime ARPU because the number of paying users in any freemium system will necessary be far lower than the number of total users, rendering ARPPU a more contextualized metric. But despite its increased relevance, lifetime ARPPU is still easily misinterpreted and applied; lifetime ARPPU is not a measure of how much the average paying user is worth because no average paying user should exist in a freemium product.

Both daily ARPPU and daily ARPU present useful pictures of patterns in monetization, but daily ARPPU has the added benefit of being more significantly affected by changes in monetization mechanics. Thus, daily ARPPU is very effective as a measure of improvement to changes to the product catalogue and to promotional offers because it is more susceptible to shocks, given that the denominator in the calculation—paying users—is so much smaller than in ARPU. Daily ARPPU provides insight into how well and how persistently changes meant to affect revenue generation perform.

Both ARPU and ARPPU can be calculated over any period of time for which data is available, but calculating values of these metrics for longer time periods than a day requires the analytics system to be able to distinguish between total users and unique users. Given that a user can interact with a product on multiple days within a prolonged time period, calculating a non-daily value of ARPU or ARPPU, such as a weekly value, requires the analytics system to first calculate unique users within that time period.

ARPU and ARPPU are best depicted as line or bar charts on different graphs, given the different scales on which they sit, as seen in Figure 4.7. A direct relationship exists between conversion, ARPU, and ARPPU; the smaller the difference between ARPU and ARPPU, the higher the conversion rate must be.

To contextualize the daily average monetization metrics, a *product catalogue distribution* can be depicted as a histogram to provide visual cues as to where revenue is being derived. The product catalogue distribution is a set of bar charts, displayed horizontally, representing the individual items within the product catalogue as either a percentage of total revenues, as illustrated in Figure 4.8, or as absolute revenue amounts. The product catalogue distribution helps the product team understand where the bulk of revenues are derived from, given a diverse product catalogue. The shape of the product catalogue distribution shouldn't necessarily match

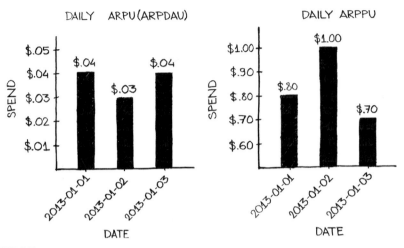

FIGURE 4.7

Daily ARPU (ARPDAU) bar chart (*left*), and ARPPU bar chart (*right*).

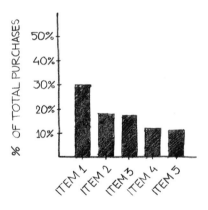

FIGURE 4.8

The product catalogue distribution by percentage of total product revenues.

the shape of the distribution of prices within the product catalogue, although price points contribute to purchasing behavior.

Aggregating the product catalogue distribution by day would create a chart too hectic to extract value from; instead, the distribution should be aggregated over a trailing time period—a week, for example—in order for the graph to capture a meaningful volume of purchase data. For more detailed daily trend analysis, the product team might create a separate report displaying daily purchases of each item within the product catalogue.

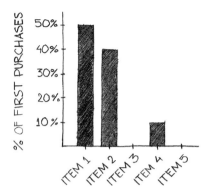

FIGURE 4.9

The first purchase distribution.

Another useful implementation of the product catalogue distribution is the *first purchase distribution*, illustrated in Figure 4.9, which graphs the items in the product catalogue as the percentage of first purchases the items represent. In other words, the number of times each item was purchased as a user's first purchase in the product is counted and divided by the total number of first purchases made in the time period being considered.

This graph is useful in determining which products most compel users to convert; it may provide valuable insights into the impetuses that convince users the product is worth contributing revenues to. This distribution is best depicted on the basis of a trailing time period.

Engagement

Engagement metrics capture user behaviors relating to product interaction. The most obvious of these metrics track length and frequency of use, both of which the product team should use in crafting the experience that takes the most advantage of the freemium model's benefits.

In the freemium model, consistent, daily use is the highest ambition: when a user interacts with a product on a daily basis, embedding the product within the user's lifestyle, then the user is likely value the product as a source of genuine delight. Put another way, when a user interacts with a product on a daily basis, the user is much more likely to apportion appreciable amounts of disposable income to it. Engagement metrics, especially session frequency and session length, not only measure the extent to which users interact with products but also help curate those interactions.

No prescribed interaction session length or daily frequency count can describe the most revenue-advantageous use case for the vast number of platforms and product genres in which the freemium model can be successfully employed. Instead, engagement metrics should be used in the develop-release-measure-iterate feedback loop to measure and maximize users' satisfaction with the product.

The onboarding funnel

A user's first session with a product is a critical determinant of the user's lifetime with the product; it is therefore worthy of the product team's when trying to optimize the user experience. In any freemium product—especially when massive scale is achieved through large-scale organic user base growth and aggressive paid acquisition—a percentage of new users will churn out during their first sessions. While this concept should be taken as a rule, effort should be expended to ensure that this percentage is as low as possible.

The *onboarding funnel* is an events-based graph of user *fall-off*, or product abandonment within the formative first moments of interaction between the user and the product. The *onboarding process* should be defined by the product team from an early stage in the development cycle; in some cases, the onboarding period is a very explicit sequence of events within the first interaction session, and in others it might be subtly implemented over multiple sessions. At a conceptual level, the purpose of the onboarding process is to introduce a new user to the product and equip the user with the knowledge necessary to interact competently with the product's feature set, given some level of compatibility between the user's needs and the product's fundamental use case.

This level of compatibility is an important point of consideration when designing the use case. An aggressive onboarding process will very quickly alert a user for whom the product's use case isn't entirely valuable that the product won't meet the user's needs. Such an aggressive salvo will cause a greater amount of churn during the onboarding process than will a more subtle process, during which users may not realize until later that the product isn't an appropriate match for their purposes.

While a mismatch in fit between the product's use case and the user's needs precludes revenue generation (or at least, mutually beneficial revenue generation), a user engaged with a product is a potential source of virality. At the same time, users who aren't satisfied with a product are more likely to serve as negative publicists for that product, especially if they feel their time has been wasted.

The net effect of these conflicting consequences must be estimated and measured during the implementation of the onboarding process; keeping users engaged when the product can't possibly meet their needs isn't necessarily the best course of action when introducing them to the product's functionality.

To create the onboarding funnel, the onboarding process must be demarcated into a specific set of event flags that create countable indicators of user activity. Auditing these events should produce, in aggregate, a decreasing behavioral map: as users churn out before reaching various events, the counts for those events decrease from the total for the events preceding them. This map can easily be superimposed onto a line chart to produce a decreasing funnel shape, as shown in

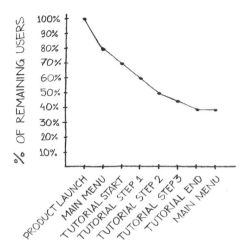

FIGURE 4.10

An onboarding funnel.

Figure 4.10. The number at the far left represents the total number of users who entered the onboarding process (new users), and the number at the far right represents the number of users who completed the onboarding process. The events that describe the onboarding process make up the space between these two points; as more events are added, the line chart grows less inflected.

Constructing the onboarding funnel from event counts, and not counts of time (e.g., a count of the number of users who remained in the product after 20 seconds), normalizes the curve for all types of behavior. Users will negotiate the onboarding process at varying speeds, and measuring engagement by time spent in the onboarding process could create false signals. But time is a valuable measure when a company seeks to understand whether churn is attributable to a mismatch between the product's use case and the user's needs, or the onboarding process's failure to explain how the product works. As such, timing should be recorded with each event flag and represented independently from the onboarding funnel to communicate to the product team how well users understand the product's feature set as it is explained.

The onboarding funnel can be thought of as a measure of intra-session retention; as its downward slope levels, it should approach day 1 retention. A large discrepancy between the end point of the onboarding funnel and day 1 retention (which measures the percentage of users who returned to the product a day after their first interaction with it) conveys a distinct mismatch between the needs of users and the product's use case. While the onboarding funnel should be used to measure how well the use case is communicated and instructed, the leap from the onboarding process to day 1 retention should be used to measure how well the product meets a real market need.

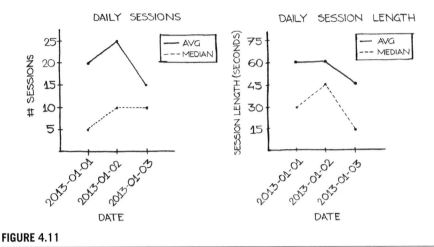

FIGURE 4.11

Line charts depicting daily session numbers (*left*) and daily session lengths (*right*).

Session metrics

Session metrics capture the length and frequency of sessions. Session metrics are used to evaluate user interaction with the product from an aggregate level; when taken alongside other indicators of user behavior and analyzed within the context of a rich events library, session metrics provide insight into how successfully the freemium model has been implemented.

Average session length is calculated, usually daily, by dividing the total length of all sessions over a specific time period (usually a period of minutes) by the total number of product sessions completed in that time period. Because session lengths can vary wildly, the *median session length* should also be tracked to indicate whether session lengths at either extreme are skewing the average.

Average sessions per day and *median sessions per day* track interaction frequency on a per-user basis (i.e., the average and median number of sessions in which users interact with the product each day). Average sessions per day is calculated by dividing the number of product sessions on a given day by the number of unique users who interacted with the product on that day. See Figure 4.11.

Because session numbers are less granular and usually exist on a more restricted scale than do session lengths (products generally experience a wider range of session lengths, in minutes, than they do session numbers), average sessions per day is less susceptible to skew than is average session length, but tracking median sessions per day is still valuable.

Both session length and session frequency metrics can be rendered as either a bar or a line graph. These graphs can then be grouped into separate charts (i.e., average and median session lengths on one chart, average and median number of sessions on another). As stated earlier, there exists no universal target number for any of the metrics; the optimal number can only be backed into through testing and experimentation.

Striking a balance between session lengths and frequency ensures that users are compelled to return to the product but not so frequently that they become bored with it. Session length and frequency metrics should be contrasted with daily churn and ARPU and examined for patterns that negatively impact the total user lifetime.

Net promoter score

The *net promoter score* is a measure of customer loyalty developed by Satmetrix and by Fred Reichheld of Bain & Company and introduced by Reichheld in his 2003 *Harvard Business Review* article, "The One Number You Need to Grow." The crux of the metric is that key insights into organic growth through word-of-mouth recommendations and repeat purchases can be gleaned by tracking only the users at the extremes of a business' satisfaction scale; those insights would be lost in a more nuanced but thorough analysis.

The foundation of the metric is the belief that customers are either *promoters*, extremely satisfied users who will serve as enthusiastic brand ambassadors as well as sources of key repeat revenue, or *detractors*, extremely dissatisfied users who will undermine brand growth by spreading unflattering testimony of a product experience. The concept's authors claim that, by taking the net difference between these two groups, a business can effectively measure the loyalty of its user base.

The net promoter score is a quantitative interpretation of qualitative data points. To calculate a net promoter score, a business must first collect the results of a single survey question that asks, "On a scale from 1 to 10, how likely are you to recommend this product to others?" The scores are then grouped into three sets: those who respond with either a 9 or a 10 are considered "promoters," those who respond with a 7 or an 8 are "neutral," and those who respond with a 6 or lower are "detractors."

Neutral responses are thrown out, and the percentage of the detractors is subtracted from the percentage of the promoters to produce the net promoter score, which spans a scale ranging from -100 to 100. Any net promoter score above zero is considered good, with scores above 50 considered exceptional. A negative score implies a user base with stronger negative sentiment than positive and which thus spreads more negative than positive testimony to potential clients.

While qualitative measurement is largely antithetical to the freemium model given the model's reliance on comprehensive measurement and instrumentation, the net promoter score can be instructive because of its focus on highly engaged users and its reliance on one decision point across which all users who respond to the questionnaire can be examined.

One of the greatest problems in conducting freemium data analysis is the incomparability of user segments due to the vast differences in their behavioral profiles. This incomparability is an asset when examining quantifiable, auditable records such as revenue, since analysis of many freemium metrics, which are highly stratified, benefits from excluding large swaths of the user base via some bimodal characteristic (usually payer or non-payer). But incomparability is a liability when attempting to draw broad, qualitative conclusions about the general appeal of the product.

A net promoter score adds depth to a product team's analysis arsenal through a qualitative measure of engagement against which the quantitative metrics can be contextualized. And because a net promoter score focuses attention on the extremes of satisfaction, it serves as a capable signal of how well the long tail of the monetization curve is developing. Likewise, a net promoter score can inform an estimation of how much value NPUs provide to the product, allowing for more enlightened decisions to be made about utilizing advertising to monetize users who haven't paid beyond some minimum threshold. If the net promoter score indicates that NPUs are serving as enthusiastic promoters for the product, then an evaluation of the benefits of advertising can be undertaken with more awareness of how it might negatively affect the product.

The net promoter score is not without its critics; arguments can be made that it is overly simplistic, and any qualitative, questionnaire-based data point is vulnerable to dishonesty and respondent bias (i.e., only the most engaged users would be willing to fill out a questionnaire in the first place). But in a freemium environment, with massive scale, these considerations are at least somewhat ameliorated by the availability of a large volume of data, which should help correct for biases. Given that most quantitative metrics are singularly focused on granular, quantitative behavioral patterns, the net promoter score, when taken within the context of the entire portfolio of minimum viable metrics, accommodates a level of balance between observed behavior and opinion on the part of the user.

In other words, the net promoter score contrasts what users with what they do, painting a more detailed picture of product engagement. A qualitative indicator of user engagement can serve as a useful waypoint in achieving the delicate balance that must be struck between frequency of use and session lengths; engagement is an outgrowth of satisfaction, which is largely subjective, and a more complete assessment of it can be made through a metric grounded in subjective opinion.

Virality

Virality, as it relates to freemium product development, describes the extent to which products are distributed without any active marketing participation from a business. Viral products "spread," or acquire new users organically, through word-of-mouth referrals or Internet-based user advocacy. A passionate user base can be far more effective at distributing a freemium product than can a well-funded marketing campaign; as such, virality is a chief concern during the development phase of a freemium product, given that marketing costs must be at least partially borne up front in a product launch.

Achieving virality is a worthwhile pursuit, but true virality is largely serendipitous and the product team's control. Virality is dependent on several factors that are not only beyond influence during the pre-launch product development phase but are also mostly unknowable. How well a product is received upon release is affected by market conditions immediately pre- and post-launch, similar products in competitors' pipelines, and user tastes. Given these exogenous influences, designing a product around some expectation of virality is imprudent; rather, a product should be engineered to facilitate virality but financial projections should be constructed, pre-launch, around a rational assumption of normal levels of organic growth.

Virality hooks

Engineering virality requires the placement of *virality hooks* within a product—mechanics or product features that connect to a third-party API and can broadcast an aspect of the user's activity. The most common implementation of virality hooks is through social networks, where the user's activity is broadcast to friends who, presumably, share similar interests with the user.

Social networks are not the sole destination of virality hooks; in fact, social networks may categorize activity generated by third-party products as spam. Additionally, notifications automatically created and sent from a freemium product to a social network tend to lack any personalization. This not only alienates the user's connections on the social network, discouraging those friends from adopting the product themselves, but also alienates the user, who believes the freemium product has abused its access to the social network. Given that such access can provide valuable demographic data about the user, respecting it is of paramount concern; if access is revoked, product development decisions lose precious context.

The difficulty faced in designing virality hooks lies in their ability to be tracked; calculating virality requires a set of inputs describing the number of people reached through viral tactics, and virality hooks must supply this number. Connecting virality hooks to social networks allows for a fair amount of transparency on the part of the product, as virality hooks can emit events when they've been triggered. But once virality hooks have been triggered, tracking the recipients' responses to those hooks—especially on some mobile platforms, where almost all information about the source of a new user is truncated—is extremely difficult. In this sense, engineering truly auditable virality hooks requires the hooks to be deeply integrated with the product.

Virality hooks thus must be designed with two independent and sometimes conflicting features in mind: auditability and effectiveness. Superficial virality hooks—for example, a viral mechanic in a mobile application that publishes a screenshot to the user's social network feed—are generally incapable of being tracked but can also be implemented with relatively little effort and utilized (usually with the push of a button) by users without presenting much friction.

The effectiveness of superficial virality hooks is difficult to measure; use counts can be compiled, but identifying users who adopt the product as a result of the virality hooks requires a level of transparency that doesn't exist on many platforms.

A deep virality hook—for example, a web-hosted social layer in an app that allows for and traces friendship invitations via email—provides for auditing but is likely to experience less use given the barrier to execution and the high level of engagement assumed before use makes sense. A blanket, untargeted broadcast of activity on a social network does not presume any interest from the parties who will be exposed to it; a personal request from a user, sent to a specific individual, does. Therefore, the possible recipients of such a hook are fewer in number, but they will most likely convert to a greater extent. A deep hook often requires more development time to implement, both in the planning and production stages. Deep hooks must be fundamentally engineered into a freemium product; they're not insignificant undertakings.

The trade-off between a deep virality hook and a superficial one is the extent to which the hook can be iterated and improved upon through the develop-release-measure-iterate feedback loop. Superficial hooks, which produce very little verifiable data, cannot be meaningfully improved by a data-driven iteration process; they are added to the nearly completed product at the latest stages of the development process and generally left alone.

Deep virality hooks do, however, produce actionable data artifacts and can be improved upon as product features, which they are. And while this flavor of hook requires more development throughout the lifetime of the product, it can be evaluated and measured, allowing for development decisions to be made on the basis of expected revenue.

Whichever option is chosen, the events library can accommodate the product user's use of a virality hook, producing a record of execution. Virality hook use, which is often referred to as *viral invitations*, can then be displayed as a top-line metric in a dashboard. This metric reveals the degree to which these mechanics are utilized by the user base and can be used as a proxy for not only organic growth (when correlated with user base growth) but also as engagement. Viral invitations are usually represented as daily counts on a line graph, as illustrated in Figure 4.12.

The success of viral invitations, which is solely represented by the number of new users who adopt the product as a result of receiving an invitation— is more difficult to trace. But when results can be capably traced, they should be used to attribute the applicable virality hook as the source of each new user. Source attribution allows users to be segmented by source, which is necessary when allocating resources to virality hook development and iteration. Virally acquired users segmented by source are usually represented with a stacked daily bar chart, where each layer of the chart represents a specific source and the chart sums to a total count of users acquired virally on a given day.

The k-factor

The most fundamental concept in measuring a product's virality is that of the *k-factor*, which is the average number of new users each user recruits into the product. A k-factor of more than 1 represents true virality, in which each user recruited into the product in turn recruits more than one new user. It also means that the viral effects of the product compound, or grow over time.

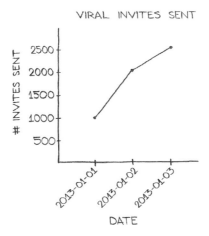

FIGURE 4.12

A line chart tracking viral invitations sent per day.

A product's virality curve depicts the number of users acquired through viral mechanics over time. When the k-factor equals 1—that is, each user introduces one additional user to the product through viral mechanics—the curve is linear. But when the k-factor sits above 1, the curve is bowed, representing geometric growth. This is because each user introduces more than one additional user to the product, and each one of those users in turn introduces more than one user to the product. In a product with a k-factor of 2, the first user of the product introduces two users to the product, each of whom introduces two new users to the product, and so on, as seen in Figure 4.13.

A k-factor is generally measured by dividing the number of users acquired virally by the number of users who were not acquired virally, both of which can be difficult to quantify precisely. The number of users acquired virally is a reflection of the number of viral invitations generated through virality hooks times the conversion rate of those invitations; when the conversion rate is not measurable (via a success indicator), then the number of total virally acquired users is not measurable. The number of users not acquired virally is derived from a diverse set of possible acquisition sources: organic discovery, word-of-mouth referrals, and paid acquisition. While paid acquisitions are at least countable (although not always attributable on a per-user basis), organic discovery and word-of-mouth referrals are essentially impossible to accurately identify.

Given the difficulties faced in attributing new users to acquisition sources, the k-factor is usually not considered a precision metric but rather a heavily informed estimate. To the extent that the inputs of the k-factor are nebulous, so too is the k-factor itself; its value is not measured in how accurately it predicts the source composition of new users but rather how it informs paid acquisition campaigns.

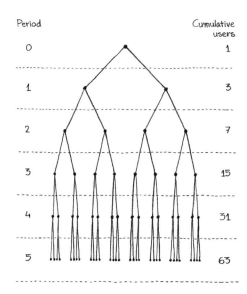

FIGURE 4.13

A model of viral growth at a k-factor of 2.

Users acquired virally are free, meaning they not only increase revenue but also decrease the average cost of acquisition on a per-user basis. This characteristic means that virality amplifies the effects of paid marketing, resulting in more acquired users than there would be without virality. When a product does not experience virality, the return on an acquisition budget—which can be fairly accurately calculated—must be weighed against the potential return on further development of virality hooks (or other product features).

Because the k-factor is an imprecise metric, it is best represented on the dashboard as a long-term product estimate rather than a daily calculation. This is usually accomplished through publishing the k-factor in numerical format alongside the "viral invitations" line graph and the "virally acquired users by source" bar chart.

When publishing an estimated metric, it is important to explain to a team that the metric is inexact and influenced by some level of error, which can be done either in writing or by coding estimated metrics with a visual indicator explained in a legend.

Using metrics in the freemium model

The freemium model's focus on metrics is satisfied only when those metrics are made available and, more importantly, put to use in the develop-release-measure-iterate feedback loop. Data can trump intuition only when it is readily available at the time decisions must be made; when it is not available as timely, easily comprehended data sets, freemium's minimum viable metrics are nothing but an intellectual exercise. Product data must be available, configurable, and actionable.

Availability is achieved through data portal centralization, allowing for access via simple, standardized desktop or mobile tools. Configurable data is data that can be aggregated around multiple dimensions and scrutinized from a number of analytical perspectives. And actionable data is timely, relatively error-free, and complete.

Data infrastructure is an obvious prerequisite to data-driven product development, but an organizational emphasis on data is as important, if not more so. Each individual on the product team must acknowledge the importance of data in the freemium decision-making process in order for data to be leveraged to its utmost informative extent. Likewise, each member of the product team should be aware of how data can be accessed and be at least familiar with a product's high-level metrics at any given point in time. Reporting is a critical operational requirement in the freemium development process, and the team must share enthusiasm and responsibility for taking full advantage of it.

Metrics and the organization

Given the required ubiquity of data and the massive scale over which data must be collected, a centralized reporting portal may be the easiest way to disseminate product metrics. The large volumes of data that must be accommodated present problems when distributing metrics calculations to desktop solutions; calculating metrics through regular batch processes and making those aggregates available through hosted dashboards speeds up the rate at which they can be accessed and absorbed. At the very least, the minimum viable metrics portfolio should be made available as pre-calculated metrics for each product being analyzed so that a baseline set of metrics, defined universally, is available throughout the organization.

The question of when to build an internal reporting infrastructure versus license third-party reporting technology often arises in freemium product development, given its orientation toward data-driven design. A custom-purpose reporting system is an expensive, time-consuming undertaking, and it is difficult to estimate the return on such a system, in terms of increased revenues, before it is fully implemented.

In almost all cases, a custom-built reporting system will perform to a higher and more granular standard than an off-the-shelf solution if the product teams are committed to data-driven development. When product teams consider reporting to be a reference point, or a source of evidence to support decisions that have already been made, then the development of a completely customized reporting system will likely never be justified unless internal attitudes toward data are changed. And when product teams are ready but not able to use data as the basis for product feature decisions, such a system will likewise go underutilized.

Interpreting data correctly in order to produce action points requires specific expertise; if that expertise is not present on a product team, then no collection of sophisticated tools, bespoke or not, can render data useful. An organization will benefit from a customized reporting infrastructure when it possesses the expertise to properly interpret metrics and implement new features based on experimentation and quantitative behavioral patterns. These two requirements relate as much to data science as they do to product development; the product team must be able to communicate clearly with the analysis team in order to interpret the results of analyses.

Freemium reporting is optimally implemented through human resources as well as technology. But legacy software development techniques don't always translate well into freemium environments; experience is not always transferable and can sometimes represent a liability. In fact, the entire product team must be able to work in small iterations, at a swift pace, as the need arises, in order to properly implement the business model. Spotting these characteristics in potential hires requires a keen eye and an understanding of the business model by those hiring new employees.

The product team should be comfortable with metrics and make them as visible as possible within the organization. Visibility in this sense goes beyond availability; metrics should be circulated internally in reports, cited in presentations, and even displayed in the office to keep teams abreast of how the company's products are performing.

Absolute transparency around metrics creates a strong sense of quantitative, data-driven focus in an organization, which is a dominant concern when developing freemium products. Intuition in a freemium environment is not necessarily a bad thing, but it must be qualified with data; by fostering an atmosphere of total data awareness and making data readily available, a freemium organization tempers any individual's urge to let intuition trump quantitative feedback.

Dashboard design

The design of a dashboard can affect how frequently it is used and how authoritative users consider it to be. Dashboard functionality needs to be intuitive, but when data is displayed too abstractly, it may not be considered definitive. Dashboard aesthetics must achieve a balance between scientific and artistic; likewise, dashboard functionality, such as aggregating metrics around various dimensions like date or geographical features, should be obvious and easy to understand.

A dashboard's *console* is its set of control functions that allows the user to limit and aggregate the data being displayed. A console generally features drop-down menus, radio buttons, checkboxes, and sliding scales to facilitate data aggregation around various data dimensions. The dimensions of the data being displayed depend on the underlying data set and the features of the product; at the very least, almost all data sets should include a *date* dimension that allows data to be limited to a specific date range.

Often, the best way to view date ranges is relative to the current date, so a mechanism that automatically reduces the data set to data points within the "last seven days," "last fourteen days," "last twenty-eight days," etc. can be useful. Dates are otherwise manipulated using a sliding menu with two selectors to specify start and end dates. Because date is such a fundamental dimension, the date selector usually appears at the top of the console.

Demographic data dimensions should also appear in the dashboard console to allow aggregation. Attributes such as a user's country, age, language, and gender allow for valuable insights about product usage to be gleaned when aggregated around their individual values. Since dimensions of this nature can take multiple values such as country and age, grouping the dimensions into age ranges or continents, for example, can render the dashboard more useful.

Where appropriate, it its also important to aggregate around platform dimensions. Segmenting data by operating system, screen resolution, and device model, for example, can highlight sources of product deficiencies or poor performance, especially as they influence engagement and monetization. Such console aggregations can also highlight platforms and devices on which the product performs especially well, potentially impacting the priority of future feature development.

Generally speaking, dashboards are most effective when they're succinct and thematic, as illustrated in Figure 4.14. An all-purpose dashboard containing dozens of graphs and charts will likely not be used as often as will several specific dashboards segmented by metric theme, since navigating a massive dashboard slows the metrics interpretation.

The dashboard should contain some sort of navigation scheme to allow for graph themes to be either added to the current set of displays or displayed independently. One theme methodology for the various metrics is the same used to define the minimum viable metrics: retention, monetization, engagement, and virality. Splitting the metrics into these groups and displaying them on separate dashboard

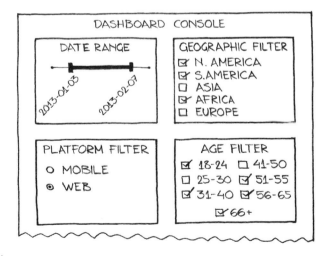

FIGURE 4.14

A dashboard console with filters for date, geography, platform, and age groups.

pages serves to keep the looks of all dashboards streamlined, preventing potential information overload.

Only so much data can be interpreted at once; if a dashboard contains too many graph items, users may be inclined to spot patterns where none exist or, conversely, become so overwhelmed by the amount of information presented that they focus on only one or two graphs. "Dashboard stuffing"—the act of putting every conceivable metric onto a dashboard under the assumption that it might be found useful either now or in the future—should be avoided. Not every metric belongs on a dashboard; some metrics are only relevant for a specific period of time or to specific people. The dashboard is a universal gauge of performance and should contain high-level metrics significant to the organization; metrics with a narrow scope should be reported to interested parties through separate reports.

Ad-hoc analysis

When a set of metrics is relevant for a limited amount of time, or when it is only relevant to a specific segment of an organization, then it doesn't belong on an all-purpose, organization-wide dashboard. When a group-specific metric is perennial and important enough to be referenced every day, then a dashboard for that specific group should be developed. But when a set of metrics is needed only for a discrete, time-constrained purpose—a presentation or due diligence on a potential partnership, for example—then adding that set of metrics to a dashboard is inappropriate. Instead, those metrics should be fetched with ad-hoc analysis.

Ad-hoc analysis is the process of querying data directly from the database in order to investigate a trend or hypothesis. Ad-hoc analysis is required when the granularity of the analysis precludes the use of dashboard data, such as when comparing user segments that are too specifically defined to be sensibly included on the dashboard.

Generally speaking, ad-hoc analysis is performed by either an analyst on the product team or by the organization's analysis group. Analysis is easiest to conduct when it is well-defined and the goals are understood. For instance, if the purpose of an analysis is simply to check for the existence of an ambiguous pattern, then the results of the analysis will surely beget more analysis, creating an analysis rabbit hole from which little actionable insight will likely be gained.

If analysis is entered into under the premise of a null hypothesis, then the results of the analysis can be used to drive decisions. Analyst resources are as valuable as any other; the analyst should take care to achieve maximum impact on the product and, eventually, on revenues.

When conducting analysis, the analyst will most likely query raw data from the data warehouse. When data structures get complicated enough, querying data can become not only cumbersome but shapeless; there may not exist one obvious, straightforward query string but rather several equally complex, inscrutable query strings, each of which derive the same resultant data. Mistakes are easily made when constructing convoluted query strings; for this reason, the analyst should have the query string reviewed by someone else familiar with the underlying data structure. The analyst should also conduct a "smell test" on the results, or a subjective evaluation of the feasibility of the results in the context of historical patterns. Most of the time, when the results of an analysis conflict dramatically with existing notions about a product, an error is present in the analysis. And even if an error isn't present, conclusions that encourage change to a model of thought always benefit from a second review, even when the conclusions are correct.

The conclusions from an analysis are usually distributed in spreadsheet format. If the analyst believes that the conclusions might need updates on a regular basis, the spreadsheet should be formatted in a way that makes such updates easy. This is best accomplished by separating into individual worksheets the outputs of the analysis from the underlying data used to derive them; this method allows new data to be pasted onto each data worksheet without changing the calculation of output statistics.

Revisions to the analysis should be indicated in the filename; a good filename convention for an analysis document is MMDDYY_AnalysisDescription_versionX, where MMDDYY represents the date the file was last modified, AnalysisDescription represents a concise description of what is being analyzed, and X represents a version number. Version control is not easily implemented with most spreadsheet software, but saving files in this manner lessens the risk of irreversible mistakes by allowing for versions to be "rolled back."

When requests for an updated analysis model happen often, the model becomes a good candidate for inclusion on a dashboard. The benefit of initiating dashboard items as ad-hoc analyses is that the analysis process checks the validity of the metrics being calculated, identifies the sources of the data points needed for calculation, and defines the best format for presenting conclusions. By the time several iterations of analysis identify a set of metrics as a candidate for dashboard inclusion, those metrics and the format they are reported in are concrete; the analyst can simply explain the query string and output to a data engineer and the new dashboard metrics can be implemented without any ambiguity. Using the analysis process as a filter for dashboard metric introduction helps deter dashboard stuffing and ensures that all metrics included on the dashboard are trustworthy and credible.

Minimum viable metrics as a source of revenue

One innovation the freemium model brings to bear is analytics as a fundamental component of the product development life cycle. Since distribution (and thus customer adoption costs) are zero, behavioral customer data is available with enough volume to develop new streams of revenue from it. The freemium model gives an analytics team the opportunity to conceptualize new sources of revenue; under traditional models, the minimum viable metrics can at best merely optimize existing revenue streams, and at worst they simply reduce expenses.

This phenomenon is an outgrowth of the inverse relationship between user base size and barrier to purchase (cost), which is illustrated in Figure 4.15. At a price

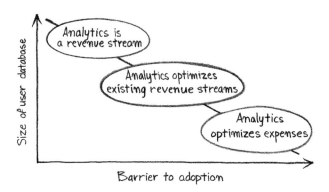

FIGURE 4.15

The analytics value continuum.

point of $0, the size of a product's potential user base is unlimited; as the price point increases, the number of potential customers decreases. This is obvious, but what is less obvious is how that relationship empowers the minimum viable metrics portfolio as a product development tool.

As a product's user base increases, the data artifacts it creates become more valuable because their volumes render them actionable. Optimizing a 1 million-user revenue stream is easier than optimizing a 100-user revenue stream; the data used to make decisions is more reliable, trends are easier to spot, and results are easier to communicate to management because *black box argumentation* is rendered unnecessary.

The phrase "black box argumentation" is defined within this context as a faith-based description of a specific result that relies on statistical or algorithmic techniques too complicated to explain to management in a presentation. These are "trust me, I'm a scientist" means of influencing a decision based on the results of an experiment or analysis, and they are very rarely persuasive—the more opaque a process is, the less likely its results are to influence decision-making. Analyses are most effective when they are based on a simple conclusion that can be clearly communicated and understood.

The freemium model facilitates the development of autonomous data products seeking green lights from management, without relying on black box argumentation, by providing large volumes of data on which to conduct straightforward analyses. This is one of the primary benefits of Big Data as a business strategy; it shifts complexity away from analysis and onto data architecture and processing, allowing results to be communicated more clearly and convincingly. Thus, within the context of the freemium model, data products are easier to pitch and implement at the organizational level, imbuing the organization's analytics team with a product development and management directive.

So the belief that analytics systems exist simply to reinforce product maxims that an organization already believes to be true doesn't apply under the freemium model; since large volumes of data serve as the foundation of the freemium model, analytics is a product driver. Analytics is not an intellectual or philosophical initiative; it is the scientific framework used to generate revenue.

This perspective is at odds with some inherited definitions of analytics, which generally fall along the lines of "a reporting system that alerts the organization to problems." In the freemium model, analytics should describe the current state of the product: its usage, its growth, revenue statistics, etc. But analytics should also be useful in delivering metadata that can be used to enhance a product's current functionality as well as to develop additional functions that may not have existed in the product's original development scope.

The question, then, is how the generation of revenue through analytics is achieved. The most obvious means of using analytics to produce new revenue is to invest in it sufficiently through hiring the right people and building out the right infrastructure. But for an analytics group to be serious about producing new revenue streams, the entire organization must be dedicated to data-driven product development. This is probably the hardest aspect of implementing the freemium model: integrating reporting and design functions under the product umbrella group as opposed to segmenting them.

Metrics can form the foundation of the freemium model only if analytics is approached with genuine intent. Analytics can't be pursued part-time or with minimal expenditure in mind; as a fundamental constituent of the product development process, analytics must be staffed, resourced, and prioritized with the same commitment as any other product-focused initiative. Thus, the minimum viable metrics portfolio represents two things: a hard launch requirement that must be met before the product can be exposed to the public, and a genuine source of new revenue.

Lifetime Customer Value

Lifetime customer value

In the freemium model, full intellectual ownership of data is the only means through which optimized improvements can be made to the product in development iterations. The concrete action points users produce should instruct the product team's efforts.

Analytics is used to increase the various behavioral metrics groups that correlate with product enjoyment. But increasing the value proposition of a product requires some insight into the extent to which a user can be expected to contribute revenues; for some users, revenue contributions are not realistic, and thus the behavioral data they produce doesn't inform revenue-oriented product iterations. To that end, in order to optimize the product value proposition to the user, the product team requires some estimation of that user's value proposition to the product. In other words, what can a specific user or group of users be expected to contribute in revenues? This measure is known as *lifetime customer value* (most commonly denoted as LTV, although the acronym doesn't correspond with the first letters of each word).

Lifetime customer value and the freemium model

LTV is defined as the present value of all future cash flows attributable to a user for a given product. Put another way, LTV is the total amount of money a user is expected to spend on a product, adjusted as if that money were received as a lump sum today. The LTV equation was most popularly defined in *Modeling Customer Lifetime Value*, a 2006 article by Gupta et al (2006) whose authors included two prominent academics in the field of LTV estimation, Bruce Hardie and Dominique Hanssens. The equation the article uses to define LTV is depicted in Figure 5.1. Hardie and another academic, Peter Fader, have contributed perhaps the greatest volume of practical, actionable literature to the academic study of lifetime customer value within the field of marketing.

This conceptual description measures LTV over a predetermined, finite period. In the case of the freemium model, as with most practical applications of LTV, the period over which a user will remain active is unknowable. And while the LTV equation does a capable job of relaying what, exactly, the LTV metric measures are, the implementation of a mechanism for calculating LTV relies very little on a mathematical equation.

$$LTV = \sum_{t=0}^{T} \frac{(P_t - C_t)\, r_t}{(1+i)^t} - AC$$

P_t = price paid by
consumer at time = t

C_t = cost of servicing
consumer at time = t

i = discount rate

r_t = probability that customer
is active at time = t

AC = acquisition cost of customer

T = total time horizon over
which LTV is measured

FIGURE 5.1

The lifetime customer value (LTV) calculation, as defined by Gupta et al.

The aggregate sum of the LTV metrics for all current and future users is known as *customer equity* (CE), which is useful mostly as a component of a firm's enterprise value. Customer equity is rarely used as a decision-making apparatus at the product level; more commonly, it is utilized by early stage technology companies to derive a transparent company valuation ahead of a round of financing. Since the value of a firm is the sum of all of its projected future revenues (in addition to various intangibles like goodwill and brand value), the customer equity value provides a quantitative framework for producing a valuation for a young company.

In a freemium scenario in which revenues are composed of, at least in part, recurring purchases such as subscription services, estimating LTV is fairly straightforward. It is simply the user's expected lifetime multiplied by the recurring price of that user's subscription. But in freemium products with very large, diverse product catalogues designed to take full advantage of freemium dynamics, estimating LTV is resource-intensive and prone to error—and potentially very rewarding.

The analytics infrastructure required to launch freemium products fulfills the preconditions for estimating LTV: behavioral data around spending patterns, demographic data, usage statistics, etc. The barrier most firms face in employing predictive LTV models is twofold: (1) experts who deliver actionable predictive models of this nature are in short supply, and (2) given their complexity, LTV models can be described using only black box argumentation, which many firms are loath to pay for.

Nonetheless, understanding LTV at a conceptual, if not quantitatively actionable, level is helpful in making marketing and, to a lesser extent, product development and prioritization decisions. LTV, as a deterministic measure of what a user will contribute to the product in its current state, explains the return on marketing efforts from a customer-centric rather than a product-centric perspective, providing depth to the process by which the product is grown and iterated upon. Whether or not a product team has the resources to predict LTV with authoritative accuracy, as a theoretical metric it serves to guide the product in the direction of highest possible return.

Making use of LTV

Commanding LTV to the degree that an accurate value can be calculated and audited isn't a necessity within the freemium model. But deriving a numerical LTV metric is a valuable task for any firm producing freemium products. The thought exercise orients development around the constraints of return on investment, and it provides the firm some guidance for developing a marketing budget. So while precision in deriving an LTV metric isn't a requirement, the process itself should be; LTV forms the backbone of marketing freemium products and helps inform decisions around continued development. The capability of calculating an accurate LTV metric is only truly useful under circumstances in which users can be shifted from one product to another based on their predicted LTVs. This practice is known as *cross-promotion*.

Cross-promotion can be between either two products owned by the same firm or one firm's product and another firm's product. The latter method is usually done in exchange for money; in effect, one firm "sells" a user to another firm based on the user's predicted LTV in the first product or on the basis of a partnership, in which both firms agree to the terms of a trade.

When a firm estimates that a cross-promoted user will generate less revenue in the product through purchases than the user's sale price or trade value, then cross-promoting that user to another firm's application is an economically rational choice. Cross-promotion is generally the domain of large firms with either diverse product catalogues (so that users can be cross-promoted within the firm's system of applications) or sophisticated analytics systems (so that the exact value of the user can be estimated with confidence before the user is sold or traded).

Understanding whether a user is a good candidate for cross-promotion to outside the firm's system of applications—in essence, sold to another firm—requires that the cross-promotion sale price exceeds the user's expected LTV and that the sale price exceeds the implicit value of keeping the user in the firm's system as a non-paying user. Recall that all users, whether they contribute revenue to the product or not, have value.

Small firms generally need not possess the infrastructure or domain expertise capable of accurately predicting LTV. But small firms—indeed, all firms—building freemium products benefit from understanding the mechanics of LTV, because understanding the principal components of LTV and the directional impact on its value allows for building products that maximize the amount of money users spend on them.

Since the freemium development process is iterative and data-driven, forward progress in LTV maximization can be measured even if the final metric isn't precisely estimated. Understanding the exact LTV value of a user is only valuable if that user is to be sold; understanding, in the abstract, what can be done to increase the LTV of a user always provides valuable insight that leads to the development of freemium products that are better monetized.

LTV can be calculated in any number of ways and, given that any predictive metric possesses at least some level of error, none are perfect. But no matter what calculation methodology is used, the primary components are always the same: retention and monetization. The retention metrics describe how long a user is predicted to remain active within a product; the monetization metrics can be extrapolated to describe how much revenue that user is expected to spend on the product.

Even though LTV is not precisely accurate, it belongs in the stable of freemium metrics because it represents the confluence of all of the minimum viable metrics, for which increased and continued accuracy should always be a goal. LTV is predictive, and any predictive model is prone to error; retention and monetization are descriptive and should be measured with complete confidence. So, in pursuing an ever more accurate LTV measurement, the product team is implicitly ensuring that its retention and monetization metrics, over which many product decisions are made, remain trustworthy. This side effect, of itself, is well worth the effort placed into modeling LTV.

LTV in, LTV out

Traditionally, the concept of LTV has been useful primarily for establishing a baseline understanding of how much money can be spent, on a per-person basis, to acquire new users. This aspect of LTV certainly holds true in the freemium model. It is a useful benchmark for setting the marketing budget, which determines how much money can be spent in user acquisition. But the dynamics of freemium product development, and the presupposition of at least a minimally effective analytics infrastructure upon launch of a freemium product, contribute another dimension of utility to the LTV metric: a customer segment benchmark. Users can be evaluated on their way into a freemium product's user base, and they can also be evaluated on their way out (i.e., upon churn), thus assisting in the segmentation process and shaping product development.

Performance user acquisition—paid marketing campaigns undertaken with the sole purpose of introducing new users into a product's user base (as opposed to building brand awareness or reengaging existing users)—is wholly dependent on at least a basic, reasonable estimate of LTV. If no quantifiable understanding exists of the amount of money any given user, acquired through any given channel, will contribute to a product, then performance user acquisition is conducted blindly without regard to return on investment. Given the dynamics of the freemium model, in which the vast majority of users are expected to not contribute to the product monetarily, blind user acquisition campaigns have the potential to result in disastrous, near-total losses.

The LTV metric is the basis for performance user acquisition because it represents the maximum price that a user can be purchased for to avoid a loss. In some cases, a firm may pursue user acquisition on a loss basis to build an initial user base or generate publicity preceding some sort of liquidity event or fund-raising initiative. In other cases, a firm may undertake a loss-producing user acquisition campaign to lift its user count ranking on a platform store to a highly prominent position, with the expectation that the product's discovery will benefit from greater visibility (and thus yield an appreciable degree of organic purchasing). But these are calculated initiatives and usually only take place on a short timeline; no marketing professional should engage in user acquisition without being able to identify an informed, defensible estimate of LTV.

For an LTV estimate to qualify as reasonable, it should be calculated around a set of behaviors that lend themselves to monetization. Demographic data such as age, gender, profession, or level of disposable income isn't enough; these describe broad characteristics that don't necessarily relate to a user's relationship with a specific product or a user's propensity to spend money on that product. Demographic data plays a role in a diverse, thorough array of features used to segment users, but it should not be relied on exclusively to derive an LTV metric.

Performance user acquisition campaigns are generally undertaken on the basis of volume, with a specific number of advertising impressions being purchased for a set price. This type of advertising campaign is known as *cost per mille* (CPM), where mille represents one thousand impressions. In a CPM campaign, an advertiser sets a *bid* price, or a price it is willing to pay for the opportunity to display an ad, and the entity brokering the advertising campaign shows only the advertiser's ad to parties willing to sell ad displays at that price or lower. A bid does not represent the price of acquiring a user in a CPM campaign; a bid in this context merely represents the price paid to show an ad.

When an ad is shown to a potential user, the user chooses whether or not to click on it; the historical proportion of people who see an ad and subsequently click on it is known as its click-through rate, or *CTR*. Once a user has clicked on an ad, that user generally must complete some further action to be considered acquired— usually either registering with the product or installing it. This final acquisition threshold (usually named by the action it is measuring, e.g., *install rate* or *registration rate*) is measured as a percentage of total users who see the ad and is almost always lower than CTR, given that some users will discover the product but have no interest in it.

Some advertising networks undertake user acquisition on a *cost per acquisition* (CPA) basis; that is, the advertiser submits bids not for an ad display but for product adoption. This means that the advertiser only pays for a user who has successfully and verifiably interacted with the product at least once. Advertising networks facilitate this by using algorithmic optimization with the aim of achieving click-through and install rates for an ad campaign that match the CPA bid submitted by the advertiser. In cost-per-acquisition campaigns, interplay between LTV and the marketing budget is straightforward: the price paid for each user's acquisition cannot exceed LTV. A full table of an advertising campaign's metrics is shown in Figure 5.2.

In the figure, CTR is measured by dividing ad clicks by ad views. Similarly, install rate is calculated by dividing ad views by installs. CPA is calculated as a

Total campaign spend	Ad Views	Ad Clicks	Installs	Click-through rate (CTR)	Install rate	Cost per acqusition (CPA)
$500	2591	1240	320	48%	12%	$1.56

FIGURE 5.2

An advertising campaign performance overview.

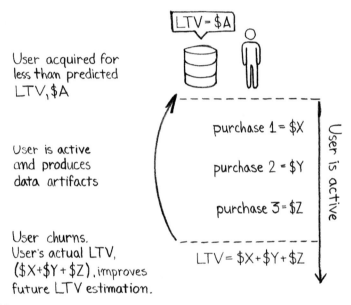

FIGURE 5.3

A diagram of LTV estimation, user lifetime, and model optimization.

function of installs: it measures how much each install costs, given the ad's performance. Performance marketing is conceptually grounded in achieving an acquisition price that is less than a product's LTV; when this does not hold true, an advertising campaign is being run at a loss.

Once a user has been acquired, the estimated LTV used to acquire that user is no longer relevant to that user's behavior; by its nature, LTV is predictive, and as a description of any particular user it is only useful in determining the price that user should be acquired for. But that user's predicted LTV becomes relevant again once that user churns out of the product; it becomes a measure of how accurate the LTV prediction mechanism was in the first place. (See Figure 5.3.)

When a user churns from a product, an actual LTV can be calculated by summing the total value of purchases over the user's lifetime. The difference between the user's actual and initially predicted LTV metrics represents the error present in the LTV estimation mechanism.

A churned user's actual LTV should be contrasted with that user's behaviors to hone the LTV estimation mechanism evaluating users entering the system. Actual LTV metrics should cycle back into the model that is used to formulate estimated LTV in order to increase its predictive capability. This cycle, whereby predictions become more accurate over time as more data becomes available to disprove those predictions, is a distinct feature of the freemium model, in which total instrumentation delivers compounding benefit.

Retention versus acquisition

One reason understanding the value of a user in a product's user base is important is that product teams should be equipped to make quantitative decisions about the lengths they should go to retain users. In almost all businesses, retaining an existing user is far more economical than acquiring a new user, and the freemium business is no exception. What is different, however, is that, given robust analytics, a respectable estimate can be made about every user's potential total value to the product, given that user's archive of behavioral data.

Acquiring a new user involves uncertainty. A person is only within the scope of a product's analysis regarding likelihood to spend once the person crosses a product's "event horizon" by interacting with the product for the first time. A user outside of that scope, for whom the product team has no meaningful understanding of likelihood to spend, represents a position on a very wide spectrum of behavioral profiles, most of which do not lead to direct contributions of revenue to the product. Thus, a user with an LTV of $0 who is engaged with the product is still more valuable to the product than a single newly acquired user, given three statements of fact:

1. The likelihood of any one newly acquired user spending money is low; the likelihood of that user spending vast sums of money approaches zero.
2. The data the product has about the existing user holds value in terms of its utility in creating more predictive models about future users. Again, the new user is a mystery; tenure cannot be predicted, and all things being equal, data about a user with a long tenure is more valuable than data from a short-tenured user (because longer tenures in freemium products are scarcer).
3. The new user must be acquired, which represents an expense. Even if the existing user was acquired through a paid campaign in the past, that cost is *sunk* and thus not relevant to the current decision point. Generally, in software, the cost of retaining a single user versus the cost of acquiring a new user is negligible.

While it is somewhat convoluted, the decision point in choosing to replace (via paid acquisition) or retain any given user will almost always favor retention. Retention contributes to LTV not only in its calculation but in its accuracy; a greater volume of data about users who have remained engaged with a product produces a more robust and actionable LTV metric.

Discounting LTV

Because LTV is a calculation of a stream of revenues over a variable length of time (the user's lifetime), its numerical value at the time of estimation isn't strictly the sum of the estimated revenue contributions projected into the future. This is because money has a *time value* owing to the opportunity cost of allocating finite resources. Money invested into one set of revenue streams is not invested into another, and thus the return of each stream of revenues must be compared in determining the true value of each stream with respect to the others. In other words, money received today is more valuable than money received in the future because money received today can be invested in interest-bearing activities. The opportunity cost of not allocating money to an activity that could produce returns must be taken into account when making financial decisions. This concept deserves consideration when formulating an LTV calculation.

The time value of money is incorporated into corporate decision-making and project financing by determining the minimum amount of money an investment should earn to make the investment preferred over not investing. This is usually quantified by calculating what is known as a *risk-free rate*, which is the rate of return an investment would generate if placed in risk-free government bonds (so-called because they face an almost nonexistent risk of defaulting). The rate of return generated by an investment (into product development, research, marketing, etc.) should exceed this risk-free rate; if it doesn't, it is not a favorable choice because investing the money into risk-free government bonds would yield a larger eventual return.

The process of assessing a stream of cash flows in terms of their values today is known as *discounting*, and the rate by which the value of a future payment is reduced to a value in the present is known as the *discount rate*. Calculating the *present value* of a stream of future cash flows is relatively simple, involving only basic algebra. The formula for the calculation is presented in Figure 5.4. The output of the formula is an amount of money that a person should consider equivalent to the value of the payment expected in the future.

$$\text{Present Value} = \sum_{n=0}^{N} \frac{\text{Payment}_n}{(1+i)^n}$$

n = period number

i = discount rate

Payment_n = nominal value of payment at time n

FIGURE 5.4

The equation to calculate the present value of a stream of future cash flows.

Like many other aspects of the LTV calculation, some controversy exists around the idea of discounting future revenues from users in order to produce a present value LTV metric. Most academic surveys of the LTV calculation advocate for discounting, especially as the surveys relate to traditional businesses such as subscription services, in which users pay the same amount on a regular basis. Likewise, many businesses of this nature can take advantage of discounting by project finance methodology: choosing the most profitable projects out of a broad portfolio of opportunities. But these characteristics don't generally apply to freemium businesses. For one, given the typical freemium product catalogue, revenues are anything but regular and consistent, thus representing a challenge in estimating the per-period value of any user's revenue contributions. Also, most freemium products are their firms' sole focus.

The decision to fund an aspect of freemium product development based on a comparison with simply leaving the money in an interest-bearing security or money market account isn't relevant, as most firms developing freemium products have a mandate, either from shareholders or investors, to fully utilize the firm's specific expertise in developing freemium products. Massive industrial conglomerates generally have capital markets groups that generate return through investment activities with the firm's capital reserves; most freemium product developers have no such facility and are instead dedicated to building freemium products.

Discounting the LTV metric presents a needless complication in making product and user acquisition decisions. When LTV is discussed henceforth in this book, the calculation undertaken is not discounted and represents a simple sum of user purchases values.

Calculating lifetime customer value

A number of quantitative methodologies exist through which an informative and actionable LTV metric can be calculated. The complexity present in an LTV calculation generally corresponds to its purposes; when used as an estimate of return on a proposed product feature to inform a development decision, LTV has to be exact only with respect to magnitude. When used to set a budget for user acquisition, however, the LTV metric should be dependable enough to produce positive returns on marketing investments.

Any LTV calculation is constructed by multiplying the expected lifetime of a user, in periods (where period can be any length of time: day, week, month, etc.) by that user's expected revenue contributions per period. This formulation is fairly intuitive and its two components can be easily explained (even if the calculations producing the components are harder to interpret), alleviating the need to engage in black box argumentation when explaining why and how the LTV metric should be used in making decisions.

The component parts of LTV, like any other relevant metric, must be computable around various dimensions for the purposes of user segmentation. A global LTV metric may be useful in making financial forecasts, but it can't substantially contribute to marketing operations. The dimensions used to aggregate the LTV metric must reconcile with those generally used when acquiring users: location, age, sex, platform, interests, etc. The level of granularity required of an LTV metric obviously depends on what can be accomplished through that granularity, but the dimensions used to calculate group LTV metrics should be driven by business need and practicality.

In this book, I discuss LTV calculation as a possible implementation of two different frameworks, each corresponding to a different level of complexity and company tolerance for ambiguity (i.e., black box argumentation). As mentioned earlier, there exists no perfect LTV calculation; any estimation of what a user might spend on a product in the future is a prediction and is thus susceptible to bias, influence from unforeseeable externalities, and user error.

But formalizing a quantitative approach to LTV estimation is important because it serves to bookend the user experience through the lens of data-driven optimization: the user is acquired into a product with an LTV determination and creates an LTV artifact upon leaving, which is then used to optimize the system. A focus on LTV from the product standpoint places an impetus on the entire development process to quantify and evaluate the user experience on the basis of financial return.

This book presents two methodological approaches to estimating LTV: the *spreadsheet method*, whereby the calculation and its required parts are manipulated entirely within desktop spreadsheet software, and the *analytics* method, whereby the calculation and all related data are housed in an analytics infrastructure and cannot be updated or altered without the assistance of an engineer. Both methods are valid for different reasons, and the appropriate choice for a given product depends on the product team's resources and the organization's tolerance for abstraction and inaccuracy.

In either case, this chapter does not identify a specific formula to use to calculate LTV; the construction of a formula is heavily related to the needs of the product being estimated for and cannot be prescribed. But each method discussed presents a framework for identifying the critical inputs to LTV and a broad, abstracted formula for deriving its value.

The spreadsheet approach

The spreadsheet approach to estimating LTV operates from the position that LTV is the average revenue per period multiplied by the average periods per user lifetime. This approach precludes the possibility of comprehensive revenue or engagement segmentation, given that spreadsheets can only accommodate a few million rows of data at most; instead, predetermined aggregates are used to calculate LTV metrics for very large, very broad user segments such as those based on country.

The advantages to this approach relate to communication and flexibility. Spreadsheets are corporate poetry; when constructed elegantly enough, they can be used to communicate sophisticated ideas to audiences who wouldn't otherwise be receptive to details. The spreadsheet approach sidesteps the black box argumentation minefield completely, since it is entirely self-contained and transparent: calculations are auditable and verifiable, and the impact of changes can be seen instantaneously.

And while the data present in a spreadsheet model may itself be aggregated output from an analytics system, it is generally not manipulated beyond simple counts or averages. The agreeability of a method's medium may seem like a trivial benefit, especially when compared to a medium's ability to produce granular results, but it shouldn't be understated; information can't be used to influence decisions unless it can be parsed and interpreted by decision-making parties. For better or worse, spreadsheets are a fundamental pillar of the modern corporate structure, and ignoring their existence doesn't change anyone's expectations about how data will be presented.

Another benefit of using a spreadsheet to calculate LTV is the spreadsheet' experimental nature; adjusting a calculation results in instant feedback and allows the relationship between variables to be observed quickly and without much development effort. This flexibility is valuable; understanding the dynamics of customer value allows for decisions about product strategy and priority to be made with return in mind. The spreadsheet approach allows the product team to model alternate scenarios or adjust assumptions without the assistance of an engineer. This means that while the spreadsheet approach's LTV calculation is potentially less precise than what could be produced programmatically,it has greater conceptual gravity within the organization because people have a better understanding of its dynamics.

The downside to the spreadsheet approach is granularity and accuracy. Given that a spreadsheet can't match the data capacity of a database, an LTV metric derived from a spreadsheet can't possibly match the breadth of one calculated programmatically from within an analytics infrastructure. This downside relates directly to the confidence with which an LTV calculation can be used to make decisions, especially those around setting budgets for customer acquisition. The spreadsheet approach thus relegates the LTV metric to a decision influencer from a decision point; a precise LTV metric is itself actionable, but a loosely estimated LTV metric is simply one element of a portfolio of data points that must be considered, especially when making a decision about user acquisition.

This trade-off between communicability and reliability appears frequently as a result of the freemium model's data-reliant nature, in which metrics are the basis of decisions but black box argumentation isn't persuasive. The spreadsheet approach is valuable in its ability to serve as a staging ground for product decisions and a way to observe the relationship between a product's mechanics and revenue, but the spreadsheet model itself cannot represent the sole basis for decisions.

Constructing the retention profile in a spreadsheet

The retention profile, as discussed in Chapter 4, presents a template for use patterns following a fairly standard decay pattern: 50 percent of the users who use the product one day after first engaging with it (day 1 retention) can be expected to return seven days after first engaging with it (day 7 retention), and 50 percent of those users can be expected to return twenty-eight days after first engaging (day 28 retention). This decay pattern isn't universally applicable, and in most cases, it probably doesn't describe the exact retention values for users one, seven, and twenty-eight days after first using a product.

But the retention profile gives the product team a framework for estimating freemium product use, which is valuable. This framework can be used to drive assumptions about use patterns before the product is launched; once the product is producing data, it is no longer necessarily needed, as user behavior can speak for itself through measurement. Thus, once a product is live, its retention profile becomes the actual observed measure of retention following first interaction, from day 1 through the end of the product's life (although, in practice, retention is often only valuable through day 365). When plotted, these measurements take the shape of a curve, and the area under the curve can be used to calculate the lifetime engagement of the average user (given that the retention metrics comprising the points on the curve are average values over a sample of the population). The curve can be constructed as measurements from any user segment; the analytics system should capture retention metrics for each user as binary count values (1 or 0, corresponding to whether or not a user interacts with the product on a given day). These counts can be summed across any number of aggregated dimensions; dividing the sums by the number of new users (DNU) for that set of aggregates provides the retention percentage for that user segment.

For the LTV calculation, the retention profile should be composed of retention values over the range of days from 1 to 365 (keeping in mind that day 365 represents the retention profile's *terminal value*) because, in order to be actionable, the LTV model should encompass a user's entire lifetime; in order to be predictive, it must describe any new user's end state.

In the spreadsheet model, the retention profile is curve-fitted onto the standard 50 percent decay pattern and projected through day 365 until enough data has been collected to supersede these assumptions. This allows for a one-year retention profile (and thus a user lifetime estimate) to be constructed from day 1 retention data only.

The first step in constructing the retention profile in a spreadsheet is building a template that can be updated in the future, when more data becomes available. The retention profile consists of only two inputs for a user segment: a timeline of days since first interaction (called *retention days*) and the percentage of the user base that interacted with the product on those given retention days (called *retention percentage*). These inputs relate to all users in the segment being considered, not just users who joined the product on a specific day; in other words, the values are summed across the entire user segment being measured, regardless of the first day of interaction.

A good way of building this template is to use the columns of the spreadsheet to represent the retention percentages and the rows of the spreadsheet to represent retention days, as shown in Figure 5.5. The benefit of this format is that additional

	A	B	C
1			**Retention Percentage**
2	Retention Day	0	100%
3		1	
4		2	
5		3	
6		4	
7		5	
8		6	
9		7	
10		8	
11		9	
12		10	

FIGURE 5.5

A spreadsheet template for retention data.

retention profiles can easily be added to the template by copying an entire column, pasting it into a blank column, and adjusting the relevant retention values.

Given the limited amount of data available, at least one of the day 1, day 7, and day 28 retention cells should be *input cells*, meaning the cell's value shouldn't be determined by a formula but rather input directly. When the product is new and has not yet collected much user data, only day 1 retention will receive input directly; days 7 and 28 are calculated from day 1 using the 50 percent decay pattern (day 7 = day 1 $\times \frac{1}{2}$, and day 28 = day 7 $\times \frac{1}{2}$). As more data becomes available, the values of all retention days for which data exists should be input directly.

The initial estimated retention profile relies on the values for days 1, 7, and 28; once these cells have values, a terminal value should be determined for day 365. There is no general decay pattern that provides a rough estimate for the percentage of users who will retain in a product through day 365 and beyond; estimating the terminal value relies solely on intuition.

A value of 1 percent for day 365 retention would reflect a reasonably committed but not fanatical user base. The estimate of day 365 retention represents the retention profile's right-most endpoint; once this has been input, the boundaries of a discrete curve have been put in place, and the curve can be constructed.

Keep in mind that day 365 retention represents the percentage of users who retain with a product for at least a year; as a terminal value, day 365 retention describes the percentage of users who interact with the product indefinitely after day 365, not specifically on day 365. In other words, the retention profile can be thought of as two separate curves. The first is the retention curve through day 365, composed of large values near the origin and descending toward zero on the x-axis as "retention days" approaches 365, and the second is the retention curve from day 365 through infinity, starting from a very small number and steadily shrinking as "retention days" approaches infinity.

The terminal value at day 365 represents the area under the second curve, and it can be shown as a discrete value at the endpoint of the first curve in a process that would be equivalent to modeling retention through infinity. This is the first of a number of computational limitations of the spreadsheet approach.

$$\text{Step-down} = \frac{.80 - .40}{7 - 1}$$

FIGURE 5.6

The equation to calculation the step-down value between day 1 and day 7 retention values.

$$fx \quad \boxed{= C3 - ((C3 - C9)/(B9 - B3))}$$

FIGURE 5.7

The step-down equation input into cell C4.

With its endpoints set, the retention profile's curve is built through a process called *linear interpolation*, whereby the known points on the curve are connected via a linear equation. Three linear equations are required: one for the line drawn between the day 1 and day 7 retention points, one for the line drawn between the day 7 and day 28 retention points, and one for the line drawn between the day 28 and day 365 retention points.

Calculating the values for each retention day between days 1, 7, 28, and 365 requires the calculation of *step-down values*, or the amounts by which retention days decrease over the limited continuums between points. A step-down value is calculated once for each linear equation; it is simply the difference between the endpoint values divided by the distance between the endpoints (in this example, the number of days between the relevant retention days). The step-down value can be thought of as a function of the slope from a linear regression. The equation in Figure 5.6 is used to calculate the step-down value for the linear equation between retention days 1 and 7, where day 1 retention is 80 percent and day 7 retention is 40 percent.

This result reveals that the retention percentage decreases by 6.7 percent for each retention day between day 1 and day 7. To apply this step-down value to the cells between the two days, the formula must be adapted to spreadsheet format and inserted into each cell in column B between rows 4 and 9. The spreadsheet formula must indicate that the step-down value is being subtracted from the cell above it; for example, it should show that day 2 retention is equal to day 1 retention minus the step-down value. Given that the step-down value should be dynamic—it should update automatically if day 1 retention is changed—the formula for the step-down value must be included in each cell. Therefore, the formula in Figure 5.7 is input into cell C4.

Using the same retention values from the example above, the new value of cell C4 (day two) is 73 percent. For this formula to retain its references, the values in the step-down formula must be made absolute; they must reference exact cells, not cells relative to the current cell's position. In most spreadsheet software, this

$$fx = C3 - ((\$C\$3 - \$C\$9) / (\$B\$9 - \$B\$3))$$

FIGURE 5.8

The step-down equation, edited to include absolute cell references.

is done with the dollar sign symbol ($). Rewriting the formula in Figure 5.7 with absolute references yields the formula in Figure 5.8.

This formula can now be copied from cell C4 to C8. The absolute references ensure that the same values are used in each cell to calculate the step-down value (which is constant across the linear equation).

The process of creating the step-down function between the two end points and using it to fill in the intermediary cells should be repeated between day 7 and day 28 retention and again between day 28 and day 365 retention to create the complete retention profile.

Calculating user lifetime from the retention profile curve

Because the retention profile curve is discrete (consider the difference between a discrete and a continuous variable), taking the area under the curve is easily accomplished: a definite integral can be thought of as the sum of the areas of a set of infinite rectangles under the curve of an equation.

In the case of the retention profile, a discrete number of rectangles are observable, the width of each representing one retention day and the height of each representing the proportion of users returning to the product on that day. The area of each rectangle is simply the proportion of returning users multiplied by the width of the rectangle (which is always a unit of one day, meaning the area is equivalent to the proportion of returning users), and the area of the retention profile is the sum of those values. The expected lifetime is therefore the sum of the values along the curve. Since each point represents a proportion of returning users per day, the resultant sum is expressed in days.

Another way of thinking about this approach is to consider a product that can only be used for two days: the day after first interaction and the day after that. If the day 1 and day 2 retention rates are both 50 percent, then 50 percent represents a probability of a future user returning on days 1 and 2 after first interacting with the product. The expected lifetime, therefore, is one day: a new user has a 50 percent probability of returning on day 1 and a 50 percent probability of returning on day 2, which, added together, equals a 100 percent probability of returning on at least one day.

The expected lifetime determined by this technique produces a value that requires special interpretation, since it doesn't represent calendar days but rather any combination of days within the retention profile. It must be thought of as the number of days that the user interacts with the product, as opposed to the total length of time that the user interacts with the product, which is a substantial distinction. This lifetime metric can be considered as the *user duration*. In finance, duration describes the weighted average lifetime over which a financial instrument delivering regular cash flows (a bond, for instance) will mature, or return its total present value.

Duration as used in the freemium context is not completely analogous to duration in finance, but as a concept it is similar; duration describes the total number of days on which a user will deliver all cash flows. Duration is much more useful in forecasting revenues—and, consequently, LTV—than a calendar days projection because it can easily be combined with the ARPDAU metric, since both are expressed in units of one day. The duration metric, therefore, comprises the lifetime component of the LTV calculation.

The retention profile should be segmented by user behavior to the greatest extent possible in order to provide a range of duration metrics. Before constructing the retention profile, thorough consideration should be given as to which segmentation approach to take, as user segments must reconcile between both user lifetime and revenue to produce valid LTV metrics. If user lifetime and revenue are segmented differently, the LTV metric won't be representative of empirical behavior; it will be a combination of varied user actions and not indicative of any probable user profile.

Since LTV values should be calculable early in the product's life, when little data exists, the best way of segmenting retention immediately after a product launch is through behavioral *triggers*—interactions with the product in the first session that correlate with day 1 retention.

These triggers are product-specific but should relate to spending behavior; a good example is a binary trigger event that simply captures whether or not a user makes a purchase within the product in the first session. This trigger can be used to segment users into two groups for which retention profiles can be constructed: those who made purchases in the first session and those who didn't. Whatever user segments are chosen, they must be applied uniformly to the revenue metrics in order to establish congruency between the LTV components.

Arranging the retention profile worksheet in the spreadsheet model to accommodate user segments is typically done by creating separate worksheets for each user segment, as depicted in Figure 5.5. Calculating user duration for each user segment is accomplished by summing column C from cell C3 (day 1 retention) to the very bottom of the column (whichever retention day is given the terminal value).

Calculating revenue with trailing ARPDAU

In order to fully form the LTV metric, revenue must be estimated as ARPDAU and applied to the duration metric. As stated earlier, ARPDAU is the appropriate metric to use in calculating LTV in terms of duration, as it is calculated in units of one day, meaning it is compatible with the duration metric (which is a number of days) in terms of its unit.

Initially, ARPDAU appears simple to calculate within the context of LTV, as it merely represents a daily average. But ARPDAU requires smoothing before its use in calculating the LTV metric is valid, even in a spreadsheet model (which isn't assumed to make sophisticated accommodations for trends or aberrant behavior). ARPDAU over the lifetime of a product, across all users, is not an instructive metric; it describes broad averages applied to various product update cycles.

A more relevant metric is *trailing ARPDAU*, which only accounts for a set number of days prior to the current day. Trailing ARPDAU should be calculated over a long enough timeline to capture a broad spectrum of behaviors, but recent enough to discard spending patterns associated with old versions of the product or from demographics that have since shifted away from the product. A trailing period of four weeks—that is, 28 days prior to the current day—is a reasonable standard for calculating trailing ARPDAU, although the appropriateness of that timeline is obviously dependent on the specific product being analyzed.

Since ARPDAU represents average spending per user, it must be calculated for a count of unique users when a trailing time horizon is used. The uniqueness requirement adds a layer of complexity to the process of deriving the metric because counting unique users for a period requires some forethought when designing the analytics system; simple sums of DAU cannot be used to calculate trailing ARPDAU because users may have interacted with the product on multiple days for the timeline being considered. The equation to calculate the trailing ARPDAU metric is shown in Figure 5.9.

The numerator of the equation, in which the total revenue for the period is divided by the unique user count, calculates a period average revenue per user. Dividing that value by the length of the period (in days) normalizes the value on the basis of one day, rendering it compatible with the duration metric.

ARPDAU must be segmented over the same behavioral conditions as duration in order to be used with duration to calculate LTV. If a behavioral trigger was used to segment retention profiles, that same trigger should be applied to the calculation of ARPDAU.

The structure of the ARPDAU worksheet is illustrated in Figure 5.10. The days of the trailing time horizon are laid out down the first column of the worksheet from most recent (one day trailing) to most distant (28 days trailing, or whatever is chosen as the maximum of the time horizon). To the right of that are columns

$$\frac{\left(\dfrac{\text{Total revenue generated in the period}}{\text{Unique users active during the period}} \right)}{\text{Length of the period in days}}$$

FIGURE 5.9

The equation to calculate trailing ARPDAU.

labeled "revenue" and "unique users," representing the component parts of trailing ARPDAU. The last column is the calculated trailing ARPDAU metric. This table template should be used for each user segment over which user duration is calculated to produce that segment's specific trailing ARPDAU value.

Note that each row represents a complete time period over which ARPDAU is calculated. For instance, the value in cell D3 would be described as two-day trailing ARPDAU, or the average revenue produced per user over the previous two days combined. The value in cell D29 would be described as 28-day trailing ARPDAU, or the average revenue produced per unique user who is active in the product over the entire period of 28 days leading up to when the values are calculated.

The revenue column value is an input for the sum of revenue generated by that user group for the period being calculated (e.g., for two-day trailing ARPDAU, it is the sum of all revenue generated in the previous two days). The unique users column contains a count input of the unique users who interacted with the product over the timeline selected.

The ARPDAU column is likewise calculated for the entire time period and contains a formula output; the formula in each cell divides the sum of the revenue generated in the given user segment by the unique users from that segment who interacted with the product over the time period. Figure 5.11 shows the formula for the D2 cell in Figure 5.10.

Since the time period over which ARPDAU is calculated is trailing, this worksheet can be updated without any changes to its template; when the values for daily revenue and unique users are pasted in, the trailing ARPDAU values automatically update.

	A	B	C	D
	Day Back	Revenue	Unique Users	Trailing ARPDAU
2	1	$ 800.00	2736	$ 0.29
3	2	$ 928.00	2182	$ 0.43
4	3	$ 876.00	2719	$ 0.32
5	4	$ 789.00	2362	$ 0.33
6	5	$ 920.00	2191	$ 0.42
7	6	$ 974.00	2286	$ 0.43
8	7	$ 715.00	2727	$ 0.26
9	8	$ 702.00	2070	$ 0.34
10	9	$ 954.00	2564	$ 0.37
11	10	$ 723.00	2355	$ 0.31
12	11	$ 732.00	2250	$ 0.32

FIGURE 5.10

A spreadsheet template for calculating trailing ARPDAU.

fx | = B2 / C2

FIGURE 5.11

The formula to calculate trailing period ARPDAU.

Structuring the LTV worksheet and deriving LTV

Once both the retention curve and trailing ARPDAU worksheets are formatted and completed, calculating LTV is straightforward: the LTV metric is simply the duration for a given user segment multiplied by the trailing ARPDAU.

Since one of the principle benefits of the spreadsheet approach to LTV calculation is transparency, an illustrative model of LTV can be created in a dedicated worksheet that explains the calculation to people not on the product team for whom the concept may be foreign.

The first and most important details to provide in the LTV worksheet are the standards by which the user groups are defined. This can be done with a simple definition of a group described in a particular worksheet. Continuing with the behavioral trigger example, the description of the user groups could be as simple as:

Group 1: Users who made a purchase in their first session
Group 2: Users who did not make a purchase in their first session

These definitions should be included at the top of each worksheet in a legend that also explains, in fairly rigorous detail, exactly how each component—trailing ARPDAU and duration—is calculated. The time period chosen for trailing ARPDAU should also be justified here, as this time period has a significant impact on the value of LTV. These clarifications may bear more weight in the decisions made as a result of LTV than the value of the LTV metric itself.

The LTV metrics are calculated by multiplying the duration value by the trailing ARPDAU value for each segment. A good graphic for LTV metrics is a grouped bar chart, where the LTV metric for each user segment is displayed as a columnar bar. These data points can be arranged in a table, as in Figure 5.12, that also includes the corresponding proportion made by each user segment. Such data provides rich context to the LTV metrics and can alleviate the need for follow-up analysis before product decisions are made on the basis of LTV.

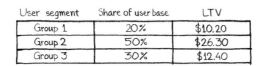

User segment	Share of user base	LTV
Group 1	20%	$10.20
Group 2	50%	$26.30
Group 3	30%	$12.40

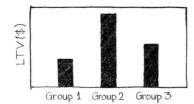

FIGURE 5.12

An example of a summary table for LTV values by user segment group.

Constructing the LTV spreadsheet model presents a valuable exercise for the product team in the earliest stages of the development process. Even when values can't be entered into the model to produce a credible LTV metric, the process of building the template and considering the user segments can help shape the direction and focus of the product's development cycle.

It should be noted that the spreadsheet approach isn't immune to suspicions of black box argumentation; even when all the data used in a calculation is made readily available, the calculation can appear cryptic. Carefully explaining the calculation keeps the focus of any LTV analysis on the value of the metric and not on the method.

An LTV-first approach to product development ensures that features will be built and prioritized with a discerning eye for optimized revenue and that, upon product launch, marketing efforts will be informed by data. The LTV spreadsheet model is the first tangible artifact a product team can produce in the early stages of development that articulates a reasonable estimate of segmented user revenues, even when the LTV is based entirely on assumptions. It is therefore worth a significant amount of effort and intellectual consideration.

ARPDAU versus projected individual revenue

The method described here for modeling LTV in a spreadsheet uses ARPDAU to describe an entire group of users composed of the segments being considered. In most cases, the group of users to be analyzed will be a subset of the entire user base, selected and segregated by some set of characteristics (very often demographic characteristics, such as country). But even when the LTV spreadsheet model as described here is broken down into distinct models of grouped segments, the individual models still represent groups of users—not individual users—and thus suffer from a clumping around averages that prevents predicting aberrant behavior. As discussed earlier, in the freemium model, the behavior of outliers is often the most revenue-relevant.

Another valid approach to measuring LTV in a spreadsheet model is simply to track cumulative spending by days since registration and then project that progression forward using a technique called *curve fitting*. An example of this technique is outlined in Figure 5.13.

This curve describes an individual user and graphs the user's cumulative in-product spending over the first few days of product interaction. When a curve is roughly fitted to the user's existing behavior, the cumulative spending appears to approach an *asymptote*, or a line that the curve continually approaches but will never cross. As more data is collected about the user's spending habits, the curve will shift, but after just a few days, a projection can be made.

A curve-fitting approach has two distinct advantages over the ARPDAU approach. The first is that the graph is intuitive and easy to explain; a brief glance at the chart in Figure 5.13 relays that the dotted line approached by the graph represents lifetime value. The second advantage is that the curve is more easily calculated for an individual user because it can be built using only spending data.

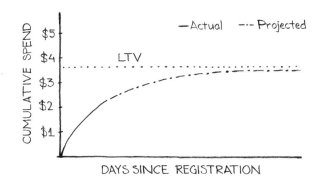

FIGURE 5.13

A fitted LTV curve.

The principal disadvantage of this approach, however, is that, given the 5% rule, any spending in the freemium model is deviant from the norm and, thus, almost impossible to predict. With respect to users who will eventually spend in a product, a fitted curve for cumulative spending at an individual level will almost always be incorrect, often dramatically so. Likewise, choosing an accurate shape for an individual's spending curve is impossible; some users may make purchases late in their use of the product, some may purchase only once at the beginning of their tenures, and so on.

The principle disadvantage of the ARPDAU method is that it tracks a group of users and not individuals. This is assuaged when the user base is large and stable. ARPDAU captures a cross-section of user spending behavior on any given day; it includes users making their first purchase on that day and users making their hundredth. When assuming that the same number of people make their first purchases on any given day as did the day before, then the ARPDAU approach doesn't need to describe the behavior of an individual user, because it describes the behavior of a group of individuals in unchanging roles.

In other words, by measuring an entire large user base in a steady state, the ARPDAU method *does* capture data about individual users, in that they are enacting patterns that are present on any given day. A user base is not always in a stable state, of course, but this can be managed by adjusting the trailing period over which ARPDAU is calculated; when the product's user base is in flux, the period should be increased to provide more data over which to calculate an average. As the user base stabilizes, the length of the period can be decreased, as almost all behavior can be considered pattern-recognizable, from a general perspective.

The analytics method

The shortcomings of the spreadsheet method are obvious: spreadsheets cannot process extremely large volumes of data, the model must be updated manually, and spreadsheet models generally do not accommodate values variability. The *analytics method* circumvents these shortcomings and is implemented programmatically alongside the product's instrumentation; as users create data artifacts, the artifacts are cycled back into the LTV estimation mechanism to calibrate the mechanism to new data.

The analytics method presents a new set of shortcomings, however, which are mostly related to an organization's realities. The first shortcoming is that an automated, programmatic LTV estimation methodology forces black box argumentation when used in making decisions; the analytics method calculates LTV metrics automatically by a completely opaque process that is difficult to explain and audit in nontechnical terms. Such opacity may not be acceptable to a firm, especially when large marketing and product development budgets are allocated on the basis of estimated LTV.

The second shortcoming is the expense of building a system of such breadth and technical intricacy. The spreadsheet method requires only spreadsheet software and a standard business intelligence stack to implement, and a spreadsheet template for modeling LTV can be completed in a few hours. The analytics method requires that a system be designed and built, usually with enough flexibility that it can serve multiple products and be expanded in the future. Such an undertaking is not trivial, could be very expensive, and could easily span months.

That said, at massive scale and when combined with a sophisticated analytics stack, the analytics method can produce very large returns by automating the management of the entire customer life cycle, from acquisition through churn. It is also capable of far more accurate predictions than the spreadsheet method, given the sophisticated statistical techniques the analytics method can employ and the vast amounts of data it can parse.

The analytics method also affords far more immediacy in analysis; as user trends change or market dynamics shift (especially in paid acquisition markets), a near-real-time LTV metric is available to capitalize on opportunities or limit expenses. When the scale of a product's user base is large enough, these optimizations can represent appreciable amounts of money.

Given the fragmented and constantly evolving nature of the system of analytics technology platforms and the almost endless intricacy with which an LTV estimation mechanism can be implemented, this book avoids any specific prescriptions for building an LTV estimation mechanism with the analytics method. Instead, the concepts forming the foundation of the method are introduced in the vernacular of the field, providing a basis for further exploration.

The truth is that the specifics of an entire predictive analytics platform exceed the scope of a discussion of LTV, given the mastery needed across a wide range of disciplines—computer science, probabilistic statistics, data structures and data management, and machine learning—in order to construct such a platform. Rather than broach these topics, the analytics method is described in conceptual terms as an alternative to the spreadsheet method.

The Pareto/NBD method

The Pareto/NBD (negative binomial distribution) model was introduced in a 1987 article by Schmittlein, Morisson, and Colombo entitled *Counting Your Customers: Who Are They and What Will They Do Next?* (Schmittlein et al. 1987). The Pareto/NBD model is perhaps the most popular model used in predicting LTV within the context of irregular revenue streams (i.e., non-subscription and non-contract business units) and has spawned a vast amount of academic literature on the subject.

Given a set of user data, the Pareto/NBD model attempts to determine two things: (1) whether or not the user is still "alive" (that is, whether or not the user has churned out of the product), and (2) the number of purchases the user is likely to make in the future, called *discounted expected transactions*, or DET (Fader et al. 2004).

The utilization of the Pareto/NBD model is contingent on a set of assumptions about the underlying user base being true:

- At any given point in time, a customer can exist in only one of two possible states with respect to the product: "alive" or "dead." Customers who are alive may make a purchase in the future; customers who are dead have permanently churned out of the product.
- The number of purchases made by a customer who is alive in a given time period varies randomly around that customer's average purchase rate as a *Poisson process*. A Poisson process is simply the function of a binomial distribution, which describes the probability of a specific event taking place within a discrete period of time.
- The transaction rate across users is heterogeneous, following a *Gamma distribution*. The Gamma distribution is the parent form of the exponential distribution with a long right tail and is often used to describe times between events and lifetimes.
- User lifetimes follow the exponential distribution.
- The point at which a customer churns out of the product is not observed; rather, it is deduced as an estimate based on a period of inactivity. Churn points are heterogeneous and follow a Gamma distribution.
- The reasons behind customer churn are varied and exist as a component of randomness in the alive or dead estimation. That is, users may churn out of the product for unknowable reasons that occur independent of other users.

Many marketing models rely on a methodology for gauging customer value called *recency, frequency, and monetary value* (RFM). This approach values a customer's future contributions to the product as a result of how recent (the recency) the last purchase was, the frequency with which the customer has made purchases in the past, and the monetary value of past purchases.

The Pareto/NBD model uses only recency and frequency as model determinants; it assumes that the size of a purchase is independent of a user's propensity to make that purchase, given the user's history of purchases. This simplification reduces the amount of data needed in employing the model; for any given user, the Pareto/NBD model requires only the number of purchases made by the user over the time period being considered, the time of the last purchase, and the time of the first interaction with the product.

Like the LTV approach taken in the spreadsheet method, users should be segmented by type before being analyzed with the Pareto/NBD model. The Pareto/NBD model produces a universal description of whatever sample it is executed over; segments should therefore be defined and identified before being measured by the model so as to not aggregate the DET value across the entire user base.

The segmentation process can be undertaken in the same way it is undertaken in the spreadsheet model, except that users must somehow be coded with their designated segment in the analytics system before their data is fed to the Pareto/NBD model. This can be accomplished without much effort, usually through an SQL command that adds a column to the users table with a segment code corresponding to a set of each user's characteristics.

To implement the Pareto/NBD model, the only data needed to produce an estimate of DET (total future purchases) is basic information about the user and the user's purchasing history, which is within the scope of even the most basic analytics systems. The Pareto/NBD model, however, produces an estimate for a point in time given a historical data set; that is, the model can make a best guess as to a user's future DET given a set of historical purchases but not based on demographic data or non-purchase behavioral triggers. This limitation means that the Pareto/NBD model is adept at estimating customer equity but not an appropriate tool for estimating the LTV metric for a new user, about which little behavioral data is available.

Because the Pareto/NBD model, as described here, produces an estimate of DET, a revenue component must be included in the model to product an LTV metric. The DET estimate is analogous to the duration metric derived in the spreadsheet approach; it describes a "present value" of a unit relating to future activity (in the case of DET, the unit is purchases; in duration, it is days). Therefore, like in the spreadsheet approach, LTV can be constructed by multiplying the determinant of future activity by the empirically observed average value of that activity.

In the case of the Pareto/NBD model, that activity is the purchase, and the average value of the activity can be calculated by taking the average purchase sizes of the user segment being considered. Like in the spreadsheet approach, the segment over which average purchase size is calculated should match the segment being considered for DET. When this is done, the final calculation to produce LTV is simply the segment DET multiplied by the average purchase size for the segment. While isolating purchase size as independent of recency and frequency may seem counterintuitive (and certainly contrary to the RFM model), Fader, Hardie, and Lee provide extensive analysis supporting this notion (Fader et al. 2004).

The regression method

Another tool commonly used to estimate LTV is regression. Regression LTV models generally extend the recency, frequency, and monetary value framework and also incorporate demographic data and early behavioral and descriptive characteristics such as acquisition source and weekday of acquisition.

A multitude of regression frameworks exist that could be reasonably applied to LTV estimation; this treatment, building upon the foundation laid in Chapter 3, focuses on the use of linear and logistic regressions. As in the Pareto/NBD method, regression models should be run against user segments and not the entire population of users.

The simplest form of an LTV estimation regression model is a linear regression using recency of previous purchase, frequency of past purchases, and average purchase price as primary independent variables, with LTV representing the dependent variable. As stated previously, additional dependent variables relating to a user's demographic characteristics or early behavior can also be coded as dummy variables to provide depth to the model.

While models of this nature are simple, they can be surprisingly accurate at producing numerical estimates of LTV metrics, although estimates tend to skew high when very large lifetime values are achieved (even with low frequency). Linear models should be tempered by a maximum possible value, which is usually the total theoretical value of the product catalogue.

Linear models are incapable of capturing a user's state (alive or dead), given that the time of state change is unknowable and the linear model cannot accommodate a binary variable. The LTV regression model can be expanded, then, into two sub-models: one to predict a user's state using a logistic regression and another to predict the value of future purchases. The logistic regression sub-model can utilize the RFM data points to produce a probability of a binary alive/dead state designation. State is important to consider when modeling LTV because it is inherently random and especially susceptible to over-regression in a linear model.

The output of a logistic regression is usually stated in an odds-ratio, or the odds that the value of the binary dependent variable is 1, given a one-unit increase in an independent variable. But most statistical packages can also state logistic regression results in probabilistic terms; they can state the probability that the dependent variable is 1, given the value of the independent variable. To predict LTV, the results of the logistic regression sub-model should be stated in probabilistic terms representing the probability that the user is alive, given the RFM independent variables.

The linear regression sub-model should, as in the simple linear model described earlier, produce a predicted value of future purchases based on the RFM data points and whatever demographic and behavioral characteristics are deemed relevant. This value, when multiplied by the probability of making future purchases produced by the logistic regression model, produces an expected value of future purchases. The sum of this value and a user's previous purchase total produces that user's LTV. When aggregated over the segment and normalized on a per-user basis, as in the Pareto/NBD method, this value can be used to benchmark the value of users belonging to the various predefined user segments within the product.

The regression method represents a compromised middle ground between the spreadsheet approach and the Pareto/NBD method; as regression is a fairly common statistical technique, and regression coefficients are easily interpreted without extensive knowledge of the model being considered, communicating the results of a regression alleviates some of the tensions of black box argumentation. And while linear methods require adjustment to conform to maximum thresholds and normal empirical patterns, they can produce accurate results. More sophisticated models can be susceptible to overfitting, especially when, as noted already, some independent variables are influenced by elements of unpredictability.

Implementing an analytics model

An analytics model, defined here as a model that is executed as a process within the analytics stack and not a model that is merely built on analytics output, is rolled out in two phases using a combination of statistical software and programmatic design. The first phase is called *parameter estimation* and is initially undertaken in a statistical package on a sample of historical data in order to train the model and determine the appropriate model coefficients and constants, or parameters. In this process, the proposed formula is run against a sample of test data to build a model approximating the relationship between the variables in the sample.

Within the statistical package, the model takes on a different form than what is usually proposed in academic literature, since at this point the model is crossing the chasm between theory and practice. Most statistical packages are semi-programmatic, meaning that standard programming nomenclature, such as loops and "if" statements, are used in many places, along with various functions for performing statistical techniques.

Some programming languages, such as Ruby and Python, have had enough statistical modules written for them that they serve as better test environments than do statistical packages, especially if the back-end of the analytics stack is written in one of these languages. The benefit of using a statistical package to define the model is the access to advanced statistical functionality; when that functionality is available within a pure programming environment (such as with Python), then use of the statistical package isn't advantageous.

Defining a model means producing a formula that can be replicated in a programming environment. Academic formulas are theoretical and mostly cryptic; they are meant to convey sets of complex processes (such as sums and integrations) in as little space as possible to provide a general understanding of an entire concept in one or two lines.

Programmatic models need not be succinct; they may span dozens or even hundreds of lines of code. In programmatic statistics, the length of code is usually negatively correlated with readability: concise, convoluted code is often inscrutable to third parties, which can slow down update processes in the future if the author of the original code leaves the product group or company. Code should be eminently clear, readable, and explanatory, especially when performing complex statistics to produce a prediction, and ideally it should be checked before being deployed by another data scientist.

Once parameter estimation is completed, the model can be fed data from outside the sample and evaluated based on performance (which is measured by how well the model's output fits historical data). If the model performs to expectations, it is translated into code (if it wasn't developed in a programming environment in the first place) and deployed to the back-end, where it is inserted into the back-end's "data loop" (the T in ETL). This means that the model is run against raw data and used to create a new aggregation, LTV. This is then represented as a new set of table columns on a reporting dashboard.

One of the most profound benefits of the analytics approach is that the model's product is made available throughout the entire analytics stack: in-product processing, reporting, aggregation, and any other processes that directly interface with analytics in the execution of business logic. This means that LTV can now be used to trigger actions such as retention campaigns or in-product promotions based on LTV.

The spreadsheet approach doesn't provide this kind of interactivity, as it sacrifices direct utility for simplicity and flexibility. The downside to this interoperability is that an inaccurate analytics model can corrupt an entire system; models must therefore be thoroughly vetted before being pushed onto the analytics stack and must be continually audited while in deployment.

Auditing an analytics model

A statistical model is built to define the relationship between variables in an existing product dynamic. But product dynamics change, and rare behavioral swings that were not captured in a model's training set can emerge after model deployment. These behavioral attributes must be accommodated for in the model; deployed models always require future attention for tuning and updating in accordance with the shifts and realities of a large, complex system of user interaction.

Auditing an analytics model is the process of maintaining its level of accuracy with respect to product data. Auditing may be done on a formal basis, wherein a model's historical output is queried and compared against a proxy metric, or it might be done on an ad-hoc or automatic basis (say, a wild swing in a model output raises a red flag and invites investigation). A model audit could result in a new process of parameter estimation against a newer or larger sample of training data or a fundamental reengineering of the model on a different conceptual basis.

The best standard against which LTV can be compared, for auditing purposes, is the final, actual LTV of users. But auditing by this standard requires more waiting time than most product teams are comfortable with to determine whether a model is valid; a user's predicted LTV can be compared only to the user's actual LTV once the user has churned out of the product, which could take months.

Early summed revenue—for instance, the amount of revenue generated by a user in the user's first week—can be used as a proxy if LTV can be adjusted to a first-week value, but this could lead to interpretation problems, especially in products where purchases are generally made later in a user's lifetime.

The best model audit technique incorporates evaluation by both proxy and actual values; wild differences in proxy metrics and the normalized predicted values can be spotted early, and the model can be reevaluated before the first group of users churns out. With respect to LTV, this is a comparison of final, actual LTV to the predicted LTV as users churn out of the product. But as users join and remain with the product, their predicted LTV should be evaluated as a function of their running total actual LTV; this can be represented in one-week increments (e.g., week 1 LTV, week 2 LTV, etc.) that are gauged against their predicted LTV, normalized for weekly periods.

The difference between a model's performance and its expected accuracy shouldn't be evaluated on a per-measurement basis; one erroneous prediction, even when extremely inaccurate, shouldn't constitute a basis for removing a model. Predictions aren't generally used on an individual basis to make decisions; rather, they are utilized as broad trends. The output of a model should be curve-fitted against actual data in the same process used in parameter estimation and the measure of standard error should be considered. If the measure of standard error exceeds the threshold of acceptability, the model should be reengineered, either with a new training set or with a completely different conceptual approach.

Parameter re-estimation is by far the most straightforward means of updating a model: the model is run against a new training set, new parameters are produced, and the new model is redeployed. This process is often automated to the extent that it occurs without any input from the product team. Optimizing parameters due to slight shifts in behavior is appropriate, however, only when the product isn't undergoing rapid or significant updates that change the way users interact with it. As the product's core use case changes, so too can the way in which LTV, at a conceptual level, is conceived. These types of changes require a model overhaul; the model should be removed from the analytics stack and reimagined to fit the new functionality or purpose of the product.

Making decisions with LTV

Like most other quantitative aspects of the freemium model, LTV is primarily a decision-making tool: it should contribute to revenue optimization, reduce uncertainty, and clarify choices. The purpose of calculating LTV, and the value in approximating as accurate an LTV metric as possible, is to drive paid user acquisition with a positive return on investment and prioritize feature development so as to maximize revenue. LTV facilitates both of these initiatives by assigning distinct monetary value to the user. On this basis, LTV is often the yardstick by which product changes are evaluated. Freemium products often exist as complex systems, and adjustments to their feature sets can result in conflicting metric results that impede product progress. The LTV metric allows the product team to make decisions by focusing on a singular performance signal: profit net of marketing costs.

LTV also serves as a bridge between the product development and management spheres through an element of shared vocabulary. Speaking in terms of the revenue benefits of a specific product feature or the projected profitability of a marketing campaign helps reduce communication barriers between the layers of an organization that often interface on uneasy terms.

By unifying the objectives of both the product team and the management team, the LTV metric removes obstructions that can otherwise produce significant delays in product planning and release. Specifically, LTV attaches a marketing constraint to the product development process, meaning that marketing considerations are made early, reducing the risk of a mismatch between product vision and marketing strategy at the point of launch.

The impact of LTV is strongest in three specific areas of operational choice. In marketing, for which the LTV metric holds primary significance, LTV provides a maximum threshold for acquisition spending in the pursuit of positive ROI acquisition campaigns. In product development, LTV informs the direction of a specific feature based on a concrete goal. And in product portfolio management, LTV provides a unit of measurement by which proposed new projects and existing projects can be allocated resources, given a strategic revenue mix. Each of these uses of LTV accomplishes different goals, but all are anchored in one core precept: that an explicit, quantifiable measure of revenue should determine strategic decisions.

LTV and marketing

The role LTV plays in making marketing decisions is fairly clear: it sets a concrete limit on the price that should be paid for a given user. This use case—appropriating a budget for user acquisition—adds substantial emphasis on the need for LTV to be calculated by user segment. User acquisition, whether undertaken through highly auditable digital ads or through traditional mediums that aren't easily tracked, such as physical billboards or television ads, is conducted with targets, usually demographic, in mind. A maximum acquisition price for a universal product LTV cannot be used to optimize marketing spend; rather, it merely describes a theoretical limit that likely isn't applicable to many users and can't inform the targeting specifications around which all marketing campaigns are structured.

The characteristics used to define a user segment and upon which the LTV is based, then, must translate into realistic marketing targets. For instance, an LTV metric for a segment consisting of users owning a specific device is useful only in a marketing context in which a campaign can be targeted on that basis; if the device in question is a specific television model, or a specific brand of computer, then those users aren't likely explicitly targetable. Thus, user segmentation, as it applies to the calculation of LTV, may need to be applied in reverse order at the organizational level: the marketing group defines the characteristics of potential users who can be filtered, and the product team segments those users within the analytics system accordingly.

This isn't to say that marketing completely dominates the segmentation process and determines how users are grouped for product development; the marketing and product development segments can exist independently of each other.

The segments can also exist within a hierarchy; because marketing segments are traditionally broad, product teams can easily subdivide them into more specific segments to optimize the user experience or ignore them altogether for product development purposes.

Because marketing segments are determined beforehand, by definition they can be made using only demographic, not behavioral, characteristics. The most common attributes used to define marketing segments are age and gender. They are also almost always based on geography, if for no other reason than to be adjusted for translation and cultural sensitivity. Given these constraints, an LTV used for marketing might be defined around three dimensions—location, age, and gender—meaning that a maximum acquisition price has been set for each combination of the three factors. Typically, a marketing segment takes the form of something like "men in the United States, aged 18–35." An example of an acquisition price segment table is shown in Figure 5.14.

Using LTV as a maximum acquisition price isn't to constrain growth; it is to maintain a strictly positive return on marketing spending. There are cases where it may make sense for a firm to spend more to acquire a user than the firm predicts to spend on a product. Such cases include a product that requires an initial seed of users, or a firm that is attempting to reach a more visible position in a platform rankings chart (which will initiate increased organic growth), or an intangible benefit that can be obtained from conducting marketing at a loss. But marketing activity undertaken blindly or without regard to top-line return isn't sustainable, and long-term marketing expenditure must be justified by the profitability of any given campaign on an LTV basis: users are acquired for less than they are expected to be worth.

It is tempting to think about the role of LTV as a proxy for overall business profit, where the difference between a user's expected LTV and acquisition cost represents a per-user profit (or loss) margin. But this is misguided; LTV is, at its heart, a marketing metric, and so it merely describes the profitability of a given

Country	Age Group	Gender	LTV
USA	18-25	F	$7.00
USA	18-25	M	$5.00
USA	26-40	M	$20.00
SWE	18-25	F	$16.00
SWE	26-40	F	$19.00
CAN	18-25	M	$17.00
CAN	18-25	F	$22.00

FIGURE 5.14

A sample acquisition price segment table.

marketing campaign. LTV is therefore a marketing mandate, not a business strategy, and because it represents expected revenues and not immediately realized revenues, it cannot be used as a proxy for firm-level profits.

The firm-level evaluation of operational profit is expressed as *revenue minus expenses*; LTV contributes to this only in the sense that it constrains marketing expenses to within the boundaries established by the firm's estimation of total lifetime user revenue contributions. But those revenue contributions are not immediate; in fact, they can materialize over very long lifetimes. Because of the mismatch in chronology—revenues accumulate over a period of indeterminable length and acquisition expenses are shouldered at the start of a user's lifetime—LTV can't be used in an accounting context to describe profit.

Similarly, marketing expenses for user acquisition spending that the LTV formula calculates constitute only one component of a firm's overall operating expenses. Other expense groups such as salaries, facilities, product development, and so on must obviously be considered when evaluating whether or not a firm is profitable. Constraining the consideration of a firm's profitability to its acquisition campaigns, in most cases, severely underestimates its total expenses.

For these reasons, LTV exceeding per-user acquisition cost is a prerequisite for overall firm profitability but does not exclusively determine it. In freemium products, the degree to which LTV exceeds user acquisition costs must be considered with respect to the *LTV minus CPA* margin, the volume of users acquired, and the size of the total user base. The fact that the expected total revenue contributions from purchased users exceeds those users' purchase prices may be undermined by low margins and low volumes that don't make up for the firm's overhead expenses.

LTV, then, should determine only marketing strategy, not company strategy; the degree to which LTV must exceed per-user acquisition prices is set at the company level and is based on growth targets and the expense structure of the entire organization—not just marketing—that user revenues must compensate for.

LTV and product development

Within the scope of a single product, the LTV metric, in conjunction with the minimum viable metrics, can be used as a diagnostic tool to identify shortcomings that wouldn't otherwise be visible without a derived measure of performance. LTV is synthetic in the sense that it is composed of multiple metric groups—retention and monetization—and can highlight poor performance by the standard of one set of metrics even if another set is performing to specification. For this reason, LTV is useful when prioritizing new feature development based on the metrics that features are expected to boost. For instance, if LTV is low but conversion and ARPDAU are reasonable, then features contributing to retention should be prioritized.

A product team is concerned with maintaining or growing product revenues, given a target range of daily user activity. In this sense, the product can be thought of as a hose: it receives an input, water (users), and produces an output, force (revenue). In this metaphor, LTV serves as a choke point that exposes a leak in the hose, given stable input (new and returning users); the leaks would be identifiable of their own accord but are much more visible when contextualized within the system and stress-tested, which is what LTV does. The magnitude of each leak in the hose is measured by the speed of the water leaving it; in the product development process, magnitude is measured by the difference between the metric's current values and historical high points. The most consequential leaks are patched first; this is the prioritization that LTV imposes on the iteration process.

Addressing metrics shortcomings using LTV as an indicator requires establishing a standard for the metrics in the first place, which should be done as early as the product feature planning stage. For a feature that exists only on paper, forecasting its impact on product metrics is fraught with uncertainty, but estimated LTVs play a vital role in the feature evaluation process; each new feature developed should be considered under the guidance of the role that feature plays in meeting overall product revenue targets.

This is why the LTV model is so important, even when it is only directionally accurate. When introducing a specific feature, comparable historical feature development can be used to estimate, with reasonable accuracy, the impact on product metrics. Even if an LTV model is useful only in predicting the magnitude of LTV change at a relative level, not an absolute level, it can still be used to prioritize feature development.

LTV and organizational priority

High LTV products (products exhibiting high and non-stratified LTV metrics across user segments) tend to be niche; users are most willing to spend money on products they feel passionate about, and user passion negatively correlates with general appeal. This dynamic introduces a strategic element to the composition of a firm's product portfolio: a diversified collection of freemium products, all exhibiting points across a wide spectrum of LTV values, may present more opportunities than a number of niche freemium products or one very large, broadly appealing freemium product.

This is because some minimal overhead is required to build and maintain a product, regardless of the size of its user base: a portfolio composed of a large number of small, niche products incurs greater fixed costs in maintenance than does a relatively smaller portfolio. A portfolio composed of a small number of broad products with large user bases, though, faces the risk that any one product falling into user base decay could disastrously disrupt revenues. The freemium product portfolio can be optimized to reduce expenses, maximize revenue, and allow for the most beneficial aspect of the web and mobile platforms: cross-promotion.

Any product's user base is transitory: at some point, it will fall into decline due to the changing nature of the market in which it competes. As discussed earlier in the chapter, all else being equal, a user in the product system is worth more than a user outside of it because of the inherent value of behavioral data. This data is useful not only when determining if a user should be cross-promoted to an existing product, but also when determining which products should be developed and launched, given a user base that can be cross-promoted into them.

A low-LTV product—a casual product with broad appeal—serves as an excellent "bank" in which to retain users before cross-promoting them into higher-LTV products with more niche use cases. As old products decline and new products launch, the retention of users within the overall product portfolio system is paramount; the need for reacquisition essentially doubles a firm's marketing costs over time. This need for low-LTV, mass-appeal products must factor into decisions made about the product catalogue and the priority of the product pipeline: a firm should structure its product portfolio to maintain the *fungibility*, or substitution properties, of its users.

User fungibility describes the extent to which users can be transitioned from one product to another without friction, or churn. Cross-promoting a user from one high-LTV product to another is often difficult; if the fundamental use cases of the products align, then they represent redundant efforts. It is therefore optimal to maintain an active low-LTV product in the catalogue to serve as an intermediary "holding product" for users before they are more appropriately cross-promoted to another product in the system (or sold to a third party through advertising). This transition should take place ideally before the initial product experiences significant decline; the more precisely this can be timed, the greater the number of users that can be retained within the system.

All of this activity requires a deep understanding of lifetime customer value—not only the LTV metrics for the active products, but also the projected values for new products. Applying this strategic thought process to the composition of the product catalogue can reduce by a significant degree the need for market expenditure; as has been established, a user is an asset, and for an early-stage technology firm producing freemium products, customer equity can represent nearly all of the enterprise's value. One aspect of preserving that value is ensuring that users always have a viable destination within the product catalogue.

The politics of LTV

Given the multiple moving parts comprising its calculation and the extent of its organizational impact, lifetime customer value can stir intense emotions. In a highly fragmented and dysfunctional company, the LTV metric might create conflicting incentives across groups: the product team wants an LTV to be projected as high as possible because it results in acquiring a large user base (which is how success may be evaluated), while the marketing team wants the opposite in order to reduce expenditure (which is also how success may be evaluated). And finance may want to decouple LTV from marketing altogether, given that a high LTV allows large revenue projections to be produced without incurring commensurate acquisition expenses.

Under ideal circumstances, and when a firm is operating with a singular focus, LTV shouldn't be a point of contention. But because it is a factor in so many decisions, LTV can easily become the subject of an intradepartmental tug-of-war, with each stakeholder attempting to influence LTV's calculation or its use. This situation highlights deep, intrinsic weaknesses in the firm's operational foundation; a nuanced calculation of LTV or a multi-group committee approach toward defining it can help to alleviate these weaknesses. Taking proactive steps can reduce the possibility that LTV becomes a battleground over influence or resource allocation in the first place.

The first step is for the firm to align each business unit behind the wisdom and prudence of collective performance marketing. When the entire firm subscribes to the notion that marketing spend should always produce a positive return, convincing a product team that metrics improvement is needed before its product can be marketed profitably isn't a deviation from precedent and therefore doesn't inspire feelings of animosity. Firm-wide metrics transparency, including for marketing spend, contributes to company-wide alignment.

The second step is to define the LTV calculation universally and charge the analytics group, not individual product groups, with maintaining it. Analytics groups generally sit outside the boundaries of the potential incentive crossfire that can materialize around LTV; furthermore, as a firm-wide platform, the analytics group should be impartial to any particular product's performance.

The third step is to gauge marketing success not by volume or budget size but by verifiable profitability, which requires the marketing group to actively manage campaigns as a function of LTV. By coupling marketing spend with LTV and measuring only quantifiable profit, the marketing group is not motivated to appropriate any more budget than can be put to effective use. This step may require creativity in evaluating non-concrete marketing spend—such as on brand awareness initiatives or industry events—but it nonetheless aligns the interests of the marketing group with those of the product group.

When LTV has become a political minefield, other, more fundamental problems with the firm's operations are at play. But because of its strategic importance, as much effort as possible should be put into preventing LTV from becoming collateral damage in an intradepartmental conflict; when LTV is held hostage by company politics, the performance of the product catalogue is put in jeopardy. With as much influence and power as LTV commands, companies should take care to place the integrity of the metric beyond dispute.

Freemium Monetization

6

The continuous monetization curve

Successful monetization in a freemium product is contingent on a small percentage of users monetizing; therefore, the design of a freemium product's catalogue of purchasable items must facilitate a workable LTV metric from the perspective of performance marketing. The LTV metric is a function of customer lifetime and typical spending behavior. But average monetization metrics, as with all average metrics in the freemium model, don't provide much insight into the realities of product use.

It is highly unlikely (if not, in most cases, impossible), that users would make consistent purchases every day of their tenures within a product. Rather, users make purchases according to their needs at specific points in time and based on the appeal of the product. These two aspects of user monetization—user need and product appeal—form the foundation of a concept in the freemium model called the *continuous monetization curve*.

Choice, preference, and spending

The theoretical basis of the continuous monetization curve is that a product catalogue should be so complete that, at any given point in their tenures with a product, users are presented with a diverse and relevant set of potential purchasable items from which to choose. This catalogue should be composed of not only static, predefined purchasable items but also of dynamic purchasable items created specifically for the needs of a particular user.

The size of the range the LTV metric can take is a function of the size of the product catalogue: a small product catalogue necessarily limits the breadth of values the LTV metric can assume, given that a small catalogue of purchasable items doesn't allow for a large number of combinations of purchases. Large product catalogues offer users choice; the larger the degree of choice afforded to a user, the more the user is given the opportunity to monetize. Keeping in mind that the vast majority of users in a freemium product will never spend money, the best way to create a dynamic in which the 5 percent can monetize to a considerable degree is to match those users' every potential whim with a potential purchase.

This phenomenon unfolded in the supermarket sector in the 1980s. In their book, *Discrete Choice Theory of Product Differentiation* (Anderson et al. 1992),

Anderson, de Palma, and Thisse describe two catalysts for the rise of the super-market format and of the diversified product catalogue around which it operates: the preference consumers place on variety over time in consumption of goods on different occasions, and the specific tastes of individual consumers with respect to brands, flavors, size, etc.

The core principle supporting the large product catalogue adopted by supermarkets—which is also significant within the realm of freemium economics—is that customers are willing to pay a price premium for the products that best suit their personal, idiosyncratic tastes. For this reason, the supermarket model is better equipped to capture consumer revenues and, combined with the effects of econo-mies of scale, has all but pushed the specialty food store model into extinction.

The dominance of the supermarket model has created an entire subset of aca-demic research around *vertical product differentiation* (VPD) and competition, the general thesis of which states that the increased fixed costs associated with chain supermarket development—land acquisition, logistics infrastructure development, and inventory supply—create natural oligopolies by making it harder for competi-tion to enter the market.

But freemium software product development isn't subject to these same con-straints; the marginal cost of selling and distributing a freemium product is $0. And while the marginal cost of developing an item in a freemium product's purchase catalogue is not zero, it relates mostly to salary and overhead expenses.

This chapter examines the monetization curve in a freemium product, focus-ing on three elements: its construction and conceptual basis, its expansion through "data products" and purchase offers relevant to specific situations, and the concept of *downstream marketing*, or user-focused retention and conversion techniques. Each of these concepts contributes to how much a freemium product is able to monetize its users and deliver revenue.

What is the continuous monetization curve?

The continuous monetization curve describes the possible extents to which users can monetize; it is a reflection of the size and depth of the product's catalogue of purchasable items. Each point along the curve is a measurement of the percentage of the total user base that will ever reach some specific lifetime customer value. When graphed, the y-axis represents percentages of the user base and the x-axis represents lifetime customer values, with the curve generally taking the form of a Pareto distribution, as seen in Figure 6.1.

The y-intercept, or the percentage of users expected to hold the most common lifetime customer value above $0, sits at a value below the conversion rate when more than one lifetime customer value in the product is possible; this is because the sum of the area under the curve represents 100 percent of paying users, and it is unlikely that all converted users (i.e., those users that directly contribute rev-enue) would have the same lifetime customer value. In other words, the curve inter-cepts the y-axis at the most common LTV, which is generally the minimum level

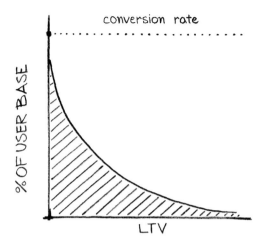

FIGURE 6.1

The continuous monetization curve.

of monetization. But unless the most common nonzero LTV is the only possible nonzero LTV, the percentage of users holding that value will not match the conversion rate; it will be lower, given further possible levels of monetization.

The curve decays from the y-intercept for increasing values on the x-axis until it forms a very long, very thin tail for extremely high lifetime customer values. The curve intercepts the x-axis at some point (usually theoretical), beyond which a level of total monetization for any user cannot be predicted.

The curve as described is actually discrete, not continuous (and, in fact, no curve of monetary values can be continuous, as monetary values are limited to two decimal points and are thus countable). Describing the curve as continuous instills a sense, within the product catalogue design, that every user who is willing to contribute monetarily to a product can be uniquely and individually served at a specific price point. This design principle is core to the freemium ethos and represents the strategic distinction between freemium and paid purchase strategy: when users believe that a product is accommodating their personal, idiosyncratic tastes, they are willing to pay a premium for that accommodation. It is this structural reality that allows freemium products to generate higher revenues than they would under other commercial models.

The continuity of the monetization curve could only be accomplished in a product that allowed purchases to be made at theoretical levels of fractions of a unit of currency, which would imply some form of time-based interest accumulation in perhaps an in-product pseudo-economy. The point is that the freemium monetization curve (as described, with LTV values plotted against percentages of the user base) should *approach* continuous form, with the product catalogue being designed with the aspiration of continuity in mind.

Engineering continuity in a product catalogue generally requires the presence of dynamic products that are not strictly designed but materialize as collections of customized features existing across a large (or infinite) number of combinations. Thus, the product catalogue is not analogous to the physical catalogues that were mailed to recipients in times gone by, such as clothing retailers; in these catalogues, customers were exposed to a discrete, limited number of clothing choices and purchases were made from within that spectrum. In the freemium model, the spectrum of purchasable items approaches continuity as the customer's ability to customize those products increases.

The most obvious customization option to fit the clothing retailer analogy is the option to choose a color (and, in fact, some clothing retailers allowed for this customization, given a variety of color options that the clothing the retailer had in stock). But if the retailers offered customers the ability to choose any color combination from the color spectrum, the size of the potential product catalogue would increase.

Likewise, if the retailer allowed customers to choose clothing size not based on predetermined configurations (such as small, medium, and large) but based on personal measurements in millimeters, the size of the potential catalogue would increase even more drastically. And if the retailer allowed the combination of these nearly open-ended factors (color and measurements), the number of items in this potential product catalogue would climb into the millions (given that possible dimensions were limited to reasonable forms), even with just a limited number of basic products.

This process—approaching continuity in the monetization curve by providing nearly endless customization and personalization options to a discrete set of core purchasable items—is what transforms the freemium product catalogue into a dynamic mechanism capable of serving users' personal tastes to such a degree that they are willing to pay a premium to participate in the product economy.

Engineering a freemium product catalogue

Product differentiation has long been a key component of retail success—the wider the spectrum of products a store offers for sale, the more likely any given customer is to find the product that best matches his or her tastes. But a second competitive component to this strategy provides value; by increasing the depth of its product catalogue, a retailer takes on additional infrastructure, logistics, and real estate costs that increase the price of competing with the retailer on the basis of product diversity. Thus, the wide product catalogue, for the so-called "mega-retailers," serves as a means of pricing competitors out of the market.

In their 1993 paper, *Dynamic Retail Price and Investment Competition* (Bagwell et al. 1997), Bagwell, Ramey, and Spulber describe a three-part *game* in which mega-retailers enter a market, compete on the basis of price while investing in core infrastructure, and then settle into a permanent share of the market, with one firm usually dominating the rest. In this game, the mega-retailers are of equivalent *quality* (or magnitude of product diversity) at the outset, and customers make their decisions based solely on price. This is because price, in the case of the mega-retailer market, signals firm maturity and stability; the firms that are able to offer the best prices on goods are considered to be the best at managing their operations and are thus considered the most likely to operate for the long term (meaning the consumer won't need to switch companies in the future, which could incur a cost).

In the freemium model, this dynamic changes. Infrastructure does not determine the size of the product catalogue beyond the minimal threshold to support *any* product catalogue, and the marginal cost of selling one unit of a digital product is $0. Similarly, the real estate costs incurred by mega-retailers are not barriers in the freemium model: the freemium "store" is distributed electronically, and thus it, too, incurs no marginal cost with an increase in the size of the catalogue of purchasable items. In the freemium model, the size of the product catalogue is not a competitive mechanism in the sense that it prices other firms out of the market; instead, it is purely a measure of quality—a measure of how capable a given firm is to meet a customer's most personalized needs.

Engineering the freemium product catalogue, then, should be undertaken with the most individualized needs of the user in mind. Projecting quality, or a high degree of customization and personalization, allows users to evaluate the product as both enduring and relevant to their needs. Product longevity is perhaps even more important in the digital marketplace than in the physical one, as the cost incurred in switching from one digital product to another may be higher than that incurred in difficult to transfer (when a product or service is shut down, they may be impossible to transfer); users are reluctant to use a product that appears immature and not market-tested because the time invested in using those products will go to waste if they are shuttered. Thus the quality (diversity) component of the freemium product catalogue strategy is paramount; it gives users confidence that the product is worth investing their time into, which in turn increases early stage retention.

Another advantage of the diverse freemium product catalogue is the increased ability to monetarily engage with users. A large, broad, nuanced product catalogue presents more opportunities for the user to extract value from the product with a transaction than does a smaller catalogue with fewer provisions for a personalized experience. To leverage the freemium model's commercial advantages, users must be given as many opportunities as possible to have their needs and tastes fulfilled. A large product catalogue is the keystone of the broad monetization curve, the breadth of which allows the freemium model to monetize. It also facilitates and capitalizes on the extended degree to which users can engage with the product.

Engineering the continuous monetization curve, then, is a matter of building a diverse assortment of opportunities with which the user can extract value from the product. These opportunities can materialize in discrete, preconfigured products or in customization options that augment and differentiate the user experience at the individual level. They can also be represented in a combination of the two, with a core set of products that can be endlessly and infinitely customized, as in the clothing catalogue example cited earlier.

These opportunities to enhance the experience are instruments of delight: they allow the users to whom the product holds the most appeal to engage with it to whatever extent they want. And the more opportunities that exist, the longer and higher the curve can reach: more possibilities manifest in higher levels of monetization and more varied levels of monetization, which produces the monetization curve's long tail.

Freemium and non-paying users

The 5% rule, as it is discussed in this book, is defined as absolute; it is not. Examples exist of freemium products that monetize far more than 5 percent of their user bases, especially products serving smaller niche markets in which they operate alone. The 5% rule is meant to establish a limit as the size of the user base reaches a very high number; in other words, the products with the broadest possible appeal will experience the lowest levels of conversion.

At first glance, a scenario in which only 5 percent of users monetize might seem non-optimal; the scenario is often described as *subsidization*, whereby monetary contributions from paying users make up for the lack of contributions by non-paying users (NPUs). In this perspective, NPUs are a cost of doing business, an unfortunate reality of the freemium model that should be reduced to as insignificant a level as possible.

But the success of a freemium product is predicated on the existence of NPUs; indeed, when the product catalogue is optimized and the product is functionally sound, a low level of conversion indicates broad product appeal. NPUs do provide value to freemium products, but that value is indirect and thus requires a thorough understanding of the model in order to quantify it. But NPUs are neither unfortunate nor a component of a freemium product that should be actively minimized; rather, they are a natural and essential core component of any freemium product's user base.

The value provided by non-paying users emerges in three ways. The first is in data, on which successful freemium implementation is dependent. The data generated by NPUs holds intrinsic value; when sophisticated statistical methods can be employed, the data can yield important insights into user behavior when the tendency to purchase is controlled for.

But even when these methods can't be employed—when NPUs and paying users must be analyzed separately because the tools to isolate their shared behaviors aren't available—the data generated by NPUs can be used to build segmentation models. Early behavioral segmentation allows the product team, at the very least, to group users into *paying/non-paying* segments that may dynamically alter the user experience. In other words, identifying a non-paying user is, for practical purposes, the equivalent of identifying a paying user.

The data generated by NPUs isn't limited to the scope of product use. Many platforms allow for users to review and rate products, with the best-received products receiving preferential treatment from the platform in terms of discoverability (e.g., the products with the highest ratings are displayed more prominently in the platform's store). Such sentiment-related meta data, when it is flattering, can contribute significantly to a product's user base growth, and it is not wholly dependent on monetization.

The second benefit non-paying users accord to freemium products is viral scale. Non-paying users increase the product's viral "surface area," or potential for generating viral growth: NPUs, while not contributing to the product monetarily themselves, may introduce friends and social contacts to the product who will.

Virality is an amorphous concept because it is difficult to measure and difficult to engineer; given its importance in scaling a user base, it should be accommodated for with every mechanic conceivable. Enthusiastic product users need not uniquely and exclusively be paying users; a user may be highly engaged with a product but not contribute to it monetarily for any number of reasons. Discouraging NPUs from using the product reduces the extent to which the product's user base can grow through virality.

The third benefit yielded by non-paying users is critical mass. Many freemium products require a minimum number of participants before they are useful; examples include platforms built around reviews, social sharing products, and location-based networks. For a product to become sustainable—to develop past the point that a lack of users threatens the utility of the product—every user who joins before critical mass has been reached, regardless of level of monetization, is not only valuable to the product but is essential to the product's viability.

Even when network effects are not fundamental to a product's success, that is, when any individual's experience is not affected by the size of the user base, a large user base serves as a signal of product quality, regardless of what percentage of that user base monetizes.

This can be deemed the *nightclub effect*: nightclub patrons who haven't paid anything for drinks still hold value to a nightclub because they serve as proof that the nightclub is worth visiting. When people enter a nearly empty nightclub, they tend to believe it isn't very good and don't generally stay for long; this doesn't change if the few people on the dance floor are holding drinks.

While the three benefits accorded by non-paying users are undeniable—especially the viral benefit—they are quantified with a great degree of uncertainty. Luckily, the presence of NPUs does not detract from a product's ability to generate revenue from paying users; in fact, NPU presence enhances it. When determining if NPUs should be presented with friction in an effort to dissuade their use of the product because of operating costs, the question is, does the presence of non-paying users provide more value (through the benefits identified) than the cost of accommodating them? For most software products, where the marginal cost of serving an additional user is almost nothing, the answer is yes, even though the value of the benefits of NPUs is difficult to precisely price. For products with a significant marginal per-user cost of operation, the question is rendered moot, as the freemium model is a bad fit for any product that experiences such a barrier to massive scale.

Ultimately, a freemium product should strive for as many non-paying users as possible to participate in its user base (given a steady rate of conversion) simply as a means of achieving scale. Identifying the benefits of NPUs is merely an intellectual exercise; because of the unique characteristics of the freemium model, it is understood that the vast majority of users will never contribute revenues to the product.

Revenue-based user segments

The monetization curve is more useful in driving design decisions in the abstract than it is as a reporting tool. Generating a monetization curve for a product based on real data is possible but difficult to graph and interpret, especially as a time series. A better means of achieving the same effect—monitoring the blend of the user base on the basis of LTV—is to group the user base into revenue-based user segments and track those over time.

Revenue-based user segments are often created using a *whale* (and lesser amphibious creatures) designation hierarchy. In a freemium product, a whale represents an active user who has surpassed a high (relative to the monetization curve), specific LTV threshold. Descending from this threshold are various other designations to indicate smaller thresholds; some commonly used examples are those of the *dolphin* and the *minnow*. These classifications are employed by the product team to describe users who have monetized to a specific level.

Sometimes the whale segment is further subdivided into whale species, which can be helpful when the monetization curve has a very long tail, making the threshold definition for a single whale segment seem arbitrary. Some common examples are the *blue whale* (the biggest whale species, relating to the highest-monetizing users), the *orca whale* (a medium-sized whale), and the *beluga whale* (a small whale).

Creating revenue-based user segments tracks the monetization of users over time with meaningful, intuitive depictions. User segments can be easily graphed by day in a stack percentage bar chart (see Figure 6.2), which draws attention to the growth or deterioration of various segments over the lifetime of the product.

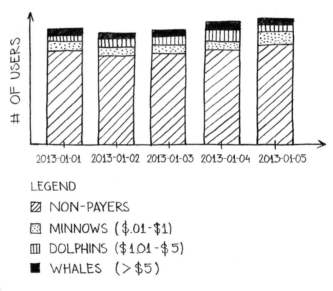

FIGURE 6.2

A chart tracking active users by user segment per day.

The segments should be represented by the percentage of DAU existing at those monetization thresholds on a daily basis; for a product with a large, stable user base, these segments should settle into fairly stable values over time.

Wild fluctuations in the values of the segments are a sign that the monetization curve has not reached an optimal level of continuity (or that the user segments thresholds are too far apart, or too numerous at the higher end of the scale). A continuous monetization curve provides many opportunities to monetize between segment thresholds, but one that is not fluid will exhibit sharp, staggered declines; these declines manifest themselves in volatility in the segmentation bar graph.

This volatility is a hindrance to product design because it doesn't produce actionable insight; a steady, continuous change in the size of active segments speaks to holes in the product catalogue or declining interest in the product, but erratic changes can't be easily interpreted in order to make decisions. Ideally, each segment should settle into a consistent range of values, changes in which can be taken as alerts that the product catalogue requires updating (i.e., a decrease in a segment at the lower end of the monetization curve means less-expensive products are losing appeal).

Some criticism has been leveled against the practice of grouping users into segments named from the animal kingdom. The practice originated in the gambling industry, wherein spendthrift gamblers were classified as "whales" and treated to an improved experience by the casino to induce further spending.

While taking cues from the gambling industry may be viewed as adopting conventions from a commercial enterprise that is largely seen as exploitative, the specific labels applied to user segments is irrelevant: the term *whale* could be replaced with *highly engaged user* and the purpose of segmentation, which is deriving data that assists in optimizing the user experience, wouldn't change. To that end, grouping users into segments named after animals is no different from the myriad other techniques employed by product teams with the goal of creating a personalized, enjoyable experience for each user.

Data products in the freemium model

The rise of Big Data and ubiquitous instrumentation in consumer products has led to the emergence of a layer of meta-products that capture information about behavior and trends and allow the information to be leveraged to enhance the user experience. These meta-products are called *data products*, and they have become a staple of large-scale software platforms that generate huge volumes of data artifacts. The insight produced by such volumes of data is not only of consequence to the developers of products for feature design purposes, it is also generally valuable to users, who can utilize the insight to self-direct their own behavioral optimizations.

The best example of this type of insight being valuable to the end-user from behavioral audits or records mining from platforms that offer only data products. Some personal finance products, for instance, connect directly to users' bank accounts and look for expenditure patterns over long time periods that the user may not have been cognizant of; others connect to users' social networks and relay information about the size and scope of the sub-networks found within. The value of such products is derived wholly from preexisting data.

Freemium data products can serve to monetize users without presenting friction. They are generally valuable to the most engaged users; they enhance the core experience and allow for it to be improved through product awareness that is available only with direct access to user data and a robust analytics infrastructure, neither of which users generally have at their disposal. In this sense, data products can be seen as more of a service—the ability to access and use an analytics platform—the scale and expense of which most individuals wouldn't be able to justify but nonetheless are still able to extract value from. Data products, then, are a means of leveraging existing, necessary analytics infrastructure to generate additional streams of revenue.

Data products essentially take two forms: tools that allow users to optimize their own experiences, such as user-centric analytics or insight products, and opt-in suggestive tools that optimize the user's experience based on the user's behavioral history. Data products don't explicitly take the form of products that a user can recognize; they may simply be implemented into a user interface as elements of the navigation or product console. As such, they might be considered product features, except that data products are generally developed with heavy input from the analytics group.

This distinction is important to recognize because the develop-release-measure-iterate feedback loop for data products is fundamentally different as a result of the analytics group's involvement. So, while the development of data products adheres to the same general guidelines as do other product features, consideration must be made for exactly how they are implemented, measured, and iterated upon.

Recommendation engines

A recommendation engine is a behavioral tool that helps guide users into the best possible product experience based on their personal demographic characteristics and the tendencies they have exhibited in the past. Unlike feature-level optimization, which is usually undertaken without any fanfare because it is based solely on user behavior, recommendation engines are opt-in, meaning users are presented with a choice and must either accept or decline it.

The opt-in nature of recommendation engines stems from the fact that opt-ins generally affect the way the product is used. One of the most popular examples of a recommendation engine is a social tool that suggests appropriate new connections in a network-based product: these often appear as panes on the periphery of the user interface and propose potential new connections to the user, based on a number of factors. If the product's network is presumed to be based on real-world connections, the proposed new contact should likewise be someone the user is likely to know in a personal or professional context, which can be estimated through an analysis of shared contacts.

A tool of this nature materializes as a recommendation engine because a social network exists to allow users to connect of their own volition to the contacts of their choosing. A product that automatically assigns connections to a user is not a network, it's an algorithmic data dissemination tool. Given that the inherent value of a social network is the network itself, curating the curation process would not be a user experience optimization but a total presupposition of user intent, the misuse of which would negate the product's purpose and render it unusable.

Far from being the core of a product, a recommendation typically takes the form of an ancillary enhancement to the product's user interface or a call to action in the product flow. For example, the "people you may know" tool described earlier might be introduced to the user during the initial onboarding period, immediately after registration; this allows the user to immediately populate the user's network and thus extract value from the service from the outset, reducing the probability of churn. After this initial introduction, the tool might sit at the border of the user interface—always accessible but not overwhelmingly conspicuous.

Recommendations can be made individually or in larger numbers, depending on the projected efficacy of the recommendation (i.e., whether or not the user is expected to accept the recommendation) and the nature of the recommended object. They can likewise take a less obvious form than a explicit recommendations; rather, they might be posed as interface options or account settings. Whatever the case, the user should be made to feel that a nonpermanent choice is being presented.

The efficacy of recommendations is easily measured: it is the ratio of proposed to accepted recommendations. This ratio isn't merely a characteristic of the algorithm that determines the recommendations; it should be used to actively improve upon the algorithm beyond some minimum acceptable threshold of appropriateness. No universal effectiveness benchmark for recommendations exists; a benchmark should be defined for the product, taking into account the nature of the recommendations. But recommendation engines that are not performing to an appropriate standard should be shuttered, as inappropriate recommendations are not necessarily benign; they can undermine the user's trust in the product and distract the user from the core experience.

Consolidating the disparate components of the recommendation engine into a user interface implement requires cooperation between the analytics team and the product team over design and logistical considerations. The analytics team will own the data delivered by the tool, but the product team should determine where it is placed, how it contributes to the product experience, and when it will be visible to users.

The product development schedule therefore must be coordinated with care across the two groups, especially when updates are required. The two groups should also come to a consensus over the definition of success before the tool is launched, and that standard should be used to determine whether the tool remains active or is removed from the product. A concrete, agreed-upon standard to be reached in a predetermined timeframe after launch can help relieve conflicting interpretations of the tool's effectiveness.

The dynamic product catalogue

The continuous product catalogue in a freemium setting isn't necessarily composed of explicitly designed items; rather, to approach continuity, the product catalogue can be rendered dynamically as a function of customizable options available for a smaller, discrete set of items. In this sense, the product catalogue can approach an infinite size, which presents problems for navigation as well as appropriateness: some product configurations will be more valid than others to certain users, based on preference. Data products can be used to ameliorate both of these issues by pre-selecting the best product customization options for the user based on behavior and sorting those products based on taste.

While an infinitely large and complex catalogue of purchasable items meets the quality requirements cited in the discussion of discrete choice theory and vertical product differentiation, it comes at the cost of usability and straightforward navigation. A product experience is enriched by diversity, but too much choice can be cumbersome, especially when the majority of choices are inappropriate for any given user. The dynamic product catalogue should capitalize on the data artifacts users create in order to tailor the specific options and the variety in the product catalogue to users' tastes and behavioral preferences.

Some product catalogues will invariably be harder than others to classify with respect to a user's past behavior, especially when the user has not spent much time with the product. This can be accommodated for by profiling users early and establishing catalogue preferences that can be matched to a minimal set of data. Once a user is profiled, the user's personal catalogue can evolve over time as the user produces data artifacts capable of informing the progression of the catalogue.

In the "people you may know" product example, this evolution might take the form of a set of contact recommendations for a user that is determined from a very broad demographic characteristic, say, the user having registered with a university email address. The product catalogue for this unique product, which is the contact recommendation engine, would change over time as the user exhibits a preference for certain types of connections, such as professional contacts or contacts from the same university. As this user's tastes become clearer, the catalogue itself changes, offering more precisely tailored products (recommendations) for which the user is likely to have a desire.

In addition to selecting dynamic product options based on appropriateness, the dynamic catalogue of purchasable items should also be capable of ranking those options based on the likelihood of the user finding them appealing. Even when finely tuned to a user's tastes, an unwieldy catalogue of purchasable items can reduce the user's propensity to buy by inviting so much analytical comparison between options that, ultimately, no choice is ever made (a form of "analysis paralysis"). Tailoring a product catalogue to a user's tastes requires pruning the catalogue to an appropriate size to maximize the likelihood that the user finds exactly what the user wants.

The benefit of limited choice is derived from the notion that the evaluation of a purchasable item is accompanied by an opportunity cost, which is foregoing the evaluation period and the purchase altogether. The evaluation period of most purchasable items is small and undertaken with only a few features, such as price, in mind. But when the options for a particular purchasable item increase, the process of comparing those options becomes more complex and requires considering more features to produce an efficacious result, given decreased differentiation. When the set of options and thus the set of comparison features grows very large, the opportunity cost of this evaluation process can exceed the utility of the eventual choice.

Such a situation is extreme, but even at lower levels of comparison, users can be led into inaction by the fear of making an incorrect decision. Thus, while purchasable items should be customizable to the extent that users feel they can buy exactly what they want, the purchasable items in the catalogue should be sufficiently differentiated so that they can make a quick comparison. The optimal size of the catalogue depends on the level of differentiation that can be achieved in variants, although enough variants must be presented to communicate a sense of diversity to the user (and satisfy the quality requirement).

At the macro level (the level of design that considers the entire user base), product catalogue continuity is a necessity because it allows for every user's tastes to be accommodated for. But at the individual level, observable continuity—when a user can deduce, given the massive size of a product catalogue, that at least one purchasable item suits the user's tastes—is less beneficial than ease of navigation. Therefore, the scope of the continuous product catalogue that is presented to the user should err on the side of being quickly and painlessly browsed through. While quality is important to communicate, and quality is communicated through a large product catalogue, the return on conspicuous quality rapidly diminishes as the product catalogue becomes cumbersome to navigate.

Productizing analytics

Predicting all possible use cases for a product during the development phase undermines the purpose of the minimum viable product model and is often futile. Use cases develop unpredictably, and, as a result, the extent to which the most engaged users will treasure a product is indeterminable until those users have been exposed to the product. The most engaged users may adopt a product as a staple of daily life, as occurs with some lightweight mobile apps.

These dedicated users can represent a powerful community of supporters and advocates whom overly aggressive monetization might alienate. As a result, their product use might be of little value; if a product space is commoditized to the point that the cost of switching between competing products is low, then even the most engaged users may not be incentivized to pay for direct use. In such a case, the enthusiasm for the product is better monetized than is actual usage, and productized analytics may offer an opportunity to strike a balance between adoption and monetization.

Productized analytics describes a meta-product that provides insight into a user's interaction with a product. Many users, especially the most engaged, may expect the functionality—even the advanced functionality—of a product to be provided for free in a market segment that is dominated by the freemium model. Whether or not these expectations are rational is irrelevant; market participants must adapt to them. By providing product users with in-depth analytics to describe their usage of the product, the developer sidesteps a potential scale-limiting monetization strategy by allowing the most engaged users to become more deeply attached to the product.

Users are generally interested in the same scope of analytics as are product teams, with the exception that users may appreciate metrics describing their interactions with other users (e.g., profile views on a social network) and real-time metrics that aren't useful for development purposes. Productized analytics can generally be extracted from the same infrastructure that produces product development analytics; however, the increased strain of making these analytics available to users (in terms of infrastructure load) may necessitate additional resource allocation to the analytics stack to ensure fidelity and availability.

As in product development, analytics tools made available to the user can be optimally delivered in a configurable dashboard. This dashboard may extend the user profile or exist as a separate functional entity, but it should be intuitively accessible and designed with simplicity of use in mind: product teams and users may engage with analytics for the same purposes, but product teams do so with informed intent. Users must be guided to analytics, and any hurdles to understanding the value in analyzing their behaviors might serve as an impediment to using the dashboard.

Pricing analytics products is often undertaken within the same freemium strictures as the source product itself, with a free tier available to entice users to become acquainted with the product and a paid tier available to those extracting the most value out of such information. Analytics products should be designed to underscore monetary value: if a user understands that streamlined product use (via analytics) can create direct, monetary value, then the user can more likely make an educated decision about purchasing analytics products. Thus, the overarching theme of the analytics tools should indicate a possibility of decreasing expenses (especially through streamlined usage) or increasing revenue.

Downstream marketing

The dynamics of the freemium model—large scale, low conversion, and a nearly continuous catalogue of purchasable items—pose discovery challenges. Specifically, items in a nearly infinite product catalogue are not readily accessible, and even highly engaged users may not be capable of staying abreast of the most recent product developments. For this reason, marketing in freemium products doesn't apply just to the process of introducing users to the product, it also applies to users already in the product's system as a means of targeting users for appropriate promotions and reengaging them with new and existing features. In this sense, marketing can be divided into two conceptual formats: upstream marketing, which describes the marketing activities undertaken to grow the user base, and downstream marketing, which describes activities targeted at the existing user base.

Downstream marketing is driven almost entirely by data, especially in freemium marketing; the ability to reengage a user or present a user with the most appropriate product promotion is contingent on an understanding of that user that can be realized only through behavioral data.

In this sense, downstream marketing is divorced from traditional marketing skillsets and is realized by applying data science to marketing principles. In essence, downstream marketing represents commercial analysis when a product's system cannot be managed as a monolith. When the product catalogue is continuous, the user base is segmented, and the levels of potential lifetime value fall across a very broad range, then the process of encouraging the user base to make purchases never ends.

Reengagement marketing

The most popular form of downstream marketing is probably reengagement marketing, or marketing efforts undertaken to bring a user back to a product that has ostensibly been abandoned. While it is not always effective, reengagement marketing is popular because it is cheap, and user acquisition is not. When a single user has apparently churned (or is considered likely to churn), the product team must weigh the cost of attempting to reengage that user against the cost of acquiring a new user.

With web-based products, reengagement campaigns are almost always delivered by email, as it is an inexpensive medium that is capable of converting with little friction by using embedded links. Emails are also incredibly easy to track, test, and iterate upon; the content of emails can be constructed in any number of combinations over which send rates, open rates, and click rates are readily and easily quantifiable.

Email campaigns are usually constructed with a template that is populated by specific user details when the campaign is launched, as shown in Figure 6.3. For a reengagement campaign, an email will typically focus on a specific call to action involving a discount or an invitation to explore an aspect of the service that the user hasn't yet accessed. Templates addressing specific situations are constructed according to the relevant situational dynamics, and the analytics system automates the delivery of emails to appropriate recipients on a regular schedule (usually nightly).

The transparency of email campaign conversion allows for continual optimization but may also create a sense of progress that isn't wholly warranted; email campaigns are notoriously ineffective, generally producing conversion rates of far less than 10 percent. The return on invested time should be tracked carefully when engaging in email reengagement campaigns—slight conversion gains may not be worth the time invested to produce them, and email content can be adjusted endlessly.

FIGURE 6.3

A sample reengagement email template, in which values surrounded by % are replaced with user data from the product database.

On mobile platforms, a more powerful alternative to email reengagement campaigns is called *push notification*. A push notification is a system message delivered ("pushed") by an application. Push notifications are received by user opt-in (at first launch, most applications request to send push notifications); if a user has selected to receive them, the user converts extraordinarily well. And while the space allotted for push notifications is small—usually not more than a few words—and thus offers little latitude for testing, tracking behavior that results from push notifications is straightforward, since the entire process takes place on a user's mobile device.

Determining when reengagement should be pursued is mostly a function of the definition of churn for that product. Users who have churned out of a product are not only largely resistant to reengagement overtures, they're also likely to consider such attempts spam, which incites negative feelings for the product and potentially damages its reputation. A company should take care, especially in email reengagement, to not communicate with users who have obviously churned completely; rather, it should connect with users when they are considered likely to churn, which is the analytics system's responsibility.

Promotional targeting

User segments are not useful merely for predicting user behavior and grouping monetization profiles; they can also be useful in categorizing users based on the stimuli the users respond to, especially as those stimuli relate to monetization. The manner in which users interact with a product's catalogue of purchasable items, and the goals users seek to achieve with a product, can be useful tools in curating an experience that best suits users' needs.

Product promotions—discounts, time-limited special offers, combination products, volume prices, and so on—are universally appreciated; that people welcome the notion of paying less for a product under special circumstances is not controversial. And in the freemium model, the opportunity exists to dynamically undertake promotional pricing strategies in perpetuity, whereby the entire product catalogue is subject to an optimal pricing framework at all times. This framework need not be a monolith; instead, it can apply to each user (or, more often, each user segment) in the manner that best optimizes product revenue.

Promotional targeting is a strategy for increasing revenue that involves setting prices so as to intersect with demand within user segments, not within the entire population of users. In practice, this intersection isn't accomplished through different prices for different user segments but rather through ongoing promotional efforts that vary by user segment. Since the marginal cost of producing products in a freemium environment is $0, products should be priced (discounted) to whatever extent results in the highest number of sales.

Promotional targeting is driven by analytics: much like in reengagement marketing, promotional targeting matches a predetermined template (in this case, a discounting template) to a user profile and presents that template where it is relevant. The determinants of the segment profiles in promotional targeting are product preference, promotional preference, and timelines. These preferences and characteristics can be derived by measuring how users react to various items in the catalogue of purchasable items and grouping them accordingly.

The unit economics of freemium products supports promotions that can be used to gauge sentiment to some of the factors listed above. For instance, a catalogue of purchasable items might include a perennial discount on a specific product to test for users' enthusiasm for sale prices. Users who respond favorably to such promotions might be grouped into a "value buyer" segment that is targeted for additional discount prices in the future. Likewise, a "combination buyer" user segment may be presented with promotions that provide combinations of purchasable items that don't normally exist in the catalogue, in order to encourage monetization. These user segments can be identified early in the product experience by permanently applying promotional techniques to various items in the purchasable catalogue.

Targeting users for discounts can also be done as a function of product preference. Users who have exhibited predilections for a specific type of product can be offered promotional pricing opportunities in order to motivate increased engagement. The opportunities presented should be grounded in the user's historical purchasing tendencies as well as the user's expected utility from the purchases. A user's purchase not only augments a sense of commitment to the product, but it also improves the user's future experience with the product. Encouraging purchases can therefore be seen as a means of boosting retention and engagement; it's not simply a strategy for increasing monetization.

Measuring downstream marketing

Downstream marketing is largely an automated endeavor; the processes designed to keep users engaged in the product and aware of the evolving catalogue of purchasable items should, for the most part, be handled by systems. But, like any system designed to operate autonomously, the systems driving downstream marketing require measurement and oversight. Complex systems can break at large scale for any number of reasons; to ensure the effectiveness of downstream marketing, it must be monitored and shortcomings must be addressed as they surface.

Monitoring downstream marketing requires the derivation of metrics that can be used to measure its success. For reengagement marketing, these metrics are fairly straightforward: number of reengagement messages sent, number of messages received, and number of messages converted into further use of the product (usually defined as another session). Metrics relating to revenue generated from reengaged users might also be tracked within a conservative time period after the correspondence is sent. For example, all revenue generated during the week after sending a reengagement campaign is attributed to that campaign. These revenue metrics are useful for measuring return on investment and making decisions about increased investment in reengagement.

Measuring dynamic promotions is more difficult. Dynamic promotions leverage the low marginal cost of product sales to create revenue where there otherwise would be none. Given this conceptual abstraction, counting all revenue generated by a promotional sale may be overly simplistic. Whether a user would have made a purchase in the absence of a promotion is unknowable; in fact, overly aggressive promotional pricing may cannibalize baseline revenues.

Because of this inherent ambiguity, tracking dynamic promotion conversion as a proxy of success may be more valuable than trying to attribute revenues to promotions. The user segments that best capture promotional revenue experience fluidity; as the product and user base mature, so too will preferences for products and receptiveness to promotions.

Aspirations for consistent conversion on promotional offers should be pursued by monitoring any dynamic mechanisms used in producing them; decreasing conversion rates (i.e., fewer people over time purchase the promotions they are exposed to) should serve as a signal that either user tastes have changed, the level of discounts offered is no longer attractive, or the user segments around which promotions are configured have evolved.

The effectiveness of dynamic promotional pricing on revenues can be measured only through A/B testing against a control group (i.e., a group that is not exposed to promotions). While reaffirming the efficacy and need of any automated system should be undertaken at regular intervals, it is not necessary on an ongoing basis. The testing sample should be derived using the same targeting logic that produces user segments for the automated promotions, and testing the technique's impact on revenue can be done using the statistical methods introduced in chapter 3. If a promotional technique isn't working—it is not producing more revenues than the baseline pricing scheme of the catalogue of purchasable items—it should be deactivated and re-conceptualized.

Downstream marketing metrics are necessarily limited in relevance; while the product team should be interested in the performance of downstream marketing techniques, very few others in an organization likely need to know much about them. Including such metrics on a high-level dashboard is therefore not necessary, but tracking these metrics on a regular basis is. Automated systems should not be left unmonitored; automation can lead to unintended consequences when implemented and forgotten.

Besides being tracked properly, automated systems should integrate a means of being shut off or paused when various metrics breach predetermined thresholds; for instance, if the conversion rate on a promotional offer exceeds a certain number—50 percent, for example—that promotion should automatically stop until it has been investigated. The logic driving automated systems operates on a limited set of *a priori* assumptions that may fall victim to unpredictable factors. A stop-loss shutdown mechanism should prevent any automated system from operating outside the bounds of predicted behavior for a meaningful amount of time.

Virality

7

The viral product

Virality was introduced briefly in the discussion of the minimum viable metrics model as one aspect of a product's user base growth. This description was intentionally left vague; the truth is that virality is a nebulous concept and is notoriously difficult to measure, despite being one of the critical sources of growth for most consumer Internet and mobile products.

What is virality?

At the user level, virality is achieved through two possible *viral mechanics*: interpersonal recommendations and in-product invitations. An interpersonal recommendation, as it relates to virality, is any invitation to join a product that takes place outside the scope of the product (i.e., it wasn't initiated by a user within the product). One example of an interpersonal recommendation as a viral mechanic is a word-of-mouth recommendation, which can't be counted or attributed to a specific user but which nonetheless contributes to the product's user base in a viral manner (and is often the most effective means of viral growth).

An in-product invitation is a proposal, initiated by an existing user to a non-user, to join the product, using some mechanism the product offers. In-product invitations often take the form of email invitations or social networking alerts; a user in a product is encouraged to invite the user's social circle into the product and is presented with a prefilled template for distributing information about the product to others. The number of in-product invitations sent should be measurable through in-product event tracking infrastructure; the number received and acted on may be difficult or impossible to measure on some platforms, such as mobile.

It is not feasible to count the number of interpersonal recommendations a product receives; however, recommendations are likely the best-converting sources of viral growth. Likewise, the number of times a product is adopted because a person was seen using it—perhaps on a tablet on a city bus, or on a laptop in a café—is similarly unknowable. But these sources of users are real, and they must be considered. This phenomenon serves as the greatest obstacle to product development as it relates to user base growth: how can virality be designed into a product if it can't be measured?

As it turns out, virality can be measured—it just can't be measured precisely. At a high level, a product is inherently viral or it isn't; viral mechanics designed as an afterthought generally can't create contrived growth trends (or, if they can, those growth trends are generally short-lived and insubstantial).

One of the basic properties of a virus is that it is self-replicating; that is, it grows, independent of any external catalysts. By definition, any agent that does not replicate autonomously is not a virus. The same general condition holds with viral growth: if a user was acquired into a product through a marketing initiative, and not from another product user, then that acquisition was not the result of virality.

Calculating virality

The principle metric associated with virality is the k-factor, or the average number of additional users introduced to the product by each user. For reasons discussed earlier, measuring the k-factor with precision, in many cases, is difficult: tracking all the means by which existing users may introduce new users to the product is problematic (if not impossible), meaning conversions cannot be reliably attributed to viral mechanics. When a product platform is surrounded by an opaque data moat, as are many mobile platforms, ascertaining how a user becomes aware of a product can be treacherously costly and laborious. On the other hand, some platforms—notably, web-based platforms—present simple and straightforward methods for tracking this information, rendering the conversion rate from product invitation mechanics easy to quantify. For instance, a web-based product can track invitations and conversions from end to end through URL parameters, meaning confusion can enter into the process only if an invited user doesn't click on an invitation link but rather types the base URL of the website directly into a browser.

When considering attribution in calculating virality, new users must be separated into three groups: those acquired through paid channels (who are removed from the virality equation completely), those acquired virally (through any means other than direct discovery and paid acquisition), and those acquired organically (those who came across the product without any influence from an existing user). Virally and organically acquired users can be thought of as the two elements of a population ratio; knowing the size of the total user population and the size of one of these user groups is sufficient to determine the product's virality.

The strategy through which virality is estimated therefore depends on the accuracy provisions of the platform. Two extremes exist on a spectrum of platform data availability: the eminently transparent extreme, at which everything is capable of being tracked and all data related to viral invitations and conversions is at the disposal of the product team, and the eminently opaque extreme, at which no data related to the user source is accessible.

Even on platforms sitting near the eminently transparent extreme, the k-factor is not wholly measurable through counts of invitations and conversions because these platform-centric metrics do not take into account the effects of interpersonal viral mechanics. (See Figure 7.1.) Counting conversions that result from in-product viral

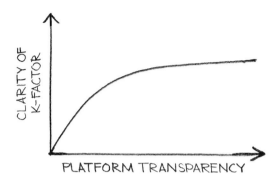

FIGURE 7.1

Platform transparency versus clarity of the k-factor.

mechanics only provides one aspect of overall product virality; to capture a conceptual viral metric, or a *global k-factor*, all users who weren't acquired organically or through paid channels should be classified as viral.

In other words, a conversion rate for viral invitations doesn't provide much insight into a product's true virality. Instead, the global k-factor should be calculated as a function of user base growth, of which viral invitations are only one contributor, with the understanding that the metric is fundamentally rooted in broad assumptions about how product use spreads within social circles. One approach to measuring the global k-factor this way is to analyze user base growth as a time series, controlling for external factors (such as media coverage and platform featuring) and natural user base decay.

When the user base is examined as a time series and broken down into periods, the global k-factor can be calculated by dividing the growth of the user base from one period by the number of users in the period preceding it, as shown in Figure 7.2. This calculation distributes the user base's decay-adjusted growth (the net of churned users), regardless of attributable source, across the entire period-one user base (and thus accounts for interpersonal viral mechanics). This k-factor reflects historically relevant total user base growth as a ratio of the number of users introduced to the product virally, as opposed to a local k-factor that relies solely on the calculation of product mechanics (like viral invitations) to grow the user base.

Calculating virality as a function of in-product viral mechanics is likewise valid but only addresses those sources of virality that are able to be measured. This approach to calculating the k-factor relies on the straightforward formula found in Figure 7.3. In the figure, I represents the average number of viral invitations a user sends and C represents the average conversion rate of those invitations. The result is the number of users converted to the product, on average, via a single user.

While the k-factor is more limited in scope than a time-series measurement of the entire user base, the invitations approach to calculating it is not without merit,

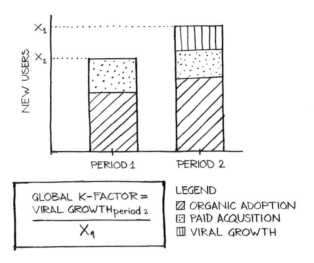

FIGURE 7.2

A two-period user base growth chart, illustrating the global k-factor calculation.

$$K = I \cdot C$$

FIGURE 7.3

An equation to calculate k-factor.

as it provides clear insight into the performance of in-product viral mechanics and is more immediately actionable with regard to product development. Where the time-series approach relates a high-level (if ambiguous) sense of overall product appeal, the invitations approach relates a very specific measurement of user enthusiasm for the product and the subsequent clarity and allure of product enticements captured therein.

The effects of compounding virality

Perhaps the most appreciable and visible benefit of virality as it pertains to user base growth (especially through paid marketing) is its compounding effect. Like interest on a financial instrument, the compounding effect of virality allows a user base to grow geometrically; such a growth pattern provides access to users that would otherwise be achievable only through organic discovery or paid acquisition, and sets the conditions for massive, profitable scale.

True virality exists at a k-factor at or above 1, meaning each user, on average, introduces more than one new user to the product. In theory, this means that a user base can grow infinitely, after being seeded with an initial set of users, as a function of its own momentum. In practice, a number of limitations exist that cap the absolute extent to which virality can grow a user base.

$$X_2 = X_1 \cdot (1 + r)$$

FIGURE 7.4

A formula to calculate growth from one period to the next.

$$X_n = X_1 \cdot (1 + r)^n$$

FIGURE 7.5

A formula to calculate growth over n periods.

$$a^x = b$$
$$X \cdot \ln(a) = \ln(b)$$

FIGURE 7.6

These two figures are equivalent.

As with compounding interest, compounding virality is rooted in exponential math, or arithmetic that is driven by some base value being multiplied by itself. The formula for calculating one-period growth, given a per-period rate of growth, is shown in Figure 7.4, where X_2 is the value of the quantity in period two, X_1 is the value of the quantity in period one, and r is the rate of growth.

Extending this logic, the formula for calculating n-period growth under conditions of a constant growth rate is shown in Figure 7.5, where n is the number of periods over which growth takes place, and X_1 is the value at the start of the growth period.

The rate of growth in these equations would be expressed in terms of per-period percentage increases; for instance, if a user base grew from 100 to 110 in one period, the variable r in Figure 7.4 would be replaced with .10, representing 10 percent growth. If the user base had grown from 100 to 200, or 100 percent growth, the variable r would be replaced with 1.0 (and thus the value within the parentheses would be $1 + 1$, or 2).

A 100 percent growth rate represents a doubling of the user base, which is a significant virality threshold and a benchmark that is often cited in terms of user base growth. A user base doubling in size is a powerful psychological motivator for a product development team and is often used in the product planning process or as motivation for investment into further development. In any case, knowing the time required, given existing growth rates, for a user base to double in size is useful when making decisions about the future course of a product.

The *doubling time* of a user base, given a consistent growth rate, can be calculated with exponential arithmetic, which allows for equations containing exponents to be rearranged using natural logarithms. To illustrate this concept, consider that the equations in Figure 7.6 are equivalent.

The doubling of a user base over n periods, where X_n is twice as large as X_1, is represented in Figure 7.7.

$$\frac{X_n}{X_1} = (1+r)^n$$

FIGURE 7.7

Calculating the growth rate needed to double a user base in n periods, given that X_n is twice as large as X_1.

$$2 = (1+r)^n$$

$$\ln(2) = n \cdot \ln(1+r)$$

FIGURE 7.8

Re-arranging Figure 7.7 using a natural logarithm yields Figure 7.8.

$$\frac{\ln(2)}{\ln(1+r)} = n$$

FIGURE 7.9

Solving Figure 7.8 for n yields Figure 7.9.

$$\frac{\ln(2)}{\ln(1+.10)} = n$$

$$\frac{.69}{.10} = n$$

$$7.27 = n$$

FIGURE 7.10

Assuming a growth rate of 10%, a user base will double in 7.27 periods.

When a user base doubles, X_n is twice as large as X_1, thus resolving to a multiple of 2. Therefore, rearranging the equation in Figure 7.7 using a natural logarithm to isolate the exponent for a doubling of the user base yields the results shown in Figure 7.8.

Dividing the natural log of 2 by the natural log of the growth factor solves for *n*, as shown in Figure 7.9.

So, given a consistent growth rate of 10 percent, a product team can calculate the number of *n* periods over which a product's user base will double by using the formula shown in Figure 7.10.

In this example, the user base will double after 7.27 periods (which would be rounded up to eight, because periods are measured only in whole denominations).

$$\frac{72}{10} = n$$

$$7.2 = n$$

FIGURE 7.11

A rough approximation of doubling time.

The general logic of this arithmetic isn't unique to the doubling of a value; using the same format, the *tripling time*, *quadrupling time*, and so on can be calculated by replacing the 2 in Figure 7.10 with the multiple of interest.

This property of exponential arithmetic is often employed using a heuristic known as the *rule of 72*, which stipulates that the doubling time of any value experiencing compounding growth can be roughly calculated by dividing the growth rate expressed as a percentage (e.g., 10%, not .10) into 72. Using the same values from the example in Figure 7.10, a rough approximation of the doubling time is calculated in Figure 7.11.

This heuristic is often used to generate estimates of doubling time in the planning stages of product development. The relationship between QUOTE and QUOTE should underline the notion that higher virality reduces the amount of time required for a user base to double. This is the chief benefit of viral mechanics and viral tendencies: they can create feedback loops that quickly increase the size of a user base.

Understanding the relationship between these variables and taking informed, proactive steps to increase r, thus decreasing n, are fundamental tactics in strategic product development. Over the course of a product's lifetime, but especially in the earliest stages, user base growth is a product team's principal concern. A firm grasp of the dynamics driving that growth efficiently and quantifiably is necessary to control it.

Virality and retention

Virality and retention exist on opposite sides of the acquisition threshold: virality describes how users are introduced to a product, and retention describes how long users remain with a product. But in essence, both sets of metrics measure the same general sense of delight users feel for a product, manifested in different ways. To that end, virality and retention generally exhibit a positively correlated relationship: products that users are inclined to return to over a long period of time are also likely to be products that users invite others to join.

At a conceptual level, the logic driving the one-directional relationship between virality and retention (i.e., strong retention increases the potential for strong virality) is fairly straightforward; users for whom a product exhibits overwhelming appeal retain with that product longer than users who don't, and thus they are presented with more opportunities to invite others into the product than non-retaining users.

In practice, this relationship may not manifest; some products are designed for individual, private use and are not conducive to viral growth no matter how strongly users feel about them, and some products do not competently implement the means for viral dissemination. But at the core of any product's use profile sits the single characteristic—delight—that contributes to both virality and retention metrics.

When these two metrics do not correlate positively—when a product exhibits strong virality but weak retention or vice versa—the positive effects are often neutralized (or even become liabilities). For instance, present strong virality but low retention, a product's user base may grow rapidly but just as quickly diminish as users churn out of the service. This scenario is problematic because churned users must be reacquired, which is difficult when they have already abandoned a service.

In the opposite situation—a product exhibits strong retention but low virality—the growth costs are not offset by the accumulation of viral users, which in some cases may completely reduce the product's ability to expand. A product cannot capitalize on either strong virality or retention unless the other metrics group exists at some minimum level.

The product development cycle should accommodate this relationship by focusing on the core experience that drives delight, rather than addressing an individual metrics group. Tactics used to boost either retention or virality—but especially virality—often detract from the product experience and appear contrived.

If a product doesn't exhibit virality, users fundamentally oppose revealing their use of the product because the product isn't useful to them, the product doesn't meet the quality threshold required to make a recommendation, or because they simply don't want people to know they use the product. None of these reasons can be attenuated by an additional viral mechanic; they must be addressed with deep core changes to the product experience.

Likewise, retention metrics underscore fundamental product delight; addressing a specific retention-day drop with a new feature or gimmick won't fix the structural shortcomings that cause users to leave a product and not return. The underlying reasoning users employ to justify leaving a product (either for another product or because the product's use case is simply irrelevant to them) won't be dismantled with artificial auxiliary product features.

It is true that retention and virality can be improved incrementally through product features that don't augment the product's core use case. But for these metrics to contribute to the user base meaningfully and sustainably, both must exist at a minimum threshold that lets a virtuous cycle develop, where retention allows for greater virality and greater virality introduces more users to the product. If one of the groups of metrics doesn't reach the minimum threshold, this symbiosis can't occur and, as pointed out, the relationship could actually have negative effects on the long-term viability of the product.

Until both the retention and virality metrics groups reach a minimum level, product development shouldn't be directed at features that address either one specifically; rather, the fundamental use case should be addressed and iterated upon, with the goal of improving all of the minimum viable metrics. Feature development undertaken to specifically address virality or retention, before the product has achieved a minimum level of performance, will likely achieve only short-term, negligible gains.

Signal versus noise

In-product viral invitations are often seen as a well that can be infinitely drawn from in pursuing virality: invitation mechanics are easy to implement, present massive potential for virally acquiring new users, and are easy to instrument and track. But invitation mechanics can be forced onto users to an extreme that not only negates their effectiveness but also produces unfavorable results through overexposure and a tone reminiscent of spam. The extent to which viral invitation mechanics are relied on should be considered (and, ideally, tested) within the full scope of their possible consequences.

One reason viral invitation mechanics should be implemented cautiously is psychological; given that a product's value proposition should be self-evident, products that frequently encourage users to make use of invitation mechanics may appear adversely selected for (because products of obviously high quality don't need to remind users to tell others about them). This realization could discourage users from sharing their use of the product at all, because they could feel like marketing agents rather than customers and because they might not want to risk their reputations on promoting a seemingly substandard product.

Copious and aggressive invitation mechanics render a strong signaling effect on the user base that contributes significantly to user sentiment for the product. But perhaps more importantly, they have a strong signaling effect on potential future users—those on the receiving end of the invitations. Numerous invitations to a service, especially from the same user, are understandably interpreted as spam and are ignored. Belligerently pestering would-be users with invitations to join a product can create permanent non-users or, worse yet, negative messengers and product denouncers.

These psychological effects are difficult, if not impossible, to offset. Users who have made determinations about a product, especially a product they perceive to have spammed them, will not likely change their minds about that product without significant input from existing users. And, given the presence of such enthusiasm, the product would almost certainly be better off if that enthusiasm were directed either toward potential users who have never been exposed to the product or inward to the existing user base, thereby increasing engagement. The effort required to convince potential users that a product is worth investigating after they have mentally dismissed it is monumental.

The second reason in-product invitation mechanics should be implemented methodically and with deliberate restraint is that users can engage with only a limited number of contacts at once in any service. When users exercise a viral invitation mechanic to lure a large number of new users into a product, the existing users' capacity for communicating with their contacts strains with each new user who accepts the invitation. The users who accept the invitation, join the service, and are then seemingly ignored by the person who invited them may feel neglected or believe that the product isn't functional; in either case, this effect increases the likelihood that they churn.

A low number of highly engaged and socially active viral users can be worth more than a high number of viral users who feel isolated. A limit on the number of viral invitations that a single user can send serves to ensure that users acquired by those invitations are given the fullest attention possible by the users who invited them, especially in social products or products where users are aware of their contacts' actions.

Additionally, when a person knows an invitation was one of a limited number that could be sent—he or she was allocated a scarce resource—that person is more likely to attach value to the invitation than if he or she knows invitations are limitless. The same is true on the current user's part when selecting invitation recipients: having only a limited number of invitations, the user is more likely to select the most appropriate contacts, personalize the invitation (to the extent made possible by the product), and potentially follow up on the invitation. This mentality substantially increases the likelihood that an invitation converts to an acquisition.

Viral invitations are well structured as mechanics that exist as passive, permanent fixtures of the user interface in terms of product implementation; aggressive pop-ups and entreaties to invite friends appear desperate and unfavorable. Invitation limits may be either explicit (e.g., the user is directly told that the in-product mechanic may be used to send a specific number of invitations) or enforced through the layout of the mechanic (e.g., the mechanic has only three fields for inputting contact email addresses).

When the user must proactively seek out an invitation mechanic, that mechanic is more likely to convert than mechanics that have been forced on the user. Given the negative effects of a rejected invitation—appearing as spam, the impression of adverse selection, etc. —the number of viral, in-product invitations should be kept to a minimum, filtering out invitations from all but the most enthusiastic and dedicated users.

Quantified virality

As noted earlier, virality is notoriously difficult to measure, much less model for predictions. A global k-factor may be easily calculated, but it is not necessarily forward-facing or predictive; the growth in one period of the non-paid user base can be influenced by any number of factors and may not presage future growth trends. And calculating the effects of viral mechanics may be impossible without an accurate mechanism for attributing a new user to a specific viral invitation.

That said, freemium product virality is important enough, in light of the cost of user acquisition and the scale needed to fully exploit the business model, that an informed attempt at modeling virality provides some value, even when it isn't entirely accurate. One reason for this value is that understanding the dynamics of virality can help improve its effects, even if that improvement can't be accurately measured. In an environment where user base growth is dependent on either viral reach or paid acquisition, modeling virality under imperfect information and assumptions can still help the product team achieve non-paid user base growth.

A second reason even imperfect virality models are valuable is that they can help draw attention to shortcomings in retention that otherwise might be overlooked. When virality is high but retention is low, the user base experiences wild swings in size as users enter and churn quickly. This phenomenon is better to witness under the auspices of virality, which provides free users, than under paid acquisition. Viral models can serve as warning signals that the product is not ready to effectively utilize paid acquisition, thus sidestepping potentially ineffective expenditure.

Virality models are predicated on a limited number of variables, all of which are conceptually simplistic. Likewise, they can be built in standard desktop spreadsheet software and don't require sophisticated statistical packages to deploy. That said, the concept of virality can be hard to grasp because of its compounding effect: it is a challenge to explain how viral growth takes shape over multiple periods. For this reason, virality models may be the most cumbersome to use in distributed decisions because, although they might exist in spreadsheet format, they're seen as a form of black box argumentation. The goal of this section is to outline the proper structure of a virality model and provide a framework for discussing virality in a way that can be easily digested.

Viral periods

The effects of virality are more or less fluid; users don't invite other users into a product by a prescribed schedule, but they do whenever it is convenient and sensible for them to do so. However, for practical purposes when calculating virality, it is analyzed in terms of *periods*. A period is any amount of time between two endpoints over which user base growth is investigated; the denomination of the period (days, months, weeks, etc.) depends only on the purpose of the analysis.

Viral periods are generally described in the abstract, as opposed to a predefined amount of time, because virality is a key factor in any robust revenue model, and revenue models can be necessitated over any number of arbitrary timelines (such as quarterly, for financial reporting). But in practice, the virality period is often designated in days: that is, one period is equal to one day.

As in calculating interest on a principal sum of money, calculating compounded virality is more precise the more granular the measurement period, which is another reason why days are preferable to longer periods. Additionally, calculating compounded viral user base growth is straightforward and more or less easy to explain on a daily basis.

Virality is expressed as the growth of the user base relative to an initial group of users who adopt the product in the same period (where period length is flexible and could be one day, one week, one month, etc.). Cohort analysis is frequently used throughout freemium product analysis; the calculation of virality is one such analytical implementation. When calculating the effects of virality from period to period, user base growth is attributed to the start of the second period; that is, new users adopted virally from an initial cohort of users in period one are considered to have joined the product at the start of period two.

The compounding effect of virality—the phenomenon of users virally acquired themselves inviting other users into a product through viral channels—creates the need for identifying viral cohorts by their *order*. The cohort acquisition order relates to how far away, in periods, a cohort is from the origin cohort (which is the cohort that spawned the viral growth). Each subsequent order of cohort—second order, third order, fourth order, etc.—is a product of the k-factor and the number of users in the cohort preceding it.

For example, if the origin cohort contains 100 users and the global k-factor is 20 percent, then the first-order cohort (in period two) is composed of 20 users. The second-order cohort, or 20 users producing a new viral cohort at a global k-factor of 20 percent, would be four users; the third-order cohort, or four users exhibiting virality at a rate of 20 percent, would be 0.8 (truncated to zero). The total size of the user base at the end of the fourth period would be 124, representing growth of 24 users through four periods of virality.

When modeling virality in a spreadsheet, the origin cohort usually sits in the top left-most cell, representing the number of users at period one. The y-axis of the spreadsheet represents ordered cohorts, and the x-axis represents periods; as ordered cohorts are added, they are inserted into the model downward and diagonally to the right. Figure 7.12 demonstrates the example discussed here, with an origin cohort of 100 users and a global k-factor of 20 percent growing through period four, as modeled in a spreadsheet.

The growth of 24 users (cell B6 through cell F10, rounded to a whole number) is larger than the global k-factor times the origin cohort (20, or 20 percent times

	A	B	C	D	E	F
1	Local K-Factor	20%				
2	Origin Cohort	100				
3						
4		Periods				
5		1	2	3	4	Total
6	Origin Cohort	100				
7	First-order Cohort		20			
8	Second-order Cohort			4		
9	Third-order Cohort				0.8	
10	Total	100	20	4	0.8	124.8

FIGURE 7.12

Viral growth for an origin cohort of 100 users and a global k-factor of 20%.

100). This is a function of the multi-order effect of virality (in other words, that virally acquired users can produce virally acquired users).

In practice, growth as modeled in Figure 7.12 is improbable; this model depicts a situation wherein users capture total virality in their first period of interaction with the product (i.e., the k-factor is manifested in the period after adoption). Delayed virality over a certain length of time after the user's initial adoption of the product is more realistic, because users must become acquainted with the product before feeling comfortable inviting others into it and because viral invitations cannot always be immediately accepted. This delay is implemented into the virality model via a concept called the *virality timeline*.

The virality timeline

The timing of acquiring users through viral channels, whether they are acquired in-product or through interpersonal recommendations, is an important consideration when modeling the effects of virality. One reason for this relates to the discussion of the time value of money in Chapter 5: the sooner users adopt a product, the sooner they may begin contributing product revenue, which can be reinvested in further product development, marketing, or savings. Whatever the case, revenue generated sooner is preferable to revenue generated later.

But a second element adds complexity to the timing of virally acquired users; in highly viral systems, when virality is "front-loaded," or takes place primarily at the beginning of a user's tenure, the compounded effects of virality manifest through user base growth near the start of the original user's tenure. This accelerated growth curve can be a boon to certain products—especially those that rely on network effects for viability, such as social networks—but it can also present scaling and user base consistency issues.

A rapidly growing user base may present technological and operational challenges to product support structures in terms of scaling, which could prove detrimental to the user experience and thus undermine the value of accelerated growth. Furthermore, a poor early user experience can repel users who may otherwise find the product useful and appealing under circumstances of slower growth, and those users may not return.

And with respect to user base consistency, a user base that grows quickly is likely to experience volatility as user cohorts churn out in large numbers at the end of their lifetimes, even with a gently declining retention curve. This presents problems with network efficacy and reliability for users, but it also renders user data difficult to interpret, as instability in the size of the user base skews the effects of real phenomena. This volatility also poses problems for forecasting future performance: when a massive cohort falls across a broad retention profile and churns out in numerous and appreciably large blocks, estimating the lifetimes of those disparate user segments is cumbersome.

Taking these factors into account, the *virality timeline*, which is the weighted-average number of virality periods over which virality manifests, must contribute to any model of virality. A virality timeline is calculated by assigning weights to each

$$\sum_{i=1}^{n} = \frac{V_i}{V_t} \cdot i$$

n = total number of
viral periods

i = current period number

V_i = number of virally
acquired users
in this period

V_t = total users
acquired virally,
all periods

FIGURE 7.13

The calculation for a weighted-average timeline as used in the virality timeline.

period's contribution to total virality relative to total virality and reducing those weights to a single number. The formula to calculate a weighted average timeline is expressed in Figure 7.13.

The virality timeline is denominated in periods and describes the average length of time over which all virally acquired users who are invited into the product by a single user adopt the product. For example, if one user virally acquires six users over three days through in-product viral invitations and interpersonal recommendations (where three users are acquired on day 1, two users are acquired on day 2, and one user is acquired on day 3), then the users' virality timeline is 1.67 days, as illustrated in Figure 7.14.

The virality timeline should be calculated for whatever user segment is being analyzed; that is, the virally acquired users for a given cohort should be aggregated on a timeline, as opposed to averaging the individual virality timelines for the users in that cohort (which would produce an average of averages). Once calculated, the virality timeline should inform a model of virality by serving as the period into which all virality is divided.

The model explored in Figure 7.12—a product with a global k-factor of 20 percent and an origin cohort of 100 users—can be extended by incorporating a virality timeline of three periods, meaning the global k-factor is distributed evenly across the three periods following product adoption. Since the global k-factor is applied to the origin cohort as a universal total and not a per-period amount of growth, the first-order virality can be expressed across the three succeeding periods, with the rest of the ordered virality cascading in a similar manner, as shown in Figure 7.15.

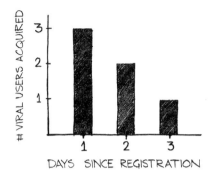

Total Viral Users Introduced: 6

Day Number	Viral users introduced	Share of total	Weight
1	3	.50	.50 x 1 = .50
2	2	.33	.33 x 2 = .66
3	1	.16	.16 x 3 = .50
Weighted Average			1.67

FIGURE 7.14

The virality timeline should be weighted to more accurately reflect when users adopt the service after being invited.

	A	B	C	D	E	F	G	H	I	J	K	L
1	Local K-Factor	20%										
2	Origin Cohort	100										
3	Virality Timeline	3										
4												
5		Periods										
6		1	2	3	4	5	6	7	8	9	10	Total
7	Origin Cohort	100										
8	First-order Cohort		6.667	6.667	6.667							
9	Second-order Cohort			0.444	0.889	1.333	0.889	0.444				
10	Third-order Cohort				0.030	0.089	0.178	0.207	0.178	0.089	0.030	
11	Total	100	6.667	7.111	7.585	1.422	1.067	0.652	0.178	0.089	0.030	124.800

FIGURE 7.15

Viral growth in a spreadsheet format, incorporating the virality timeline.

Note that virality is distributed across three periods for the first-order cohort (row 8) but five periods for the second-order cohort (row 9); this is because, as the cohorts progress, virality timelines for successive cohorts overlap. In other words, in period 5, viral users are being created for periods 2, 3, and 4 across the first-order

$$f_x\;\boxed{=(C8 \cdot B1/B3)+(D8 \cdot B1/B3)+(E8 \cdot B1/B3)}$$

FIGURE 7.16

The formula for calculating viral users acquired for overlapping virality timelines.

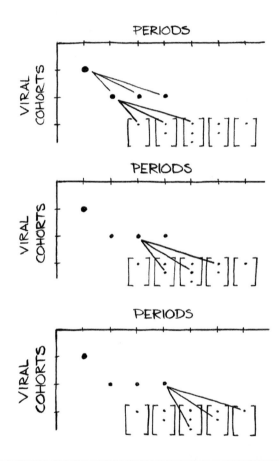

FIGURE 7.17

A visual depiction of viral growth across cohorts.

cohort virality timelines. This is manifested in cell F9 from Figure 7.15 by using the formula in Figure 7.16.

As the cohorts in Figure 7.15 advance, the total length of each row increases by 2: the length of the virality timeline, which is 3, minus 1. The logic of this structure is illustrated in Figure 7.17.

Period 1 = 100 Users

Period 2 = $100 \cdot \left[1 + \left(\left(\frac{.20}{3} \right) \cdot \left(1 + \frac{100}{100,000} \right) \right) \right] - 100 = 6$

Period 3 = $106 \cdot \left[1 + \left(\left(\frac{.20}{3} \right) \cdot \left(1 - \frac{106}{100,000} \right) \right) \right] - 100 = 13$

Period 4 = $119 \cdot \left[1 + \left(\left(\frac{.20}{3} \right) \cdot \left(1 - \frac{119}{100,000} \right) \right) \right] - 100 = 21$

FIGURE 7.18

As the user base grows, virality should be adjusted by diminishing potential future growth given a saturation point.

Saturation

Up to this point, virality has been described as a powerful force that, once achieved, is propelled indefinitely by its own momentum. But the reality is that an upper bound exists on the number of users to which any product can offer a meaningful experience. Even the most viral product has a threshold past which adoption will slow as a result of increasing exposure within the demographic matrix for which it is most appealing. This threshold is known as *saturation*, and it represents the maximum reach of a product through viral means.

In terms of virality, saturation is defined as the scope of market penetration a product can accomplish before no new users can be expected to adopt the product from a viral campaign; it quantifies the boundary of growth that a product could expect to experience virality. And while this number may be difficult to estimate with any accuracy, it is an important component of any virality model because it serves to ground viral assumptions in reality.

Projections of virality don't contribute to a realistic picture of potential product growth if they are not constrained by any limits. Even products with universal consumer appeal slow in growth as they reach large levels of market penetration. A saturation metric tempers a model of virality by serving as a sort of gravitational force exerted on viral expectations.

The easiest way to implement saturation into a model of virality is to consider it a limiting factor based on the percentage of the total user base already reached through viral channels. That is, at any specific point, the potential viral growth rate is reduced by the extent to which the user base has progressed toward the saturation point. As a concrete example, given the conditions laid out earlier, of a product with an origin cohort of 100 users, a global k-factor of 20 percent, and a virality timeline of three periods, a saturation level of 100,000 users would have the effect on first-order viral growth as described in the equation in Figure 7.18.

In the figure, the ratio of users within the saturation threshold yet to be reached is expressed for periods 2, 3, and 4 in the third element in brackets as $\left(1 - \left(\frac{Cumulative\,Users}{Saturation\,Level} \right) \right)$. This ratio is used to reduce the extent to which virality can still occur. As the number of users already reached grows, the ratio increases, and when it reaches 1, the saturation equation resolves to 0, resulting in a viral growth value of 0.

The practical effect of saturation on virality is that growth slows as the number of potential new recruits into the product decreases. This growth limitation forms a sigmoid shape to the user base curve over time: as virality takes root, the curve will inflect upward, and as the product reaches saturation, the curve will inflect downward, as in Figure 7.19.

Estimating saturation is a valuable exercise even outside the context of virality. Another way to describe saturation is market size, and it is a relevant metric at the planning stage of any product. Saturation represents a product's total, realistic potential user base; it is a fundamental component of a revenue projection or viability study. Quantifying saturation involves estimating the size of the demographics to which the product is likely to appeal. When a product is location-dependent— a city-centric directory service, for example—saturation starts at a concrete value, which is the population of the geography under consideration. In such cases, estimating saturation as a "top-down" approach is sensible: the starting value is the relevant population metric, which is decremented as specific demographics are discounted as being inappropriate for the service.

In other cases, where a product's relevant users aren't defined by a discrete population metric but rather by how well the product fits with an existing need, a "bottom-up" approach to estimating saturation may be more appropriate. This involves estimating the size of various demographics for which the product is likely to hold appeal and adding those population sizes together to form a total potential user base.

Estimating saturation may appear as an impractical intellectual exercise—and to some degree, it is—but virality itself is amorphous and difficult to concretely predict. While the estimation for saturation is not exact, it can be used in a methodical process that at least places restraints on a force that otherwise can be modeled to illogical extremes. Endless virality is not a realistic assumption, but given its

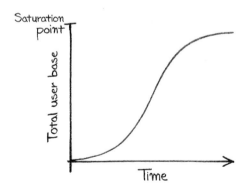

FIGURE 7.19

A graph of user base growth assumes a sigmoid shape as it reaches its saturation point.

significance, a firm must attempt to incorporate it into a model of user base growth. Saturation provides a parameter to any such estimation that serves to contain its aspirational nature.

Modeling viral growth rates

Building a reasonable model of virality first requires incorporating the component elements of viral growth discussed so far into a model of viral growth rates that can be used to drive a model of absolute user numbers. This *viral rates* model contains ordered viral growth values, which are the rates of accumulation of the user base per period. The viral growth rates model is a middle layer of logic that preempts the virality model to ease interpretation and to allow for making modifications to the viral values without having to edit the formulas in the viral rate worksheet.

Developing the viral rates model in a spreadsheet begins with recognizing the virality inputs—the global k-factor and the virality timeline—as well as determining the number of ordered cohorts over which virality should be tracked. The idea behind tracking ordered virality is that the members of the first-order cohort of virality, or the cohort invited to the product directly by the origin cohort, will themselves introduce users to the product through viral channels, and so on.

The purpose of the viral rates sheet is to answer the question, "When a user joins the product through a non-viral channel, how does virality cascade from that user over a finite number of cohorts to contribute to the overall growth of the user base?" The answer is a discrete number representing the total number of users over whatever number of cohorts are tracked, whom any one user virally introduces to the user base. This number is different from the k-factor, which represents the number of users any one user will *directly* introduce to the product. The viral rates sheet output is the total number of users a given user indirectly or directly introduces to the product as a result of compounding virality.

Tracking virality over a predetermined number of ordered cohorts isn't strictly necessary; when the global k-factor is less than 1, the total number can be calculated using a converging infinite geometric series, as expressed in Figure 7.20. In other words, the formula in the figure gives the total number of users, aggregated over an infinite number of ordered cohorts, whom any one user will introduce to the product, given a global k-factor of less than 1. (When the k-factor is greater than 1, the values will not converge, since they approach infinity.)

But the purpose of a model is to see the progression of a metric over time and to use those time-based values to estimate something else: typically, revenue.

$$\text{Total Viral Users} = \frac{1}{\text{Global k-factor}}$$

FIGURE 7.20

Calculating the total number of viral users when k-factor is greater than 1.

	A	B	C	D	E	F	G	H	I	J	K	L
1	Local K-Factor	20%										
2	Virality Timeline	3										
3												
4		Periods										
5		1	2	3	4	5	6	7	8	9	10	Total
6	Origin Cohort	100%										
7	First-order Cohort		6.67%	6.67%	6.67%							
8	Second-order Cohort		0.44%		0.89%	1.33%	0.89%	0.44%				
9	Third-order Cohort				0.03%	0.09%	0.18%	0.21%	0.18%	0.09%	0.03%	
10	Total	100%	6.67%	7.11%	7.59%	1.42%	1.07%	0.65%	0.18%	0.09%	0.03%	124.80%

FIGURE 7.21

The virality rates worksheet.

Therefore, the total number of eventual users isn't as important as the growth of the user base on a per-period basis. The viral rates sheet, then, should be laid out as a matrix, formatted as shown in Figure 7.21, with the number of periods being tracked running across the x-axis at the top and the ordered cohorts running down the y-axis at the bottom.

Cell B6 represents the origin cohort, or the cohort of users introduced to the product via non-viral means. This cohort is expressed as 100 percent because it symbolizes the entirety of the origin cohort; by expressing the values in the spreadsheets as proportions of the origin cohort, the end result can be multiplied by an absolute cohort size to produce a value denominated in users.

Row 7 represents the first-order cohort, or the first group of users introduced to the product through virality by the origin cohort. The 6.7 percent values are derived from the local k-factor of 20 percent multiplied by the origin cohort of 100 percent, then divided by 3 (because virality is manifested over the three-period virality timeline: $100 * \dfrac{.20}{3} = 6.7$).

Row 8, the second-order cohort, follows the same pattern: 6.7 percent is multiplied by the local k-factor of 20 percent then divided by the virality timeline of 3 to illustrate the percentage of users (relative to the origin cohort) virally introduced to the product by the first-order cohort. This row extends for five cells, as opposed to three, for reasons discussed earlier: the virality timelines for the first-order cohort overlap. The third-order cohort, in row 9, progresses similar to the second-order cohort.

Row 10 is where the virality percentages are aggregated vertically by period; cell L10 is the sum of these aggregates and represents the total virality coefficient, or the number of subsequent users virally introduced to the product by each user. Subtracting 1 from the value in L10 (in other words, backing out the origin cohort) produces a value of 24.8 percent, which represents the local k-factor compounded over two ordered cohorts.

The numbers in Figure 7.21 are similar to those in Figure 7.15, with the key distinction that, in Figure 7.21, the values are percentages. This is an important point; the virality rates spreadsheet is an abstraction, meaning it represents user growth in percentage. The virality coefficient in cell L10 can be multiplied by any number of users joining the product in order to produce the total number of resultant users who are introduced to the product over 10 periods across three viral cohorts.

Increasing the complexity of the model by extending the y-axis with additional cohorts and the x-axis with additional periods increases the virality coefficient but by rapidly diminishing amounts.

Building the viral model

The model of viral growth rates provides a timeline over which viral users are adopted relative to an origin cohort. The viral model should provide a timeline of total users in the user base, with each period in the model introducing a new origin cohort as well as viral users originating from previous origin cohorts.

The virality model is structured in a spreadsheet in the same general format as the virality rates model: the y-axis represents ordered cohorts and the x-axis represents periods (again, usually days). The conceptual difference in the models is that the viral growth rates model represents the viral growth rates from a single cohort over the course of a predetermined number of ordered cohorts; the virality model aggregates these growth rates per-period into absolute user numbers. In other words, the virality model outputs the actual number of users who can be expected to join the product through viral channels per period.

The virality model does not take the downward-sloping diagonal line shape of the virality rates model because it is not following the viral growth of a single cohort. Instead, it takes the shape of an upside-down plateau, as the number of users representing each ordered cohort is stacked in reverse order from the origin cohort. The first row of the virality model is thus the origin cohort for that day, or the number of new product users acquired through non-viral channels.

The number of periods covered in the virality model should span whatever length of time is being considered for projecting the size of the user base. In many cases, this will be one quarter, two quarters, or a year. When the period length is one day and the timespan of the model is one year, the width of the matrix should be set to 365 columns. The height of the matrix should match the height of the virality rates model matrix. The first row should be filled with the number of users in each origin cohort on each day. In some models, this number might be constant, representing an expectation of a constant number of new users from organic and paid channels. In other models, the number might decline over time, spike intermittently to reflect media coverage, or assume any number of shapes that new user values can follow over the lifetime of a product.

On the viral growth worksheet in Figure 7.22, each row after the origin row reflects the number of users from the nth-order cohort being added on that day. The value in each cell is derived from the growth rate in the viral growth rates worksheet, based on the ordered cohort and period of that cell; the ordered cohort number should be taken from the current row and looked up in the viral growth rates lookup table.

The value of cell C4 in Figure 7.23, which represents the first-order viral cohort invited to the product from the origin cohort in period 1, is the product of two

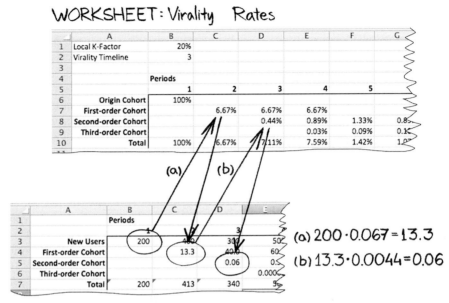

WORKSHEET: Virality Rates

	A	B	C	D	E	F	G
1	Local K-Factor	20%					
2	Virality Timeline	3					
3							
4		Periods					
5		1	2	3	4	5	
6	Origin Cohort	100%					
7	First-order Cohort		6.67%	6.67%	6.67%		
8	Second-order Cohort			0.44%	0.89%	1.33%	0.8
9	Third-order Cohort				0.03%	0.09%	0.1
10	Total	100%	6.67%	7.11%	7.59%	1.42%	1.0

(a)   (b)

	A	B	C	D	E
1		Periods			
2		1	2	3	
3	New Users	200	450	300	50
4	First-order Cohort		13.3	40.0	60
5	Second-order Cohort			0.06	0
6	Third-order Cohort				0.000
7	Total	200	413	340	5

(a) $200 \cdot 0.067 = 13.3$

(b) $13.3 \cdot 0.0044 = 0.06$

WORKSHEET: Viral Growth

FIGURE 7.22

Reconciling the viral growth rates sheet with the virality sheet.

fx $= C3 \cdot \text{'Virality Rates'!} \$C\$7 + B3 \cdot \text{'Virality Rates'!} \$D7$

FIGURE 7.23

The formula for cell D4 in Figure 7.21.

numbers: the size of the origin cohort and a viral growth rate. The first number is looked up in the viral growth worksheet and found in cell B3. The second number is looked up in the virality rates worksheet and is based on period and cohort number; in this case, the value is found in cell C7 on the virality rates worksheet, representing period 2 for the first-order cohort.

Similar to the way the virality rates worksheet is organized, as cells progress to the right in the viral growth worksheet, the virality timelines of preceding periods overlap and must be summed. For example, the formula in Figure 7.23 that produces the value in cell D4 from the viral growth worksheet in Figure 7.22 adds two values together: the period 2 virality for the origin cohort in cell B3, and the period 1 virality for the origin cohort in cell C3. This pattern continues along the row; because the virality rates sheet extends to 10 periods, the number of terms added together for each ordered cohort in the virality worksheet increases until it reaches

	A	B	C	D	E	F	G
1		Periods					
2		1	2	3	4	5	Total
3	New Users	200	400	300	500	450	
4	First-order Cohort		13.3	40.0	60.0	80.0	
5	Second-order Cohort			0.06	0.30	0.80	
6	Third-order Cohort				0.00002	0.00014	
7	Total	200	413	340	560	531	2044

FIGURE 7.24

A complete five-period viral growth worksheet.

$$f_x \quad =(SUM(F3:F6) \cdot (1-(SUM(\$B\$7:E7)/100000)))$$

FIGURE 7.25

The formula for cell F7 in Figure 7.24.

10. (The number in the right-hand-most column represents the overlapping virality for the previous 10 periods.)

At this point, the viral growth worksheet represents the absolute number of users acquired through viral channels, by ordered cohort, per period, as illustrated in Figure 7.24. The bottom row of the matrix contains the sum of each column, representing the overall per-period count of new users, or the origin cohort plus the users acquired virally in the ordered cohorts tracked. But as discussed, these per-period sums must be reduced by the saturation threshold, given the cumulative users recruited into the product up to that point. As this cumulative number increases, the proportion of potential product users who have yet to be reached decreases.

To implement saturation, the sums at the bottom of the columns must be reduced. The formula in cell F7 from Figure 7.24, which holds the total number of saturation-adjusted users acquired in period 5, is given in Figure 7.25, with a saturation level of 100,000 users.

Note that reducing the sums, as opposed to the component rows, may lead to confusion. Reducing each row of the period columns with the formula exhibited in Figure 7.25 would produce a more straightforward and intuitive sum at the foot of each column, but it would also render the formulas within the virality matrix much harder to read. The updated virality worksheet, accommodating for saturating, is depicted in Figure 7.26.

The summed columns in Figure 7.26 represent absolute, per-period numbers of users acquired virally. These values can be incorporated into a broader model of the user base (which would need to include returning users to be complete) to present a considered, if somewhat static (and divorced from exogenous effects) picture of the product's user base over time.

	A	B	C	D	E	F	G
1		Periods					
2		1	2	3	4	5	Total
3	New Users	200	400	300	500	450	
4	First-order Cohort		13.3	40.0	60.0	80.0	
5	Second-order Cohort			0.06	0.30	0.80	
6	Third-order Cohort				0.00002	0.00014	
7	Total	200	413	338	555	523	2028

FIGURE 7.26

The updated virality worksheet, with per-period sums reduced by a saturation ratio.

Engineering virality

Although it is an inexact science, measuring and quantifying virality may be the easiest aspect of managing a product's virality. Virality is a fickle beast, and often, overt, contrived efforts at instilling virality in a product are fruitless. Moreover, they may alienate the user base, instilling in it a sense that, rather than being served by the product, the product exists to be served by them. A company should not assume its users to be marketing channels; when a user contributes to a product's marketing efforts, the user does so as an enthusiast, not a customer.

But, given how fundamental virality is to the freemium model (short of a substantial marketing budget, it is the only viable path to massive scale), it is essential to control, or at the very least create, the opportunity for virality. While virality can't be expertly and predictably willed into existence, a broken virality framework—overwrought viral features, aggressive invitation mechanics, or an isolated user base—won't contribute to growth. Over the course of product development, a company must strike a balance in pursuit of virality; it must invest sufficient time in developing a virality architecture with the potential to provide value, while not over-investing time into viral features for which return cannot be reliably estimated.

To that end, engineering freemium virality is accomplished with the same conceptual logic as engineering monetization: provide users with the tools and latitude to engage, and the most zealous and enthusiastic users will do so willingly.

The viral product

At the heart of any viral growth pattern is a product that inherently invokes and rewards connectivity. Products that are useful only at the individual level can be shared and enthused upon, but long-term, sustained viral growth is a function of the fundamental necessity and advantageous benefits of a product network.

One means of achieving sustained growth is through in-product social features that add value to the core of a product experience. These features generally fall into three categories: *collaborative*, which allows for shared product use; *competitive*, which gives users opportunities to rank themselves against other users; and *communicative*, which allows for users to share and discuss ideas. These three feature categories broadly form a sense of community within a product's user base. When users believe that their membership to a community augments the product experience, they are more likely to recruit for a product than if overwhelming delight is the requirement for such proactive, enthusiastic sharing.

The operational concern in implementing features within this scope, however, is experience enhancement: if the features don't truly improve the experience but merely facilitate potential virality, then they aren't likely to engender significant user base growth and could instead alienate users by diverting attention away from the product's fundamental use case. Ill-conceived social functionality, often developed late in the design process to address a specific lack of virality, may potentially cause more harm than good.

The success of social features is often directly and positively correlated to how early in the development process they are conceived. A product is either social in nature or it is not, and the presence of social features does not form the exclusive basis of this distinction. A product is likewise either viral or it is not; that is, it either supports sustained, continued virality through its fundamental use case, or it benefits only from short-term, tenuous viral growth through superficial invitation mechanics.

The viral product is a product with a fundamental use case designed with the objective of collaboration, competition, or communication in mind. Without at least one of these objectives driving the user experience, a product cannot be viral; rather, it can merely benefit from specific viral mechanics and user excitement. But when the core experience is designed with one of the three objectives as the backdrop, users are compelled to recruit additional users into the product to enhance their own experience.

The risk with such a tack, of course, is that the user doesn't recognize the value in the product from the outset, or that the user simply has no network from which to draw. A viral product, or a social product, is only as effective as the user's network is available. If the product does not offer an experience that can be undertaken at the individual level, then it won't inspire virality and won't capture the interest of users acquired organically or through paid channels.

The prototypical categorical example of such a product is the social network, which is useless to a user without a minimal, relevant group of people with whom the user can connect. A product may be viral at its core, but when network effects are a product's basic experience—the product is merely a tool that can extract value from a preexisting network—then the product will fail to gain traction from users without those networks.

Such a design decision—whether to architect the product as inherently viral or as an individually relevant product with attendant virality features—requires careful consideration of the demographics the product will appeal to. This design decision may also require a multi-staged approach to roll out at launch: while users may not have preexisting networks relevant to the product to begin with, a product might facilitate the creation of new networks through discovery and interaction.

In such a case, the product may be designed with two launch stages in mind: the first introducing a personal experience and establishing the fundamentals of the use case, and the second reconciling those use cases into a network that enhances the experience for all users. Such an approach sets the stage for collaboration, competition, and communication from the initial launch, but it manifests the product as an isolated experience; in the second stage, social features are added as an experience layer on top of the core functionality of the product. In essence, this strategy lays the foundation for a network to form around a notional nucleus in the first stage and then introduces the in-product infrastructure for that network to take shape in the second stage. But this essentially requires the creation of two products, and the development of a product predicated on the adoption and success of a subsequent product invites a high degree of risk.

At the conceptual level, the viral product is subject to a harsher set of preconditions to success than is a product that can be used by a user in a vacuum; the viral product's use case must not only meet a real need, but a preexisting network must also serve it and manifest that need. And while the viral product benefits from inherent virality (and thus fairly effortless user base growth), it also risks a structural lack of potential for momentum.

Viral networks

The network connecting people is the propagation medium for any viral campaign. Networks are sometimes based on physical boundaries, such as location-based services, but often they're built around loose affiliations of commonality, such as online communities or forums. And while many people belong to a number of networks and can thus propagate viral products on a number of fronts, most networks are fairly isolated and limited; notions and sentiments cannot bridge the void between one network and another without an impetus.

While saturation represents the total potential market for a product based on demographics and tastes, the pace and extent of virality is set by the networks through which virality can be transmitted. Understanding which viral networks potential users participate in and how those networks can be penetrated is an important part of developing and incorporating viral mechanics. Likewise, for interpersonal product recommendations to take root and produce appreciable virality, a product's users must have interpersonal networks.

Viral networks effectively act as restraints on the propagation routes of viral campaigns; the natural silos potential users are segmented into prevent viral campaigns from being transmitted evenly throughout the entire population of users a product might appeal to (its saturation population). This restriction manifests in more money needed to construct virality features—each network may have to be accommodated—and in diminished returns on the effects of compounding virality. In other words, since each viral network must be seeded with an initial set of users the virality will propagate from, more effort is required to manifest virality than if the entire saturation population could be reached within one network. This limitation requires consideration during the product development cycle and the product's management after its launch; small networks may provide less value than larger ones do because compounded virality is not as likely to occur. If the saturation population is seen not as a monolith but as a collection of networks through which virality can be propagated, then the largest and most interconnected networks should be given priority within the product.

Additionally, seeding a small network with users through paid acquisition may cost as much as seeding a large network, yet the reach of a smaller network is, by definition, more limited. Thus, the commitment to pursuing virality on a specific network should take into consideration the total size of that network; viral mechanics require development time and must be implemented sensibly, with an eye toward return on investment.

Similarly, networks must be evaluated by the potential revenue quality of their users, or the demographic attributes of users on a network related to likelihood to monetize. Some networks may provide incredible viral growth and distribution at a large scale but represent a fundamental, measurable unlikelihood to deliver revenue. Networks exhibiting a homogeneous specific demographic attribute, such as age, are the most likely ones to sit at an extreme of revenue quality. The degree to which such networks can contribute users with disposable income should be evaluated before viral mechanics tailored to those networks are developed.

That said, the opposite may also be true: a network's characteristics may provide favorable conditions for virality that serve to reduce the effective cost of a marketing campaign. Networks composed of highly connected early adopters, although generally small, are fertile ground for the propagation of new products and services through viral channels. These networks also tend to feature users with large amounts of disposable income and lower barriers to monetization (such as the lack of a stigma around purchasing virtual products or services). In such cases, however, impressive virality should not be mistaken for widespread, universal appeal; early adopters tend to exist on a separate plane of product appreciation than does the general public, and their behavior with respect to new products can just as easily expose a passing fad as affirm a long-term trend.

Geographic networks may be the most rigidly isolated and therefore the least cost-effective to penetrate, especially at the city level. Products related to a city, such as city-level directories or social networks oriented toward local activity, suffer from strict virality barriers that can vastly increase the costs of marketing. Products of this nature require extreme virality to offset the effort required in seeding a user base at the local level. Geographic boundaries are perhaps the most cumbersome constraints on viral growth; local products may face the highest marketing costs, as each limited market contributes to marketing overhead.

Increasing viral invitations

One strategy for increasing virality is to simply increase the way that virality throughput is achieved, which is the transmission of viral invitations. As discussed earlier, the effects of increasing the volume of invitations sent are not entirely beneficial: highly prolific viral mechanics may be indistinguishable from spam, despite the best of intentions on the part of the developer. And potential users may interpret spam from a product as a signal that the product is not legitimate or is of poor quality.

The appearance of spam can be mitigated even when viral invitations are made frictionless. One method of doing so is to simply control the viral invitations any given user is permitted to send, by channel, recipient, or otherwise. By preventing a user from sending the same viral invitation to the same user or group of users more than once, the product can still maintain a high number of viral invitation mechanics while dodging potential misuse or abuse. Diversifying the format and transmission channels of viral invitations diminishes the likelihood of those invitations being considered spam, while still providing very enthusiastic users with a platform for broadcasting their use of the product. In essence, broadening the invitation channels shifts the onus of responsible use from the product to the user.

One way to increase the number of viral invitations that can be sent is by incentivizing the mechanic with an explicit reward for the user upon sending a viral invitation. This is often done by providing premium functionality for free in exchange for sending the invitation; for example, a freemium product offering premium services with a subscription model might offer one free month of access in exchange for inviting someone to the service.

This approach is fairly simple to implement and carries with it the positive signal of the initial user actively attempting to unlock further functionality from the product. On the downside, users are not necessarily incentivized to choose appropriate recipients, as they are rewarded for the invitation, not the conversion.

Many products therefore reward the invitation only upon success; that is, the user collects the reward when recipients of the invitations adopt the product, which is often defined as registering with the product. This approach may reduce the total number of invitations sent, but it likely results in those invitations being more thoughtfully sent, thus yielding more new users. Many times these mechanics reward the invitation recipient, with the goal of inuring both users to the premium feature in order to encourage continued purchases.

Another approach to incentivizing the invitation mechanic is to *gamify* the use of the product. Gamification is an approach to product design that rewards users with designations, titles, and product-specific, trophy-like keepsakes for meeting specific engagement benchmarks. Gamification fosters virality by giving users an interesting, often entertaining focal point through which to broadcast their use of a product. Gamifying the product incentivizes users to announce the achievements they have unlocked, not just to other existing users of the product, but to outsiders who may feel compelled to investigate the product for fear of being excluded.

Increasing the velocity and volume of viral invitations sent is not, of course, a goal unto itself; it is rather the means by which virality can be increased, and if conversion dips substantially as the number of invitations sent increases, the net effect could be neutral or negative. Making incremental improvements to existing viral mechanics may produce better overall virality than does adding new mechanics alongside the existing viral toolkit, especially if the viral infrastructure is varied and not overly aggressive.

Once a product has launched, incremental, individual performance improvements to a large number of disparate viral mechanics is more likely to add to increased virality than a single new mechanic is. The most enthusiastic users (for whom the product should be selecting in crafting viral mechanics) probably already understand existing mechanics, so simply making the mechanics easier and more entertaining to use could produce instant results. Users may also feel that the addition of new viral mechanics reduces the users' value to that of a marketing channel; post-launch, the product should take pains to ensure that enthusiastic users don't feel exploited. Likewise, users are more committed to products they deem as being committed to them, and the use of development time and resources on features that do not enhance the user experience detracts from that sentiment.

Increasing viral conversions

The viral invitations conversion rate represents the second set of territories on which virality can increase. As opposed to increasing the volume of viral invitations sent, increasing the invitation conversion rate does not introduce attendant risk: by improving invitations so there are more conversions (given that the number of invitations remains constant), the product does not produce new tension by looking like spam or by changing the perception of user base exploitation.

That said, increasing the conversion rate of viral invitations may be less easily achieved than increasing the number of invitations sent. A/B testing is the principle approach to improving the likelihood of producing a new user with a viral invitation. As discussed earlier, A/B testing evaluates various nuanced versions of content based on their conversion rates. And while A/B testing does allow for specific invitation metrics to be optimized, the fertility of this source of increased virality erodes after a relatively limited period of time as the easiest and most obvious tests are conducted.

A second approach to increasing the conversion rate of viral invitations is incentivizing adoption by rewarding either the person sending the invitation, the person receiving the invitation, or both. When the sender is rewarded only upon the receiver's conversion, the sender is incentivized to select the people most likely to convert. And when the receiver is rewarded for joining the service, that person is more likely to act on the invitation. As in the tactic employed when attempting to increase the number of viral invitations sent, the reward given upon conversion is usually free access to premium functionality.

Establishing an element of functionality that is premium in name but offered as a reward for conversion may effectively reduce the size of the product catalogue if the viral mechanic through which the reward is received is used frequently. This is why rewards are usually time-constrained for subscription services offering, for example, one free month of premium service. For non-subscription services, or services where the reward would be permanently applied to the user's account, some consideration should be made to what, exactly, is rewarded to both the person sending and the person receiving the invitation when the invited person adopts the product. The benefits of virality must be weighed against the possible cannibalization of revenues.

If a viral mechanic is popular, and many people joining the product receive free functionality, then the structure of the product's value proposition changes: a large portion of the user base sees the rewarded functionality as free, which may alienate those users who were not acquired through the viral mechanic and must pay for it. Likewise, the users who did receive the functionality as a free reward will come to expect that functionality, and perhaps similar functionality, for free in the future. The dynamics of a product catalogue can shift dramatically when large swaths of the user base are given access to some aspect of the product for free.

A third method to increase conversion rates in viral invitations is to instill in the sender the sense that invitations hold intrinsic value and thus should be sent strategically. This method may be conceptually similar to rewarding conversion, but it is applied, at a fundamental level, to the user's understanding of the product's use case, and it is often manifested by a restriction on the number of invitations a user can send. If the product's value proposition is a function of the quality of the user's network, then a limited number of invitations may inspire the user to qualify the people to whom invitations are sent on the basis of their likelihood to enjoy the product.

Such a perception from the user is powerful; the scarcity tactic attempts to prevent users from making impulse decisions on whom to invite into the product and to instead carefully and strategically evaluate each invitee. One effect of this approach may be an elongated virality timeline, as users consult people before inviting them, or simply deliberate more thoroughly on each invitation.

Artificial scarcity techniques need not be permanent, and they can be rolled out over time in accordance with product use to ensure that the most engaged users are given the latitude to serve as promoters for the product and that users carefully consider who will receive their viral invitations. The user can be granted additional invitations by continued use, or, if the size of a user's network itself can be portrayed as product functionality, additional viral invitations can form part of the product's monetization strategy (e.g., the user is given a limited number of free invitations but must purchase additional invitations). When invoked this way, artificial scarcity would achieve the same effect as the reward mechanism but approach it from the opposite position.

Unlike the strategies for increasing the number of viral invitations sent (which can produce negative effects and therefore must be undertaken with discipline), strategies for increasing conversion do not generally pose product perception risks and can therefore be undertaken in unison in pursuit of higher virality. But, generally speaking, the conversion rate for invitations and the number of invitation mechanics available are inversely correlated: the more viral invitations sent, the lower the proportion of invitations accepted.

Growth

Facilitating a large user base

User acquisition and growth cannot be neglected in the freemium model. While the freemium business model is itself a component of a user acquisition strategy—a free product will have broader price appeal than a paid product—it is not the only tactic required in building a user base.

Product growth is difficult and necessitates much consideration, both before and after the launch. Strategic growth is the process by which a large user base is facilitated and recruited during the development phase and throughout the life cycle of the product. Just as fundamental use case decisions must be made early in the viral product development process to support future virality, so such decisions must be made with respect to appeal for a product with a large user base in order to support future user base growth.

Strategic growth

Decisions in the earliest stages of development about a freemium product's appeal may set the tone for the product's eventual success. Scale is the fundamental pillar around which freemium products are built: the size of the user base must be large enough so that the small percentage of users who contribute to revenue constitute a meaningful enough number to justify not charging for the product. This has to be accounted for in the planning and design stages of the product.

After launch, strategic growth as a conceptual procedure constitutes a metrics-based, analytical approach to iterating upon the product's marketing initiatives and early user experience with a singular focus on growing the user base. Just as product development is undertaken in iterations with a focus on engagement, virality, and revenue metrics, marketing is executed on the basis of rapid iteration of both the product and the marketing initiatives in response to growth metrics.

Strategic growth is essentially a quantitative framework for measuring and improving upon the product's ability to acquire and retain users. Long-term retention is not strictly a growth concern; it is rather a function of the match between the user's needs and the product's fundamental use case.

Early stage retention, however, can generally be improved upon in iterations as mechanics present in the first session are enhanced and perfected. In the context of strategic growth, *early stage retention* is defined as the percentage of people returning to the product for a second session. In essence, strategic growth as a concept seeks to optimize the first session to produce a higher percentage of people returning for a second one.

Demographic targeting and saturation

The strategic decisions of greatest significance, made in the earliest stages of product design, likely revolve around demographic targeting. Targeting in this sense does not specifically relate to user acquisition, or which demographics will be advertised to. Rather, it refers to tastes—selecting the demographic groups to whom the product will eventually offer the most appeal.

Demographic targeting in the conception and design stage does not mold the end product's ultimate use case; rather, it influences the product's form, function, and general aesthetic to best fit the demographics likely to contribute revenue to that use case. And while universal appeal puts a product in the best possible position for reaching scale, the intersection of a use case and a competitive marketplace rendering a product appealing to every demographic is unrealistic. Demographics should be identified as most likely to appreciate a product as well as contribute revenue to it.

Demographic targeting will inevitably take place in a product's life cycle; the question is what that targeting affects. If targeting is done early in the design and conception phase of product development, then the product can be crafted to appeal most strongly to the demographics likely to pay for it. If targeting is saved until after the product has been developed, it can be used only to optimize marketing campaigns.

Given a defined and fairly concrete use case, a product will have an intrinsic addressable market size whether or not the product is designed with the demographics comprising that market in mind. Besides, developing an understanding of the market size, which is essentially the product's saturation metric, during the design phase results in a product that is better suited to the demographics most attracted to it.

Waiting to consider the saturation metric until after the product is developed requires a marketing plan tailored to demographic groups and adaptable to a product designed to have a broad market. The opposite approach—conceptualizing a product around a broad target demographic and fitting the marketing narrative to the product—produces a less convoluted marketing message and a product experience that better serves its core constituents.

Deciding upon the product's target market from the inception of the design process and molding the product to meet that market's tastes results in an optimized experience for the people who would have most enjoyed the product had those considerations not been made. Waiting until the marketing process to engage in such deliberation merely delivers a substandard experience to everyone: the key demographic receives a product that has been deliberately made vague, thus not serving its target's specific tastes and preferences, and the ancillary demographics receive a product with a fundamental use case that only obliquely meets its needs.

The success of the freemium model is contingent on massive scale, but no product use case has all-inclusive, worldwide appeal. When a firm operates under the assumption that a product cannot be found useful by every person on the planet, it can consider which demographic groups might find a product most useful early in the development process and deliver a product that has been more thoughtfully designed with those characteristics in mind. If that demographic consideration is only made with respect to marketing, then the degree to which the product satisfies the core demographics may be reduced.

The tradeoff, of course, is that other potential users may find a product more useful if it has been designed for universal appeal. This tradeoff is a downside of using demographic targeting in product development instead of marketing strategy; it means the design of the product caters to those least likely to contribute revenue, which runs decidedly counter to freemium principles.

A free product does not discriminate on the basis of price against any particular demographic group; it represents the utmost extent of accessibility. By designing a freemium product to accommodate the users who are most likely to capture delight from it, the product merely increases its potential, which is limited to generate revenue.

Optimizing the onboarding process

The onboarding process is the point in freemium product use where the greatest number of users churn. This is due to any number of factors: a fundamental mismatch between the users' needs and the product's use case, a mismatch between the marketing message used to acquire the user and the user's initial experience, early, aggressive tactics to monetize users or force them to surrender personal information, and too many others to articulate.

But the onboarding process also represents the point in the product life cycle through which the most users pass; it is the one part of the product that every user experiences. It therefore logically follows that improvements to the onboarding process yield the largest relative results in terms of percentage of the user base retained. A 1 percent improvement to retention at the earliest stage of the product experience yields more than a 1 percent improvement at some point further into the life cycle by matter of fact

Optimizing the onboarding experience, then, involves defining each point in the first session, or any period starting with the very beginning of a user's tenure, and tracking the degree to which users from the initial total user base have churned by that point. This is represented by and accomplished through the onboarding funnel graph. Each point in the onboarding process is represented by a bar graph, and the difference in height from one bar to the next represents churn from 100 percent of the original cohort.

The onboarding process is optimized by a fluid progression of iterations focusing on reducing the vertical distance between bars on the onboarding funnel graph until the descent from start to finish is as small as possible. Generally, optimization begins by defining a starting point and an ending point to the onboarding process: if the onboarding process is defined as the entire first session, or some meaningful number of n sessions from the beginning of the user's tenure, then the end point is represented by the beginning of session $n + 1$.

The starting point of the onboarding process is usually defined as the beginning of the first session; if it isn't (such as when a point exists in the first session before which users can't reasonably be considered acquired), then loading times in the first session should be taken into account, as they generally have a large impact on early churn.

The start of the first session does not coincide with the initialization of the product, but this fact should not be taken for granted; even in products where acquisition is considered contingent on some event taking place, such as registration (without which the product is useless), introducing a segue between initialization and the acquisition threshold, one that offers some insight into the product's value proposition, can have a meaningful impact on total churn. Users may need only a minor amount of convincing to decide to surrender personal information or otherwise take some required action before they can begin using a product.

Each iteration of the onboarding optimization process should focus on reducing the decrease between events in the onboarding funnel. This is usually and most capably accomplished with A/B testing: one or more event variants that inspire large drops in the funnel are introduced, and users are separated into different onboarding tracks, with each track containing a different version of the event. Once data is available, the variant that experienced the smallest drop is elected as the replacement (or, if none of the variants offer an improvement, the original is retained), and the process is repeated on another event.

It is important to note that A/B tests for the onboarding process should isolate only one event, not combinations of events at multiple points in the onboarding funnel. The results of two tests, each containing different combinations of multiple event test variants, can't be compared easily, and the effect of an early event variant on a later event might not be predictable. Tests should run end to end and evaluate only one set of variants for a single event.

Especially large drops between successive events in the onboarding funnel should be investigated through intermediary events; when investigating the reasons for a large drop in user progression, isolating the precise source of the event before beginning the testing process generally saves time. Reducing the product progression between events helps to isolate the points of contention and eliminate ambiguity about user progress. And tracking more data is usually less labor- and time-intensive than implementing multiple rounds of tests, each of which requires a minimal amount of time to accumulate sufficient results.

Optimizing the onboarding funnel may be done continually from product launch through shuttering; it is not a task exclusive to the period immediately following a launch. Market and user base dynamics can, over time, change the way users experience the product upon initial adoption, and while the bulk of improvements to the onboarding process are usually made soon after product launch, awareness of user progression throughout the onboarding process is always worthwhile.

Optimizing product copy

The amount of written text that accompanies a product launch is often underestimated: advertising copy, the product's description in platform stores and on the web, the text in launch and loading screens, and the content of emails sent to journalists, potential new users, and users within the developer's existing product catalogue add up to a substantial amount of written material that can affect how potential and new users interpret the product. This text, often written in disjointed sessions, sometimes without an eye for overall thematic and stylistic cohesion, can be as significant in terms of user sentiment as the product's graphical assets, which generally receive more scrutiny.

Product copy is any written text directed at potential users or new users that is used to describe the product. Product copy is most often associated with advertising, but it is used in a number of other materials, most of which fall under the umbrella description of marketing assets. And while ads may be tested to optimize performance, the rest of the materials comprising this group are often not. The fact is that these materials are not disparate, independent components of the product; they form a communicative whole and should be composed with that in mind. Contradictory or highly disjointed product copy distributed across a number of marketing assets can confuse and mislead potential users.

The first step in optimizing product copy for performance is compiling it all in a single location, ideally in a place the product can dynamically access, such as a database table, without requiring development resources to propagate changes. Centralizing product copy makes glaring contradictions or differences in tone across the component parts easier to spot; a general theme and common verbiage should be determined and applied across the entire portfolio of product copy assets. Stark differences in the quality of texts or the specific terms used to describe the product, which the user can see throughout the acquisition process and early onboarding process, can engender a perception of product ambiguity or simply confusion.

Once the product copy assets have been compiled, their individual levels of efficacy should be tested as contributors to an overall process in the same way the onboarding process is tested. Unlike the onboarding process, however, the chronology of the user's exposure to product copy doesn't follow a strict timeline. That is, a potential user may or may not have seen an advertisement for a product before arriving at a website for it. Likewise, a potential user may or may not have seen the product's website before arriving at its entry in a platform store. As a result of this uncertainty, various elements of product copy are not A/B tested as a result of any level of drop-off in a funnel but rather of their own accord. Since chronology is ignored in the testing process, the pieces of copy can be A/B tested simultaneously, assuming the variants for each piece of copy adhere to the common verbiage determined in the writing process.

Because the purpose of unifying the theme and language of product copy is cohesion and not necessarily how well the theme or vocabulary perform, a separate

A/B testing regimen might explore how well alternative elements perform. In such a test, it is best to compare only varying themes in the copy seen by everyone—usually a product description at the point of adoption, either in the product itself or on its listing in a platform store—and extrapolate the best-performing variant out to the remaining copy items.

Product copy is important to unify and test because, in most cases, it is the first aspect of the product a potential user is exposed to and because the distribution of product copy is neither predictable nor controlled by the developer. Spikes in product exposure, such as from platform featuring or coverage in a high-profile trade magazine or newspaper, can quickly bring a product to the attention of a massive number of potential new users. If product copy has been tested and optimized up to that point, the small conversion improvements achieved (in the 1 to 2 percent range) can result in tens of thousands of additional new users following an exposure event.

That said, there is a diminishing rate of return past a certain point for product copy testing, as there is with any testing regimen. Generally, testing a theme and one to three variants of each piece of copy are sufficient in optimizing the copy portfolio to an acceptable standard. As the user base grows, the number of potential users exposed to product copy without any other contextual background on the product, such as exposure to a viral invitation, shrinks relative to the total number of people who have seen the product, and efforts at optimization are more effectively directed at the onboarding process.

Paid user acquisition

Paid user acquisition is a fundamental freemium development topic; growing a user base in a competitive marketplace more often than not requires performance marketing initiatives to seed the initial cohort and facilitate continued growth. These performance marketing initiatives require the heavy analytics structure described in Chapter 2 and an organization's focus on lifetime customer value management, as outlined in Chapter 5.

User acquisition, then, is somewhat of a barrier to entry in certain market segments dominated by freemium products, where products compete on not only quality but on the robustness of their support infrastructures. Large players can price small players out of a user acquisition market, thus making it harder for small players to initiate user base growth.

User acquisition and the various marketplaces in which users can be purchased—advertised to in an attempt to entice them to adopt a product—can essentially be thought of as commodity purchasing strategies. And indeed, users of freemium apps share much in common with the commodities traded on spot markets, with one fundamental difference: quality. Regulated commodity markets standardize the quality of commodities traded on them, whereas each user purchased through paid acquisition possesses unknowable marginal value (or LTV) to the buyer.

This presents a massive scale advantage in paid user acquisition: while the marginal value of users is unknowable, the value of the entire population per acquisition channel converges around a universal mean, and the closer to the population size a buyer can set purchasing limits, the more information the buyer has about the LTVs of the purchased users. And implicit in the ability to make large purchase orders on individual acquisition channels is possession of the expensive infrastructure already mentioned, which endows the large buyers with information about the purchased commodities (users) and the markets themselves, such as seasonality and intra-day price swings.

Competing in a product marketplace on the basis of paid user acquisition should be preceded by deep introspective recognition of the developer's business limitations. If the developer cannot predict LTV, cannot afford to purchase a large volume of users on a daily basis, and does not possess the infrastructure to assess the efficacy of various networks, then participating in paid user acquisition beyond an absolute minimum level cannot reliably be done at a profit. A requisite exercise in a developer's pursuit of strategic growth is recognizing its own disadvantages in a competitive market.

Misconceptions about paid user acquisition

The data-driven nature of the freemium model dictates the way certain functional groups within an organization interact with each other during the product design and development process. Because analytics is a revenue driver and not a cost center in the freemium model, it isn't implemented after a product launch as a means to reduce losses. Rather, initiating analytics should coincide with the launch of the minimum viable product and run in parallel with product iterations as a means of optimizing the user experience and increasing revenue.

The develop-release-measure-iterate feedback loop can potentially be seen as an intrusion into the creative process of designing software by measurement and analysis. But enmity for the freemium design process is misplaced when applied to paid user acquisition. Paid user acquisition has nothing to do with the creative versus wholly data-driven design debate; it occurs outside the bounds of the freemium model and should always be determined by economic limits when pursuing an optimal revenue outcome. In any given situation, paid user acquisition is either profitable or it isn't. There is no nuance.

That said, there are two common misconceptions about paid user acquisition that presume a relationship between the design process of a product and the necessity of performance marketing for growing a user base. The first misconception is that exceptional products don't require paid user acquisition because they are viral by nature. While the most viral software products in the world probably require very little ongoing paid user acquisition, even highly viral products still require an initial seed of users with which to achieve virality, and the larger that initial seed is, the faster and more widespread the viral effects will propagate.

Every virality model is predicated on the same basic set of inputs: global k-factor, the virality timeline, and saturation. The total number of virally acquired users per period is a function of the global k-factor and the virality timeline; total user base growth is a function of saturation. If a product is truly viral—its global k-factor is greater than 1—then virality compounds user base growth by facilitating higher-ordered cohort viral conversions, as illustrated in Figure 7.17.

Thus, truly viral products are the best candidates for paid user acquisition: not only does virality serve as a supplement to an acquisition budget (because it reduces the effective cost per acquisition of a user), but it increases the size of the viral invitation pool and creates a compounding dynamic. When the LTV–CPA spread is positive, virality doesn't negate the revenue benefit of paid user acquisition or somehow render it unnecessary; it amplifies its positive impact on revenues.

The second misconception about performance marketing is that the money spent on paid user acquisition would always be put to better use funding additional product development. A less absolute version of this statement wouldn't be contestable; but, as it is written, this belief contrasts with the core tenet of iterative, freemium product development, which posits that resources should always be allocated to the initiative of highest return. In some cases, that could be further product development. But to say that product development is always the most profitable recipient of resources is to ignore that these decisions should be justified by quantifiable support, made on the basis of projected revenue contribution, and not simply a bias for product development.

Measuring the revenue effects of product development versus paid acquisition (given an equivalent budget for both) requires two things: a quantitative framework for predicting revenue from a freemium product, and a reasonable assessment of how the marketplace for a given product will evolve over the proposed development timeline.

A quantitative framework for revenue prediction is something most businesses put together before undertaking any projects and therefore shouldn't be difficult to acquire. Without a framework, ROI estimates can't be made, which makes it impossible to finance projects (or financing is done haphazardly).

An understanding of the evolution of the marketplace in the coming weeks (or months, in some cases) is harder to come by and represents a significant risk. What if a competitor releases a new product in that time? What if cost of user acquisition rises precipitously? While these factors are not unique to the decision at hand nor to freemium developers, they are made more acute when a development team is deciding upon revenues now versus revenues in the future based on incomplete information. Most developers have a reasonably concrete grasp of their product's current metrics; they can compile a sensibly accurate lifetime customer value for users who would be acquired today through paid acquisition. But it is impossible to do the same for users acquired organically (which is the assumption) in, for example, two weeks' time.

So the decision to pursue product development over paid acquisition represents an admission that the organization believes it can extract more revenues from an improved product at some point in the future than it can from the current product, given the equal cost of product development and user acquisition and an understanding of the evolution of the product's marketplace over the course of product development.

Put another way, determining whether a budget should be allocated to product development or user acquisition on the basis of revenue benefit requires an evaluation process. Product development may produce a more desirable outcome in some cases, or even in most, but to say it is always the most ROI-effective course of action is to ignore the necessity of sober, objective analysis in making decisions.

Advertising exchanges

Online display advertising, which is essentially any advertisement seen on a website, is the primary means by which publishers monetize their products on the web. A publisher, in this sense, is anyone who produces content and makes that content available on the Internet; in cases where that content is in high demand, advertising might be the publisher's exclusive source of revenue. When that content serves a niche, advertising may merely supplement the revenues that come from charging for access to the content (such as subscription fees or per-item prices).

During the earliest stages of online advertising, publishers packaged and sold their own advertising inventory (the physical space on their websites that can be filled with advertisements) directly to advertisers on a bulk basis. Publishers used *forward contracts*, or agreements for the buyers to buy specific numbers of impressions (almost always on a CPM basis) at a predetermined price at a certain point in the future. This system is known as direct buying, and it still persists to some extent. It is a viable strategy when an advertising campaign's demographic is less important than the advertisement's context (for instance, on a website that can only display ads related to sports and must purchase those ads specifically and exclusively).

The direct buying model is labor-intensive for the publisher; it must employ a sales team to interact with purchasers, and negotiations over pricing and purchasing agreements must be undertaken manually. Likewise, the process is inefficient: large blocks of ad inventory may go unsold when there is a mismatch between the bulk amounts of impressions buyers are willing to purchase and the bulk amounts of impressions the publisher has available to sell. Given the overhead of making a sale, publishers under the direct buying model have no incentive to sell impressions in small amounts, as the transaction and operational costs could eclipse sales revenues.

For these reasons, direct buying has mostly given way to the *ad exchange* model. An ad exchange is a technology platform that seeks to match buyers (advertisers) and sellers (publishers) of advertising impressions in a centralized marketplace through *real-time bidding*, where ad impressions are sold individually in near-real time. The ad impressions are based on various characteristics about the user, the content in question, and the time of day. That is, instead of purchasing impressions in bulk through a forward contract based on a predetermined projection of value, advertisers bid on each impression based on the market dynamics at that moment.

The ad exchange model orients the purchasing of impressions away from context and toward audience. The advantages of this model relate to optimization: because bidding takes place in real time, advertisers can more accurately control their spending, and because inventory is sold on a per-unit basis, publishers can prevent inventory from going unsold by decreasing their prices. The ad exchange model is not the exclusive domain of online advertising; rather, it has extended to nearly all forms of digital advertising, including ads on mobile platforms.

An ad exchange charges a fee to handle the transaction between an advertiser and a publisher. The ad exchange adds value to the process with the technology it provides to both parties and the liquidity it provides to the publisher (via access to a number of advertisers and the sales volume of individual impressions). When an advertiser elects to work directly with the ad exchange, that is, to directly manage the bidding process on ad impressions, the advertiser is said to have a *seat* at that exchange. Without a seat at an ad exchange, an advertiser must purchase ads through an intermediary, which might not offer full or direct access to the available impressions on the exchange.

Ad exchanges offer targeting capabilities to advertisers that are not necessarily restricted to the content on which the impression is being served. The most valuable targeting capabilities are historical user characteristics, or information about the user's history or state that may assist the advertiser in determining whether or not that user is a good candidate for a specific ad. Some advertisers use these characteristics to engage in what is known as *re-targeting*, or advertising a product or service to a user whom an advertiser knows has accessed it in the past. User characteristics essentially provide a means of serving the best possible ad to a user on a per-impression basis.

The basic transactional structure underpinning the ad exchange model begins with a user engaging with a specific publisher's content (which could be a website, a mobile application, etc.) where ad impressions are being sold. When the user opens the content, the publisher immediately sends the ad exchange three pieces of information: the specific piece of content the user is viewing, any information about the user the publisher is allowed to share, and the minimum price the publisher is willing to accept for the impression.

The exchange presents this information to advertisers, who then return two pieces of information to the exchange (unless they don't wish to participate in the auction): their bid on the impression and the ad they would like to serve in that placement.

In a real-time bidding environment, the highest bidder wins the ad placement. After accepting the bid, the ad exchange passes the ad content to the publisher and handles the transaction logistics (payments, reporting, etc.). The entire process, from the user first viewing the content to the publisher serving the ad content in the placement, must be executed in a fraction of a second. An ad exchange of reasonable volume must therefore be capable of processing tens or hundreds of thousands of such transactions per second, which poses substantial infrastructure requirements. As such, only a few major ad exchanges exist.

No matter what the platform is, ads form the foundation of paid user acquisition in freemium marketing (except for paid search, which is discussed separately). On mobile devices, advertising for applications can take one of two forms, web-based ads and in-application ads, that can direct users to either platform application stores or mobile websites. On the desktop web, ads can also direct to websites or platform stores for desktop software.

The acquisition cost is the average amount of money paid for an ad that resulted in a user adopting the product. On mobile devices, this cost is sometimes quoted and charged on a cost-per-install basis; on the web, prices are often quoted and charged to users on a cost-per-mille basis, meaning the advertiser calculates its per-user acquisition cost (*cost per install*) by dividing the total amount of money spent on an advertising campaign by the number of users acquired through that campaign.

Demand-side platforms

The ad exchange model is presented as a system of four parties: the user, the publisher, the ad exchange, and the advertiser. But in reality, the system is often made of six parties, with intermediaries representing the publishers and advertisers to the ad exchanges. The intermediaries that represent advertisers are known as *demand-side platforms*, or DSPs.

A DSP automates the process of purchasing ad impressions while also making the process transparent. Without a DSP, an advertiser must sell ads through an *ad network*, or an entity that purchases advertising inventory in bulk directly from publishers and sells it to advertisers. Ad networks exist in two forms: *blind networks*, which do not provide contextual information about ad impressions purchased to advertisers, and *vertical networks*, which often represent publications they own and specialize in premium inventory. Ad networks require advertisers to purchase bulk impressions on a forward basis (meaning simply that prices are set now for quantities to be delivered in the future).

The advantages that DSPs offer are economies of scale in terms of overhead management and logistics, and the ability to optimize advertising strategy in real time. DSPs also offer tools that can help advertisers track their ads' performance (through metrics like click-through rate), predict targeting efficacy, track historical data about the exchange, and unify external data sets with advertising market meta data. These all assist the advertiser with decisions about ad placement, optimal bid pricing, topical relevance, and other highly technical endeavors that small advertisers may not be equipped to undertake.

An additional advantage is that DSPs can offer advertisers access to multiple ad exchanges and manage performance across those exchanges. This increase in access to inventory gives the advertiser real-time bidding capabilities and allows the advertiser to set bids based on the goal of the advertising campaign, rather than on the expected value of the purchased ad impression.

Advertisers set these bids by establishing targets for *effective* prices, or the prices paid, on a per-mille basis, for individually purchased impressions. For example, the effective cost per mille (eCPM) is the average price of individual advertisements placed (since each placement is made individually in real time, not in bulk). Advertisers would have a difficult time achieving effective goals without access to a large pool of ad impressions.

DSPs generally offer more transparency and sophistication with respect to targeting content and demographics, which is a key issue with ad impressions. DSPs can often semantically analyze and classify content before placing ads into it; this helps to match ads to the content they're most appropriate for (and most likely to convert in).

Given that the principle value a DSP offers to an advertiser is its technology stack and analytics infrastructure, some high-volume advertisers opt to build technology platforms internally that exist essentially as proprietary DSPs. The advantage of an internal platform for managing advertising purchasing is the access to insight into the algorithms used to best match advertisements with impressions, which DSPs closely guard.

But operating an internal DSP, or advertising optimization framework, requires a seat on each exchange from whom the advertiser purchases, and seats are often granted based not just on advertising volume (which generally must be in the order of millions of dollars per month to quality), but also on the quality of advertising the advertiser brings to the exchange. Thus, the development of internal DSP functionality may not be feasible for all but the largest advertisers, who are capable of dedicating massive resources to infrastructure deployment and managing a sufficient volume of regular impression purchases to qualify for seats on multiple exchanges.

Supply-side platforms

The intermediaries that represent content publishers, or the parties selling ad impressions, are known as *supply-side platforms*, or SSPs. An SSP helps a publisher maximize its *advertising yield*, or maximizing revenue in the process of selling fixed-number, fixed expiration-date commodities.

Yield management is an interesting and fairly new focus within economics that attempts to model optimization scenarios for perishable goods that can be priced with flexibility. Yield management strategies have been employed to great success in the airline and hotel industries, which seek to maximize the revenue they generate by predicting demand, segmenting users, and implementing fluid price models. Industries and product groups that can benefit from yield management tactics exhibit five basic characteristics:

- Excess or unsold inventory cannot be saved or sold in the future. An ad impression that is not served to a user is not accessible again once that user leaves the content.
- The customer pool is stratified across multiple demand curves and price elasticity constraints. Some customers are willing to pay a price premium for

what they deem to be a higher quality experience, and some customers make their decisions to purchase based solely on price.

- Inventory sales orders can be taken on a forward contract basis when future demand is uncertain. Content publishers can either sell their ad impressions ahead of time or wait to sell them in real-time on an exchange.
- Sellers are free to turn down purchase offers on the basis of price in expectation of higher future offers. Content publishers can accept forward contract purchase orders on their future ad inventory or reject them in anticipation of increased future demand.

SSPs assist publishers with the mechanics of optimizing their yield by analyzing patterns in demand and the behavior of advertisers who frequently make offers on their inventory. Since a publisher always has the option to sell fixed-term inventory to advertisers on a forward contract basis, SSPs assist publishers in determining how they can best structure their inventory sales between bulk forward contracts and real-time, per-impression exchange bids.

Although publishers commit to forward contracts in advance (and may incur significant penalties if they do not meet the volume terms of those contracts), at the instance of each impression, the publisher is presented with the choice of whether to place the impression on an ad exchange or to use it toward the fulfillment of an outstanding bulk contract. Thus, when contracts are open, the share of a contract that an impression represents serves as an opportunity cost against which the revenue gained from selling that impression on exchange must be weighed, reduced by the demand risk of being unable to fulfill the entirety of the contract as a result of withholding the impression from the contracted party. Balseiro et al. (2011) present this in as a decision tree undertaken by a publisher at the point of each impression, which is illustrated in Figure 8.1.

Figure 8.2 depicts a similar model, adapted to the parameters of the freemium model and grounded in the logic of cross-promotion as described in Chapter 5. This decision tree extends the tree depicted in Figure 8.1 and takes into account the concept of user churn as a result of advertising; that is, when one product is advertised in another product, the possibility of churn from the source product must be compensated for by either a sufficiently high sale price or a sufficiently low predicted LTV.

While they are similar to DSPs, SSPs also provide publishers with an analytics infrastructure and reporting services that they can use to analyze their own inventory and optimize their operations. This infrastructure allows publishers to gather data about the demand for their inventory, in real time, and set price floors accordingly. This infrastructure may also allow publishers to block certain types of ads from appearing alongside their content and help them predict demand in both the near- and mid-term.

Paid search

Paid search advertising is an auction-based advertising model used in displaying contextual ads on search engine results. Instead of bidding on target user

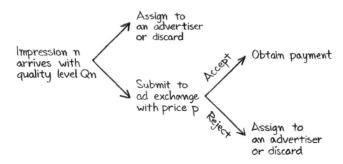

FIGURE 8.1

A per-impression advertising decision tree, as described by Balseiro et al.

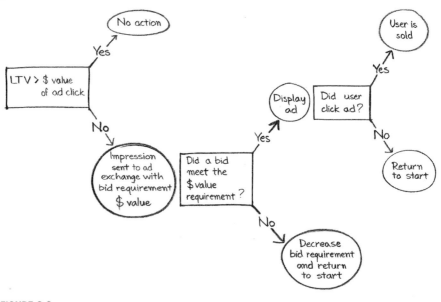

FIGURE 8.2

An extended decision tree model compensating for user churn.

demographics or specific placements, advertisers bid on keywords; when those key-words are searched for, the search engine operates an auction to determine which ads are displayed alongside results. Search engine results pages generally feature multiple ad placements, with the most valuable being "above the fold," or above the point at which a user must scroll to see additional content on the page. Search engines may also syndicate their ad placements across third-party websites and feature ad placements in their freely available tools.

Paid search ads are almost always text-based and the search engine contextually analyzes them for relevance. Ads are represented as links to websites; clicking on an ad takes the user to the advertised website. Paid search ads are most often undertaken on a cost-per-click (CPC) basis, where advertisers set bid prices on ads based on the value of a click, but cost-per-action (CPA) and cost-per-mille (CPM) pricing options are also typically offered.

The paid search dynamic merges the DSP, the ad exchange, the SSP, and the publisher role into one, creating a three-party model: the search engine, the user, and the advertiser. Search engines typically offer a rich suite of tools to advertisers in order to target and optimize the advertisers' campaigns; when an advertiser creates an ad, the advertiser provides ad copy, targeting guidelines (such as geography, language, and other restrictions), and a maximum bid per identified keyword. The *market depth* of a specific keyword at a specific point in time represents the number of advertisers bidding for access to ad impressions served alongside the keyword's search results. When market depth is greater than 1, the search engine must apply ranking logic to decide how to allocate ad placements.

Jansen and Mullen (2008) identify GoTo.com, which was later renamed Overture and acquired by Yahoo!, as having developed the first paid search auction marketplace in 1998. The initial incarnation of this auction model took the form of a generalized first price (GFP) auction; the advertiser with the highest bid took the best placement and paid exactly its bid, the advertiser with the second-highest bid took the second-best placement and paid exactly its bid, and so forth. This led to inefficiencies in the marketplace, wherein advertisers would engage in time- and labor-intensive bidding wars that ultimately decreased the revenue generated by the advertising marketplace.

In February 2002, both Google and Overture launched paid search marketplaces structured around a generalized second price (GSP) auction model. Under GSP conditions, the highest bidder wins the auction but pays the bid put forth by the second highest bidder, the second-highest bidder pays the bid put forth by the third-highest bidder, and so on; if the number of bidders exceeds or exactly matches the number of ad placements, then the lowest bidder pays the minimum bid price (the reserve price). Usually some margin amount is added to the price charged to each bidder.

The purpose of the GSP, which is a form of what is known as a Vickrey auction, is to give participants the incentive to place bids based on what the object's value is to them. Since no participant knows the bids of the other participants, they cannot game the auction system by strategically outbidding the others. An example of a GSP auction is presented in Figure 8.3. In the figure, the ad placements on the page are arranged in order of priority: placement 1 is worth the most, placement 2 the second most, and placement 3 the least.

In May 2002, Google added an additional layer of complexity to the GSP model by introducing a quality ranking component to its ad placement ranking algorithm. This component is known as the "quality score," and it takes into account four factors: the click-through rate of the ad in question, a measure of the perceived quality

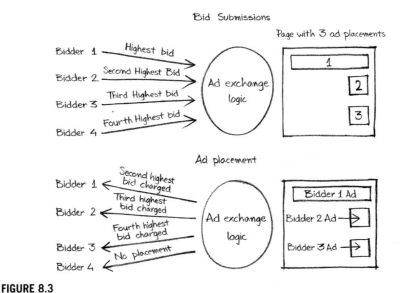

FIGURE 8.3

A GSP auction model.

of the destination website to which the ad leads, a measure of the destination website's relevance to the keyword being bid on, and the value of the bid itself. The quality score's purpose is to improve the ad experience for the user.

Because the search engine in the paid search model assumes the responsibilities of the DSP, the SSP, and the ad exchange from the ad exchange model, some operational efficiencies that emerge as frictions between moving parts are eliminated. For instance, the search engine is incentivized to offer advertisers robust analytics and targeting mechanisms in the search engine's suite of advertising tools to optimize the advertiser's yield and encourage continued use. And because the search engine has full agency over ad impressions supply data as well as user information, no tensions between the publisher and advertiser can arise over information asymmetries.

That said, because of the pervasiveness and reach of search engines and the competitive landscape in which they operate, the quality of the user experience plays a larger role in impressions allocation in paid search than it does in other advertising models. Search engines are incentivized to favor the user experience over sub-optimal ad placement service (in terms of ad quality, site quality, or relevance). This is because such a strategy preserves not only long-term advertising business, which is contingent on ad quality (given the nature of the advertising format), but also its positioning relative to other search engines. Thus advertisers with niche appeal may have trouble meeting aggressive campaign goals through paid search, as the number of placements available to niche topics is a function of the number of keyword searches executed within that niche.

$$eCPA = \frac{CPA}{(1 + k - factor)}$$

FIGURE 8.4

The formula to calculate eCPA.

Virality and user acquisition

Since the principal benefit of virality is non-paid user base growth, virality necessarily changes an organization's paid user acquisition calculus with respect to growth goals and acquisition budgeting. As defined in Chapter 4, the k-factor describes the number of additional users an existing user virally introduces to a product; this number augments the aggregate effect of user acquisition and can therefore be used to derive a more precise projection of how many total users will be acquired in a campaign and at what individual price.

When reduced by the k-factor, the cost paid per user introduced into the product is known as *eCPA*, or *effective cost per acquisition*. The calculation to derive eCPA is fundamentally the same as the one used to derive CPA: it is the total amount of money spent on a campaign divided by the total number of users acquired by that campaign. The difference in the calculation of eCPA is the degree of separation considered: CPA is calculated on a direct acquisition basis, whereas eCPA takes into account the users introduced to the product indirectly through virality.

Because the calculations use the same set of inputs, eCPA can be calculated simply as a reduction of CPA by a product's k-factor; that is, it is the degree to which the acquisition cost decreases as a result of the product's ability to spread through viral mechanics. And since the k-factor cannot be negative, it always reduces CPA. The calculation for eCPA is illustrated in Figure 8.4.

Adding the k-factor to 1 in the denominator of the equation incorporates the additional users acquired virally into the per-user price paid in the campaign. For instance, when the k-factor is 1 (i.e., each user introduces an additional user to the product virally), the CPA is effectively halved.

Another approach to adjusting the user acquisition dynamic to accommodate the k-factor is to use it to increase the calculated LTV of a product (as an *effective lifetime customer value*, or *eLTV*). This line of thought dictates that the revenue generated by users initiated into a product through viral mechanics by another user should be attributed to the original user. But three compelling arguments against this approach render the eCPA model more appropriate.

The first argument is that LTV should be segmented by various factors—geography, behavioral history, etc. —and the eLTV model works under the assumption that the profiles of users acquired virally match the profiles of the users who introduced them. This assumption is difficult to justify when considered against the potential means through which virality can take root: social media networks, word of mouth, and even chance encounters in public (such as on public transport). Given the variability in how viral mechanics produce user base growth, attributing a portion of one user's LTV to another user's as a result of viral introduction is impossible before the virally acquired users have been adopted.

The second argument is that, by attributing the expected revenues from one user to another, the organization engenders a dangerous opportunity to overestimate a product's performance. Costs are concrete, as are user counts; even if the k-factor is overestimated (thereby producing an unrealistically low eCPA), because virality is generally calculated over a fairly limited timeline, the eCPA calculation can be audited and retroactively updated in short order. But LTV is a longer-term metric, usually realized over months; adjusting an unrealistically optimistic eLTV is impractical and could lead to imprudent budgeting and a false sense of revenue security.

And the last argument is that LTV is very specifically and narrowly defined as the estimated revenues a user directly contributes to a product. Augmenting LTV by a growth factor changes this definition and renders it more difficult to calculate, communicate, and use as a decision-making tool.

Mobile user acquisition

User acquisition on mobile platforms is undertaken under a different set of parameters than those on the web and through other mediums. While the mechanics and intermediaries of user acquisition on mobile platforms remain the same as those already identified, the dynamics of the system are much less precise. For one, far less information is knowable about a user on a mobile platform prior to a purchase than is known on the web.

Second, a user purchased from with a mobile application, and not through content serving advertising, purchased under certain quality implications, specifically, that users are sold only from an application when they have not converted. These two fundamental differences between mobile user acquisition and acquisition on other channels are effectively represented by the laws of large numbers and adverse selection.

In the context of mobile user acquisition, the term "selling users" refers to advertising mechanics within one application that prompt the user to install another. These advertising mechanics are operated by ad exchanges, and when a user clicks on such a prompt, they are removed from the application they are using and brought to the second application's profile in the platform's application store.

Whether or not the user installs the second application, the session in the first application has ended. Depending on the format of the agreement between the second application and the ad exchange, the second application may then pay the ad exchange for the user it received, and the ad exchange will subsequently pay the first application.

Mobile user acquisition and the law of large numbers

The law of large numbers states that the larger the number of experiments conducted under a static set of parameters and in an unmodified environment, the closer the average of the results will converge toward the expected value of the experiment. In the case of mobile user acquisition, the expected value of the experiment, which is the purchase of a user, is unknown. Thus, the more users purchased on a specific network, the greater confidence the developer can have that the average LTVs of those purchased users represent an LTV average for that channel.

The opposite is also true: when a developer buys few users from a specific channel, the developer knows very little about the expected LTV of users on the network. When a user is purchased from a mobile ad network, the developer knows only three things about the purchase:

- The purchased user has a mobile device and has installed at least one application;
- The user's mobile device model and geographic location are known (other information such as gender and age may be known on some networks); and
- The developer of the application where that user came from was willing to sell that user for a specific amount of money.

These three data points imply nothing about a user's predilection for making in-application purchases. Considering the role subjective taste plays in whether or not a person enjoys a mobile application, mobile acquisition purchases are essentially made "blind."

When a mobile developer acquires a user, it cannot predict how much money that user will spend in its application. The determinants of a user's lifetime in-product spend are essentially random variables:

- The user's current financial status (and expected near-term future financial status);
- The user's preferences in terms of application category;
- The amount of free time the user has (and expects to have in the future) to engage with the mobile device; and
- The extent to which the user may find in-application, virtual purchases socially acceptable and financially responsible.

No mobile user acquisition networks filter for these variables because these variables are not measurable. (The last variable can be measured by proxy of past spend, but this data isn't available when a user is purchased from a network.)

Thus the notion that any developer can predict, with any reliability or accuracy, the LTV of a single user purchased from a single channel is invalid, given the lack of insight into the characteristics of the user that dictate a predilection to making in-application purchases.

The layer of haze obfuscating the contours of the mobile user acquisition market is only penetrable by huge sample sizes, as dictated by the law of large numbers. And those huge sample sizes are expensive to acquire and maintain; only the very largest firms command the economy of scale necessary to build a system that can approach the full utilization of acquisition data in predicting LTV by network.

Mobile user acquisition and adverse selection

Adverse selection further complicates the economics of mobile user acquisition. As mentioned earlier, one of the few data points known about a user, immediately after the user is acquired by a mobile application, is that the user was put up for sale. Unlike on the web and in other media formats, where content is often monetized exclusively by advertising, in-application purchase is the dominant form of monetization for mobile applications. And an in-application purchase is zero-sum at the level of a single user: the purchases a user makes in one application are purchases not made in another.

Two circumstances exist under which an app developer would be incentivized to sell a user: (1) The application monetizes exclusively by selling users; it does not offer in-application purchases, and (2) the developer does offer in-application purchases, but the user in question is not considered likely to make purchases totaling to more than the application could receive for selling the user (as discussed earlier in the chapter with respect to yield management).

The first case represents more applications, but the second case represents more users; that is, the majority of users sold on mobile acquisition networks are done so through the applications with the largest user bases, by the developers that have the most resources to analyze user behavior and predilection for purchasing. In other words, users bought from mobile acquisition networks are sold to those networks precisely because they are considered to have a low probability of generating revenue. This is adverse selection: the information asymmetry about users between buyers and sellers produces a situation where the users being sold are the ones least likely to be of value.

An open market should correct for such an information asymmetry, that is, demand for users on these markets should be dictated by the value they provide, thus setting the average cost per acquisition at a market clearing price under equilibrium. But this doesn't happen in mobile user acquisition, because buyers do not act rationally.

A developer dependent on acquisition networks for user base growth (i.e., a developer whose application isn't experiencing organic or viral growth) has no choice but to continue to buy users once it has started, whether or not the quality of those users is high. The developer also may not be able to distinguish between bad users and a bad application that doesn't monetize, but in either case, the developer cannot do anything to allay its dependency on paid acquisition until it has improved its application through iteration cycles.

When a developer does not possess the analytics infrastructure to constantly iterate and test improvements to application mechanics and instead believes the quality of the acquired users is to blame for poor performance, it likewise has no option but to continue to acquire paid users in the hopes that the quality will improve. And even when a developer does have the infrastructure and business capacity for continual improvement, it cannot stop acquiring users unless the application reaches appreciable organic discovery potential.

Users available to be acquired on mobile networks are a blend of non-converting users from applications published by savvy developers with sophisticated analytics systems and users randomly sold from applications by developers that possess no analytics infrastructure; this blend is not revealed by acquisition networks. Lack of insight into this blend of users, and the adverse selection present when the seller can evaluate the revenue capacity of its users, creates a situation in which user acquisition on mobile platforms is essentially conducted, at low volumes of users, without any means of predicting a result.

Alternative user acquisition

As user acquisition describes a firm's initiatives in recruiting users into a product, it is often considered strictly as a paid endeavor, as other pursuits of user adoption fall under the umbrella term of "marketing." But in the freemium model, the development of a user base, from adoption to optimized initial experience, is simply the broad notion of growth: the procedures and strategies employed to acquire and retain users at the earliest point in the adoption funnel.

In this sense, and because the concept of growth is supported by a unified analytics infrastructure in the freemium model, paid and alternative user acquisitions are interrelated: they represent the same set of challenges and opportunities to compound growth, and both can be tracked, instrumented, and optimized. In applying the same analytical and return-oriented approach to alternative acquisition as is used in paid acquisition, a freemium developer can ensure that its resources are being allocated to deliver to the product what matters most: growth of the user base.

Above all, a freemium developer should orient its operations to achieve profitable, consistent and reliable growth. One of the challenges presented by alternative user acquisition efforts is that they rarely provide the reliability and consistency required in making forward-looking budgeting forecasts, and their profitability can be muddied by the impression that alternative efforts do not incur costs. But the dynamics of freemium product development, and especially of the aggressive pursuit of product growth, assign a cost to every organizational action and inaction; for alternative user acquisition, that cost often shows in the opportunity cost of unrealized projects.

The goal of an organization's growth team, then, is to implement analytics throughout its operations to such an extent that the best possible allocation of resources, with the goal of profitable, continuous, and reliable growth, can be achieved through thoughtful, well-informed analysis, regardless of where those resources go with respect to paid or alternative user acquisition.

Cross-promotion, virality, and discovery

Cross-promotion and virality have been covered at length in this text, and, in addition to *discovery*, represent what is generally considered to be *organic* growth, or growth that occurs without being explicitly paid for. But while these forms of growth can be employed without direct budgetary outlays (beyond development and testing time), they all bear fairly quantifiable opportunity costs that must be recognized and appreciated.

Discovery is the means by which users, of their own accord, find and adopt a product; it usually takes place through some sort of search mechanism, such as a search engine or search function on a platform application store. Users may discover a product by searching for it by name or simply by seeking out products with certain characteristics and then browsing the results.

Of the three sources of organic growth, discovery is the most authentically organic in the sense that it occurs with almost no direct influence from the product developer beyond the thought that goes into naming conventions and product descriptions. As a result, discovery is very hard to instrument and improve on; when a user proactively seeks out a product, the only aspects of the product that impact discovery are the product's name and whatever information is available about the product through the search mechanism used. These pieces of information are so fundamental that the effects of changing them are hard to gauge and measure post-launch.

Testing the appeal of product names is possible by proxy—say, through measuring the click-through rates of advertisements, each one bearing a different potential product name—but the results can't be meaningfully extrapolated onto live, post-launch performance. Product descriptions can be more easily tested and iterated upon, but given that product descriptions are usually most valuable when succinct and authentically descriptive of what the product does, the degree to which optimized product descriptions can drive additional discovery is fairly minimal.

Cross-promotion, as discussed earlier, is the process by which a developer entices users of one of its products to adopt another of its products. And while cross-promotion can be a powerful tool in growing the user base of a new product quickly, it often results in a zero-sum transfer of a user within the broader product system, not a net new user. Cross-promotion must thus be undertaken with an eye toward the revenue profiles of both products involved in the transaction; users should be cross-promoted to products in which they are considered likely to spend additional money, or to products that are complementary enough that continued use of the departure product can be predicted with some certainty.

Cross-promotion, then, while eminently capable of being analytically considered, presents a direct risk to the developer in terms of potential revenue loss: if a user is transfers to another product and churns out due to a preference mismatch, the opportunity to capture additional revenues from the first product may also be lost. Defining a user's tastes within a product the user has already interacted with is difficult enough; attempting to define them relative to a product the user has never used adds another dimension of complexity to the process.

Finally, virality presents opportunity costs to growth in the form of alienated potential users and premature exposure. As discussed earlier, aggressive virality mechanics can have a negative impact on non-users' perceptions of the product, as the necessity of intrusive and flagrant measures in growing a user base are seen as the exclusive domain of products without obvious and unmistakable quality. In other words, conspicuous virality tactics can be interpreted as negative quality signals (which can potentially impede growth) by users who have yet to adopt a product.

Likewise, users may bristle and feel exploited when overly relied upon as a viral marketing channel, especially when they are used to propagate viral invitations without their explicit approval. A heavy-handed virality mechanic's success in growing the user base must be measured as a function of its gross effect, which is difficult to quantify to begin with, but becomes even more so when users churn out of a product over issues of trust abuse. That said, the most viral products reap rewards from virality that far exceed the associated costs, but those products are viral by nature and not reliant on specific mechanics to drive growth.

Organic growth must be viewed as a force that is not unequivocally beneficial but rather introduces frictions to overall growth that are simply not wholly apparent as explicit costs, as is paid user acquisition. Even discovery, which is the most genuinely organic of the three approaches, introduces attendant opportunity costs to the product, especially when significant effort is expended on managing the degree to which a product's name and description are optimized for appeal.

Because organic growth is difficult to predict, it can lead to models of growth that drastically diverge from reality and produce significant negative impact on budget projections. Overestimated organic growth is the most common misapprehension as it relates to these three channels—but especially virality—and it can lull a developer into a false sense of security, resulting in insufficient planning for paid acquisition.

Freemium growth forecasts are therefore most sensibly modeled using paid acquisition as the primary anchor of growth, with organic growth channels calculated as a certain percentage of users acquired through paid channels. This approach orients the model toward the factors that can be best predicted and offers fuller flexibility in revising models when market conditions (such as acquisition prices) change. Building forecasts primarily oriented around organic growth drivers requires making broad and fundamentally untestable assumptions about the performance of the product, rather than using historically auditable market conditions, and introduces an unfortunate element of uncertainty into budgeting decisions.

Search engine optimization

Search engine optimization is the process by which publishers adapt and refine their content to increase its exposure to search engines. Search engine optimization has been a phenomenon on the web since the earliest days of natural search, as content publishers sought to increase the extent to which keyword-relevant searches delivered traffic to their websites. The concept has become important on mobile systems, as the traffic delivered to products in platform stores increases in significance.

No distinction is made between the types of searches on the web and those on mobile platforms; rather, distinctions are made between search engines and platform stores. Mobile web search engine optimization is essentially the same as it is for desktop web search engine optimization. And as platform stores are generally unified for all devices on which they can operate, optimizing for keyword search on one platform usually reaps the same benefits for all platforms.

Search engine optimization is accomplished by tailoring content to appeal best to the algorithms powering keyword search. And while the specifics of keyword-matching algorithms are highly guarded by search engines as proprietary secrets, they all reward the same basic characteristics: relevance to the keyword being searched for, and perceived quality of the destination website.

Keyword relevance is fairly straightforward to measure and improve on; if the searched keyword appears frequently in a text, it will likely be considered relevant to the text's content. Added emphasis may be placed on title keywords and subheading keywords; the text that is most prominent will likely be the most heavily associated with the content. The degree to which a keyword exists in a piece of content should be measured for the keywords aspired to; the denser a specific keyword's presence in the content, the more likely that keyword is to be associated with it.

Perceived quality is a far more ambiguous determination, and it is also harder to curate for, especially on platform stores. Many search engines use the extent to which other websites link to the considered website as a proxy for quality, assuming that links reflect how much others find a website's content interesting and informative. Likewise, various website characteristics are taken into account to assess its intent and reliability, such as how often the website is updated and the amount of text on each page, although video may be assessed as more valuable than text in some cases.

The perceived quality of platform stores is largely measured through the frequency and recency of updates and product ratings by users. User ratings are eminently important on platform stores, not only because they affect search placement but because they have a profound impact on a potential user's likelihood to download a product. And while user ratings are perhaps the most transparent and meritocratic means of evaluating a product, they also allow users to exert influence on the direction of product development and in-product pricing schemes.

Once a product is released, maintaining the status quo in terms of feature development becomes a real concern, as no product change will be universally accepted as good, yet even one negative rating can adversely affect a product's discoverability (platform stores penalize it by listing it lower in search results). This phenomenon should play a role in freemium product development for platform stores: for the purposes of preserving user feedback ratings, incremental releases, even when introducing new functionality, are preferable to dramatic changes in the product's feature set.

The number of downloads a product has achieved in platform stores is an element of perceived quality that can have an impact on its position in keyword search results. Popularity, for better or worse, is generally considered a measure of universal relevance; thus, as products gain prominence, they receive additional exposure in platform stores, creating a virtuous cycle of adoption momentum.

This is part of the logic behind "burst" product launches, or product launches seeded with a large paid acquisition campaign. Increased downloads are complemented by increased exposure in keyword search as well as increased prominence in league tables tracking platform store downloads, which bring additional attention to the product.

Specific pages of content on the web that are indexed and returned as search results by search engines are called *landing pages*. Landing pages can be updated, tested, and measured rather painlessly; often, a change involves nothing more technical than a file transfer or an update in a content management system. This ease of production and curation allows for evaluating optimization strategies against each other; multiple strategies (in terms of the structure of content and density of certain keywords) can be implemented across individual landing pages, and those that perform the best can be considered superior and implemented elsewhere.

Updating product descriptions on platform stores is often more tedious than it is on the web. But how effective the content is in generating traffic from keyword searches on the web is broadly applicable to generating traffic on other platforms; if a specific set of keywords or content works exceptionally well on the web, it is more likely to perform well on other platforms as well, as opposed to keywords or content that perform poorly on the web.

Even when a product is being developed for a platform store, search engine optimization on the web can be undertaken as a multi-platform agenda: specific strategies can be tested on the web, where the cost of experimentation is merely the time invested into crafting the websites, and the strategy that performs the best can be applied to platform stores, where a burst campaign budget will be disbursed.

Traditional media

Traditional media channels—radio, television, newspaper, and magazines—have served as capable means by which software-based freemium products have gotten new users. The fundamental disadvantage of traditional media over Internet-based media is, of course, the transmission disconnect: traditional media serves only to inform a person about the product, not to allow the person to immediately adopt the product. After viewing a traditional media advertisement, potential new users must still seek out the product on their own; conversion, therefore, is prone to performing more poorly in traditional media than on Internet-based channels.

Related to the transmission disconnect, tracking traditional media is also difficult. Since users must go through discovery channels or visit the product's website to adopt the product, it is difficult to discern between the users who were influenced to seek the product out and those who found the product organically. Some traditional media advertisements supply product location information that has been modified in order to track the ad's performance (such as a unique URL embedded in a QR code in print media), but these tactics can create confusion among potential users and are only marginally effective, at best.

Since traditional media advertisements can't be accurately attributed, the most common technique for measuring their effects is simply comparing user adoption over two similar periods, with one of the periods following a traditional media campaign. The periods compared should be similar in length and where in the weekly and monthly cycles they occur. For instance, if a traditional media campaign is run on the last Monday of a month, the analysis period following the campaign should be compared to the same period a month earlier (i.e., following the last Monday of the previous month), given that monthly growth has been relatively stable.

If monthly growth was rapid, the comparison won't be valid; in that case, comparing the period to the same period a week earlier, rather than a month earlier, would be more sensible but still prone to error. Likewise, if some event took place the preceding week that disrupted the normal level of user adoption, a week-to-week comparison would be rendered useless. The problem with comparing periods is that external influences on user behavior are difficult to understand, much less isolate. Using this method to gauge the effectiveness of traditional media campaigns may provide some basic insight in the case of an overwhelmingly successful campaign but is by not an authoritative means of doing so.

Another method of attribution is the registration poll, in which users are asked during the registration process to select from a predefined set of options how they were made aware of the product. Running the registration poll for ahead of the traditional media campaign will provide baselines values for each particular response (e.g., 20 percent of users discover a product through Internet ads) as well as a baseline value for the percentage of new users who respond to such surveys at all (assuming a response is optional).

Given that the campaign's target audience is as likely to respond to registration poll as is the product's user base (which is not always a fair expectation), then upon the campaign's launch, the baseline values should change enough to provide clues into how many users came from the traditional media advertising.

The lack of a clear attribution channel in traditional media is problematic because this lack prevents the developer from measuring the return on investment into that channel. If a user acquired from traditional media campaigns can't be unequivocally identified, the efficacy of the money allocated to a traditional media campaign can't be evaluated. The pursuit of scale in the freemium model, which is of paramount importance, is predicated on the forward momentum provided by the undercurrent of profitable marketing.

Executing marketing campaigns without insight into or regard for performance runs counter to the conceptual core of the freemium business model, which holds that heightened instrumentation and analytical capacity can deliver more revenue from a larger user base than can a premium price barrier from a smaller user base. Traditional media has long been the bastion of brand advertising, where large corporations established and frequently reiterated the connection between their brand and some wide category of good or service: soap or toothpaste or insurance, and so on. This is an effective means of advertising when that intellectual connection between a brand and its category of product is valuable as well as important.

But freemium products are not categories of goods that users are confronted with every day, multiple times per day, as in the grocery store or at the mall. Freemium goods are platforms and services, and since a freemium product's price point of $0 reduces a user's barrier to moving between products, users can make easily make informed decisions around quality, rendering subconscious brand sentimentality impotent.

While traditional media is certainly not any worse an advertising medium of than online channels, it is simply not suited to the freemium model's data demands unless more transparent channels have been completely exhausted to the point of inefficiency. A freemium product exhibiting a high enough level of virality can reach the threshold of its viral networks without actually reaching its saturation point. In such a case, and given a high monetization profile, traditional media may be the only recourse by which to reach users in the product's demographic targets who are not in the population reached by online paid acquisition channels.

A product with very broad appeal to demographic groups segmented across varying degrees of technology savvy could be a good candidate for traditional media. And in such a case, the profitability of continued reach, while difficult to measure precisely, would probably be ensured through the viral nature of the product.

References

Aaker, D.A., Kumar, V., Day, G.S., 2003. Marketing Research, eigth ed. Wiley, New York.

Anderson, S., Thisse, J.F., Palma, A., 1992. Discrete Choice Theory of Product Differentiation. MIT Press, Cambridge, Mass.

Andrews, K.R., 1980. The Concept of Corporate Strategy. Irwin, Homewood, IL.

Bagwell, K., Ramey, G., Spulber, D., 1997. Dynamic retail price and investment competition. Rand J. Econ. 28, 207–227.

Balseiro, B., Feldman, J., Mirrokni, V., Muthukrishnan, S., 2011. Yield Optimization of Display Advertising with Ad Exchange. Paper presented at the ACM Conference on Electronic Commerce.

Bauer, H.H., Hammerschmidt, M., Braehler, M., 2003. The customer lifetime value concept and its contribution to corporate valuation. Yearb. Mark. Consum. Res. 1, 47–67.

Dekimpe, M.G., Hanssens, D.M., 2010. Time series models in marketing: some recent developments. Mark. JRM 1, 24–29.

Draper, N.R., Smith, H., 1998. Applied Regression Analysis, third ed. Wiley, New York.

Edelman, B., Ostrovsky, M., Schwarz, M., 2005. Internet Advertising and the Generalized Second Price Auction: Selling Billions of Dollars Worth of Keywords. NBER working paper, 11765.

Ellickson, P., 2000. Vertical Product Differentiation and Competition in the Supermarket Industry. Doctoral dissertation. Retrieved from DSpace@MIT.

Fader, P., Hardie, B., Berger, P., 2004. Customer-Base Analysis with Discrete-Time Transaction Data. Unpublished working paper.

Fader, P., Hardie, B., Lee, K.L., 2005. Counting your customers the easy way: an alternative to the Pareto/NBD Model. Mark. Sci. 24, 275–284.

Fader, P., Hardie, B., Shang, J., 2010. Customer-base analysis in a discrete-time noncontractual setting. Mark. Sci. 29, 1086–1108.

Gupta, S., Lehmann, D.R., 2003. Customers as assets. J. Interact. Mark. 17 (1), 9–24.

Gupta, S., Hanssens, D., Hardie, B., Kahn, W., Kumar, V., Lin, N., et al. 2006. Modeling customer lifetime value. J. Serv. Res. 9 (2), 139–155.

Johnson, R., Bhattacharyya, G., 1985. Statistics: Principles and Methods. John Wiley & Sons Publisher, Hoboken, N.J.

Kumar, V., Ramani, G., 2003. Taking customer lifetime value analysis to the next level. J. Integr. Commun., 27–33.

Kumar, V., Ramani, G., Bohling, T., 2004. Customer lifetime value approaches and best practice applications. J. Interact. Mark. 18 (3), 60–72.

Marshall, A., 1997. Principles of Economics. Prometheus Books, Amherst, N.Y.

Monroe, K.B., 1990. Pricing: Making Profitable Decisions, second ed. McGraw-Hill, New York.

Payne, A., Holt, S., 2001. Diagnosing customer value: integrating the value process and relationship marketing. Br. J. Manag. 12, 159–182.

Pfeifer, P.E., Haskins, M.R., Conroy, R.M., 2005. Customer lifetime value, customer profitability, and the treatment of acquisition spending. J. Managerial Issues 17 (1), 11–25.

Pigou, A.C., 1920. The Economics of Welfare. Macmillan and Co, London.

Reis, E., 2011. The Lean Startup. Penguin Books, New York.

Schmittlein, D.C., Morrison, D.G., Colombo, R., 1987. Counting your customers: who are they and what will they do next? Manag. Sci. 33, 1.

Sydsæter, K., Strøm, A., Berck, P., 1993. Economists' Mathematical Manual, second ed. Springer-Verlag, Berlin.

Whittaker, J., 1990. Graphical Models in Applied Multivariate Analysis. Wiley, Chichester.

Woodruff, R.B., 1997. Customer value: the next source of competitive advantage. J. Acad. Mark. Sci. 25 (2), 139–153.

Woodruff, R.B., Gardial, S.F., 1996. Know Your Customer: New Approaches to Customer Value and Satisfaction. Wiley, Cambridge.

———, 2005. RFM and CLV: using iso-value curves for customer base analysis. J. Mark. Res. 42, 415–430.

———, 2007. Does sutton apply to supermarkets? RAND J. Econ. 38, 43–59.

Index

Note: Page numbers followed by "*f*" refer to figures respectively.

229